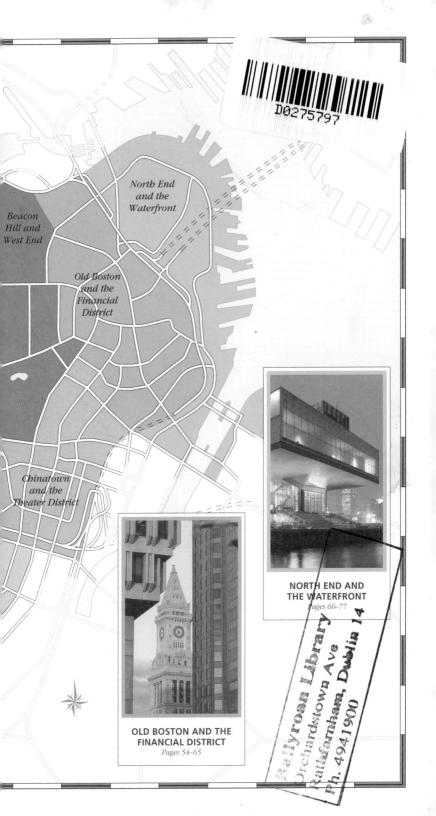

Beacon
Hill and
West End

North End
and the
Waterfront

Old Boston
and the
Financial
District

Chinatown
and the
Theater District

**NORTH END AND
THE WATERFRONT**
Pages 66–77

**OLD BOSTON AND THE
FINANCIAL DISTRICT**
Pages 54–65

D0275797

EYEWITNESS TRAVEL
BOSTON

EYEWITNESS TRAVEL

BOSTON

MAIN CONTRIBUTORS:
TOM BROSS, PATRICIA HARRIS, AND DAVID LYON

DK

LONDON, NEW YORK,
MELBOURNE, MUNICH AND DELHI
www.dk.com

PROJECT EDITOR Marcus Hardy
ART EDITOR Nicola Rodway
EDITOR Simon Hall
U.S. EDITOR Mary Sutherland
DESIGNERS Elly King, Nikala Sim
MAP CO-ORDINATORS Dave Pugh, Casper Morris
DTP Maite Lantaron
PICTURE RESEARCHER Brigitte Arora
PRODUCTION Michelle Thomas

CONTRIBUTORS
Tom Bross, Brett Cook, Patricia Harris, Carolyn Heller,
David Lyon, Juliette Rogers, Kem Sawyer

PHOTOGRAPHERS
Demetrio Carrasco, Linda Whitwam

ILLUSTRATORS
Stephen Conlin, Gary Cross, Richard Draper, Chris Orr & Associates,
Robbie Polley, John Woodcock

MAPS
Ben Bowles, Rob Clynes, Sam Johnston,
James Macdonald (Colourmap Scanning Ltd)

Reproduced by Colourscan, Singapore
Printed and bound by South China Printing Co. Ltd., China

First published in Great Britain in 2001
by Dorling Kindersley Limited
80 Strand, London WC2R 0RL

12 13 14 10 9 8 7 6 5 4 3 2

**Reprinted with revisions 2003, 2004, 2005, 2006, 2007, 2008,
2009, 2011**

Copyright © 2001, 2011 Dorling Kindersley Limited, London
A Penguin Company

ISBN: 978-1-40535-947-4

FLOORS ARE REFERRED TO THROUGHOUT IN ACCORDANCE WITH
AMERICAN USAGE; IE THE "FIRST FLOOR" IS THE FLOOR AT
GROUND LEVEL.

*Front cover main image: The red brick Old State House,
Boston, Massachusetts*

MIX
Paper from
responsible sources
FSC™ C018179

**The information in every
DK Eyewitness Travel Guide is checked regularly.**
Every effort has been made to ensure that this book is as up-to-date
as possible at the time of going to press. Some details, however,
such as telephone numbers, opening hours, prices, gallery hanging
arrangements, and travel information are liable to change. The
publishers cannot accept responsibility for any consequences arising
from the use of this book, nor for any material on third party
websites, and cannot guarantee that any website address in this
book will be a suitable source of travel information. We value the
views and suggestions of our readers very highly. Please write to:
Publisher, DK Eyewitness Travel Guides, Dorling Kindersley,
80 Strand, London WC2R 0RL, Great Britain,
or email: travelguides@dk.com.

◁ **Rowes Wharf, part of new development along Boston's waterfront**

CONTENTS

HOW TO USE THIS
GUIDE **6**

**Tiffany window in the Arlington
Street Church, Back Bay**

INTRODUCING
BOSTON

FOUR GREAT DAYS
IN BOSTON **10**

PUTTING BOSTON
ON THE MAP **12**

THE HISTORY OF
BOSTON **16**

**Federal-style houses, Beacon Hill
district** *(see pp42–5)*

BOSTON AT
A GLANCE **26**

BOSTON THROUGH
THE YEAR **34**

**BOSTON
AREA BY AREA**

BEACON HILL AND
WEST END **40**

OLD BOSTON AND
THE FINANCIAL
DISTRICT **54**

NORTH END AND
THE WATERFRONT **66**

CHINATOWN AND
THE THEATER
DISTRICT **78**

View of the Back Bay skyline, with the John Hancock Tower *(see p97)*

**TRAVELERS'
NEEDS**

WHERE TO STAY **130**

RESTAURANTS,
CAFÉS, AND BARS **138**

SHOPPING IN
BOSTON **152**

ENTERTAINMENT IN
BOSTON **158**

SPORTS AND OUTDOOR
ACTIVITIES **164**

CHILDREN'S
BOSTON
168

SURVIVAL GUIDE

PRACTICAL
INFORMATION **174**

TRAVEL
INFORMATION **180**

BOSTON STREET
FINDER **186**

GENERAL INDEX **192**

ACKNOWLEDGMENTS
205

Pumpkins for sale, a
regular sight in the fall

Memorial Church steeple,
Harvard Yard *(see pp110–11)*

BACK BAY AND
SOUTH END **88**

FARTHER
AFIELD **100**

THREE GUIDED
WALKS **120**

Trinity Church, Back Bay
(see pp94–5)

HOW TO USE THIS GUIDE

This guide will help you get the most from your visit to Boston, providing expert recommendations and detailed practical information. The opening section, *Introducing Boston*, maps the city and sets it in its geographical, historical, and cultural context. *Boston at a Glance* is an overview of the city's main attractions. Section two, *Boston Area by Area*, starts on page 38 and describes all the important

Window at First Baptist Church
(see p92)

sights plus three recommended walks, using maps, photographs, and detailed illustrations. The sights are arranged in two groups: those in Boston's central districts, and those a little farther afield. Tips for hotels, restaurants, shopping, entertainment, and sports can be found in *Travelers' Needs*, while the final section, *Survival Guide*, contains practical advice on everything from public transportation and telephones to personal safety.

FINDING YOUR WAY AROUND THE SIGHTSEEING SECTION

Each of the six sightseeing areas is color-coded for easy reference. Every chapter opens with an introduction to the area it covers, describing its history and character. For central districts, this is followed by a

Street-by-Street map illustrating a particularly interesting part of the area; for sights farther away, by a regional map. A simple numbering system relates sights to the maps. Important sights are covered by several pages.

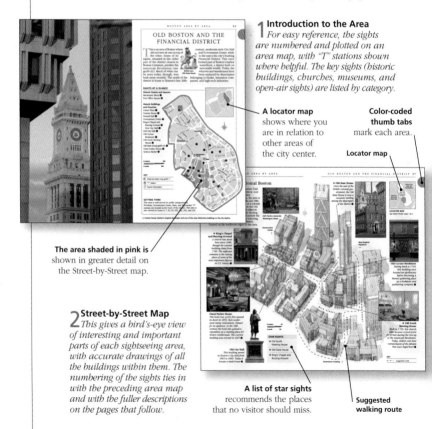

1 Introduction to the Area
For easy reference, the sights are numbered and plotted on an area map, with "T" stations shown where helpful. The key sights (historic buildings, churches, museums, and open-air sights) are listed by category.

A locator map shows where you are in relation to other areas of the city center.

Color-coded thumb tabs mark each area.

Locator map

The area shaded in pink is shown in greater detail on the Street-by-Street map.

2 Street-by-Street Map
This gives a bird's-eye view of interesting and important parts of each sightseeing area, with accurate drawings of all the buildings within them. The numbering of the sights ties in with the preceding area map and with the fuller descriptions on the pages that follow.

A list of star sights recommends the places that no visitor should miss.

Suggested walking route

BOSTON AREA MAP

The colored areas shown on this map *(see inside front cover)* are the five main sightseeing areas of central Boston (excluding the *Farther Afield* section.) Each is covered in a full chapter in the *Boston Area by Area* section *(pp39–127)*. The areas are also highlighted on other maps throughout the book. In *Boston at a Glance (pp26–37)*, for example, they help you to locate the most important sights that no visitor should miss. The maps' colored borders match the colored thumb tabs at the top corner of each page.

Numbers refer to each sight's position on the area map and its place in the chapter.

Practical information lists all the information you need to visit every sight, including a map reference to the *Street Finder* maps *(pp186–191)*.

3 Detailed information on each sight

All the important sights are described individually. They are listed to follow the numbering on the area map at the start of the section. The key to the symbols summarizing practical information is on the back flap.

A visitors' checklist provides the practical information you will need to plan your visit.

Story boxes provide details on famous people or historical events.

4 Boston's Major Sights

These are given more extensive coverage, sometimes two or more full pages. Historic buildings are dissected to reveal their interiors; museums and galleries have color-coded floor plans to help you find important exhibits.

Stars indicate the most interesting sights.

Captions provide more detailed information about specific sights.

INTRODUCING BOSTON

FOUR GREAT DAYS IN BOSTON 10–11

PUTTING BOSTON ON THE MAP 12–15

THE HISTORY OF BOSTON 16–25

BOSTON AT A GLANCE 26–33

BOSTON THROUGH THE YEAR 34–37

FOUR GREAT DAYS IN BOSTON

As well as being compact and walkable, Boston also has an extensive subway system (the "T"), which makes neighboring Cambridge easily accessible. These four suggested days offer morning and afternoon opportunities to enjoy the city's prime historical and cultural attractions,

Bronze duck in the Public Garden

with eclectic shopping as an added bonus. All the places mentioned here are cross-referenced to other parts of the guide so you can ponder more detailed information then tailor each day's outing to your personal interests. Price guidelines include transportation, food, and admission charges.

Bell tower and steeple of Old North Church

HISTORIC BOSTON

- Historic North End
- A walk along the waterfront
- Elegant Old State House
- King's Chapel

TWO ADULTS allow at least $80

Morning
Start in the **North End** (see pp68–9), Boston's oldest neighborhood. Hanover Street is full of Italian cafés and bakeries and east from here is the **Paul Revere Mall** (see p72), where an equestrian statue commemorates the patriot. Continue to the lovely 18th-century **Old North Church** (see p71), followed by a stroll through **Christoper Columbus Park** (see p73) for great harbor vistas. For lunch, head to **Quincy Market** (see p64) or **Durgin Park** (see p143), with its local specialties.

Afternoon
Refreshed, head to the **Old State House** (see pp60–61), the one-time seat of the British colonial government. Nearby is the simple **King's Chapel and Burial Ground** (see p58). Continue to the **Old South Meeting House** (see p59), where rousing speeches led to The Boston Tea Party (see p75). End the day relaxing in popular **Boston Common** (see pp46–7).

CULTURE & FRESH AIR

- Impressive Trinity Church
- Masterpieces in the Museum of Fine Arts
- Isabella Stewart Gardner Museum
- Boston skyline from Back Bay Fens parkland

TWO ADULTS allow at least $110–125

Morning
Start the day on the lovely open space that constitutes **Copley Square** (see p96), which is dominated by the beautiful 1877 Neo-Romanesque **Trinity Church** (see pp94–5), with its soaring interior spaces richly decorated with murals and stained-glass windows. Then, for a bit of morning retail therapy, walk a short distance to either of two up-scale urban malls: **Copley Place** (see p99) or the **Prudential Center**

Stained glass, Trinity Church

(see p98), where all your needs are catered for under one roof. In addition, **Boylston Street** (see p96) and parallel **Newbury Street** (see p93) also overflow with some of the city's most stylish stores and fashion boutiques. At the Copley "T" station, board a train for the **Museum of Fine Arts, Boston** (see pp104–7), the largest art museum in New England, with collections ranging from the ancient world to the 20th century. After allowing ample time to roam the galleries, head to the upper level of the West Wing to enjoy a leisurely lunch in Bravo, the MFA's classy restaurant with walls, as one might expect, adorned with a rotating exhibition of some of the museum's contemporary artworks.

Afternoon
After lunch, head to another Boston cultural treasure nearby: the **Isabella Stewart Gardner Museum** (see p103). Here, European masterpieces are among the

Boston Symphony Orchestra performing

highlights of the collection. After all this culture, take a breath of fresh air and enjoy a stroll amid the waterways, marshes, and footbridges of Back Bay Fens, one of the jewels of the area known as **The Emerald Necklace** *(see p103)*. This rambling parkland also has enchanting views of Boston's soaring skyline. If you would like to extend this cultural day into the evening, make your way to Symphony Hall, the acoustically fine-tuned home of the acclaimed **Boston Symphony Orchestra** *(see p160)*, for a classical music fest. Or, just a block away, audiences regularly fill Jordan Hall for concerts and recitals presented by students of the **New England Conservatory of Music** *(see p160)*. Alternatively, if you are in the mood for drama, Boston University's **Huntington Theatre** *(see p160)* stages first-rate productions, while the **Colonial Theater** *(see p160)*, in the Theater District, presents tours of recent Broadway hits.

Grand architecture at Harvard Yard

Museums *(see p112–14)*. Head to the Sackler, a museum dedicated to Asian and Near Eastern art that is currently housing a selection of exhibits from all of the Harvard art museums until the Fogg reopens in 2012 or 2013. Make your way back to Harvard Square, where **Sandrine's Bistro** *(see p149)* offers a good-value lunch.

John Harvard Statue

Afternoon

After lunch, visit the Harvard Museum of Natural History to see the scientifically accurate glass flowers. For another cultural experience, ride a No. 1 bus to the **MIT Campus** *(see p121)* to savor avant-garde 20th-century architecture and Alexander Calder's 12-m (40-ft) high stabile *La Grande Voile*. Catch the subway back to central Boston from Kendall Station.

CAMBRIDGE ACADEMIA

- **Bustling Harvard Square**
- **Harvard Yard architecture**
- **European masterpieces in the Harvard University Museums**
- **MIT campus and museums**

TWO ADULTS allow at least $95

Morning

Catch a Red Line train across the river to the college town of **Cambridge** *(see p108)*, emerging at Harvard Square. This is the site of the nation's oldest and most prestigious university. Immerse yourself in the scholarly atmosphere by visiting **Harvard Yard** *(see pp110–11)*, surrounded by lecture halls and dormitories that cover a broad spectrum of American architecture. From here head to the eminent **Harvard University**

A FAMILY DAY

- **Get wet on the Boston Duck Tour**
- **Swan Boat lagoon "cruise"**
- **Tropical fish in the New England Aquarium**
- **Hand's-on fun in the Children's Museum**

FAMILY OF FOUR allow $235

Morning

Get children acquainted with this kid-friendly city by joining **Boston Duck Tours** *(see p185)*, which provides narrated sightseeing tours in World War II-era amphibious vehicles. The downtown tour includes the Charles River, an exciting way to view the city's skyline. Then stroll through the **Boston Public Garden** *(see pp46–7)*, locale of bronze duck sculptures. Real ducks also swim on the park's lagoon, and you can join them aboard a pedal-powered Swan Boat. Take the subway from Arlington "T" station to Aquarium "T" station, where the **New England Aquarium** *(see pp76–7)* has a huge tank full of tropical fish, sharks and stingrays. For lunch, enjoy a sandwich on home-made bread from **Sel de la Terre** *(see p144)*.

Afternoon

Walk across the bridge to the highly interactive **Children's Museum** *(see p75)*. Permanent features include a rock-climbing wall, a construction zone, a maze, and a science playground.

Swan boats in Boston Public Garden

Putting Boston on the Map

C A N A D A

Boston is situated along the United States' northeastern Atlantic coast on Massachusetts Bay. Founded in the early 17th century around a large natural harbor at the mouth of the Charles River, the modern city now covers an area of 49 sq miles (127 sq km) and has a population of 600,000. Boston is the capital of Massachusetts and a major center of American history, culture, and learning.

TORONTO
Lester B. Pearson

Lake Ontario

Watertown

NEW YORK

Hamilton

St. Catharines
Niagara Falls Buffalo

Rochester

Syracuse

Lake Erie

90

90

UNITED STATES OF AMERICA

NORTH AMERICA

CANADA

UNITED STATES
OF
AMERICA

Boston

*ATLANTIC
OCEAN*

MEXICO

*Gulf of
Mexico*

*PACIFIC
OCEAN*

Caribbean Sea

SOUTH AMERICA

Elmira Binghamton

17

PENNSYLVANIA

Scranton 84

81

Milton 80

Delaware

Susquehanna

81

78

Allentown

Harrisburg

76

KEY

	Greater Boston
✈	Airport
═	Highway
═	Major road
▬	Railroad
- -	International border
	Shipping route
- -	State line

Philadelphia Camd
Philadelphia

83

Wilmington

MARYLAND 95

**NEW
JERSEY**

270

Baltimore

Dover

*Delaware
Bay*

Washington-
Dulles

Baltimore-
Washington

WASHINGTON DC

Annapolis

DELAWARE

66

13

0 kilometers   100

0 miles   50

VIRGINIA

Satellite image of the Greater Boston area

MAINE

Waterville

Augusta

Auburn

Portland

Concord

Portsmouth

NEW
HAMPSHIRE

VERMONT

Albany · Troy

Gloucester

Logan
International
BOSTON

MASSACHUSETTS

Worcester

Springfield

Provincetown

Cape
Cod

Hartford

CONNECTICUT

Poughkeepsie

Providence

RHODE
ISLAND

Martha's
Vineyard

Nantucket
Island

New Haven

Bridgeport
Long Island Sound

Long Island

NEW YORK
CITY

LaGuardia

Newark

John F. Kennedy (JFK)

ATLANTIC
OCEAN

Liverpool
Southampton
Gibraltar

lantic City

San Juan
Panama

Recife
Rio de
Janeiro

Cape
Town

BOSTON AND ENVIRONS

Amesbury

Newburyport

Nashua · Hudson

Haverhill

Lawrence

Gloucester

Fitchburg

Lowell

Peabody

Leominster

Atlantic
Ocean

Waltham

BOSTON

Logan
International

Marlborough

Framingham

Quincy

Weymouth

Worcester

See next page

Brockton

Woonsocket

Bridgewater

Plymouth

Taunton

0 kilometers   15

0 miles   15

Greater Boston

The city of Boston is made up of 20 separate districts, with the central city focused around the harbor on the Shawmut Peninsula. Much of the city lies within Suffolk County, although the greater Boston area also covers parts of Norfolk and Middlesex Counties. Boston is well served by major road, rail, air, and sea links, and has a good public transportation system, including a modern subway network.

MASSACHUSETTS

BILLERICA
WILMINGTON
PINEHURST
READING
WOBURN
WINCHESTER
LEXINGTON
MEDFORD
LINCOLN
ARLINGTON
WALTHAM
SUDBURY
WESTON
WATERTOWN
CAMBRIDGE
WAYLAND
NEWTON
MARLBOROUGH
BROOKLINE
NATICK
WELLESLEY
Albany
NEEDHAM
MILTON
FRAMINGHAM
DEDHAM
SHERBORN
NORWOOD
MEDFIELD
Charles
CANTON
STOUGHTON

KEY

■	Central Boston
□	Greater Boston
✈	Airport
🚉	Railroad station
—	Highway
▬	Major road
=	Minor road
—	Railroad line

0 kilometers 4

0 miles 4

THE HISTORY OF BOSTON

*E*vidence of human occupation in Massachusetts dates from
around 7500 B.C. By around A.D. 500 Algonquin Indians
were widespread in the region. Hunter-gatherers, they fished,
farmed beans and pumpkins, and hunted moose and deer. They
were made up of seven tribes, the closest geographically to present-
day Boston being the Massachusetts, Wampanoags, and Nipmucks.

Other tribes in the region included the Nausets around Cape Cod, the Pennacooks farther north, and Pocumtucs and Mohicans to the west. Their dialects came from the same language, and their physical features were similar. Each tribe lived in close-knit communities of approximately 250 people.

Artist's impression of the Viking Leif Erikson's ship

THE FIRST EUROPEANS
During the Age of the Vikings, Norsemen from Scandinavia adventured far from home, reaching North America. The coastal land of Vinland discovered by Leif Erikson in around A.D. 1000 may well have been on the Massachusetts coast. French and Spanish fishermen fished here in the mid-15th century and the Italian-born explorer John Cabot led an English expedition to the New England coast once in 1497 and again in 1498. A few years later Miguel Cortereal sailed from Portugal to Massachusetts, where his ship was wrecked. His name was found carved on a granite rock with the year 1511. Throughout the 16th

century, the English, French, Portuguese, Spanish, and Italians explored the East Coast, whaling, fishing, and trading with the natives. In 1602 the Englishman Bartholomew Gosnold sailed to Massachusetts, landing on the peninsula he called Cape Cod and traversing the island he would name Martha's Vineyard after his daughter. He returned to England with furs from the natives and sassafras to be used medicinally. In 1607 James I of England offered land in the New World to two companies. What is now Virginia he gave to the London company, led by Captain John Smith. To a group from Plymouth, England, he assigned New England and land as far south as what is now Delaware. The Plymouth Company set out in 1607 to found a colony along the Kennebec River in present-day Maine, but the harsh winter led the company to return to England. John Smith's Virginia expedition was more successful. In May 1607 he arrived in Jamestown, where he founded a permanent colony.

TIMELINE

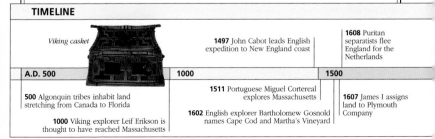

Viking casket

1497 John Cabot leads English expedition to New England coast

1608 Puritan separatists flee England for the Netherlands

A.D. 500 | **1000** | **1500**

500 Algonquin tribes inhabit land stretching from Canada to Florida

1511 Portuguese Miguel Cortereal explores Massachusetts

1602 English explorer Bartholomew Gosnold names Cape Cod and Martha's Vineyard

1607 James I assigns land to Plymouth Company

1000 Viking explorer Leif Erikson is thought to have reached Massachusetts

◁ **Inhabitants of Boston watching the Battle of Bunker Hill** *(see p20)*

The first Thanksgiving at Plymouth, Massachusetts, celebrated by the Pilgrim Fathers in 1621

THE PILGRIM FATHERS

In 1614 John Smith traveled to the northeast and published his findings in a book entitled *A Description of New England*. This land would become a haven for people who were victims of religious persecution, especially Puritans, who did not adhere to all the beliefs and rituals of the Church of England. One group of Puritan separatists had already left England to seek greater freedom in The Netherlands, but had faced economic hardship there. Lured by Captain Smith's reports, they returned to England to seek a grant for land in the New World. Joining other Puritans led by William Bradford, they set out from Plymouth in two ships, the *Mayflower* and the *Speedwell*. Quickly discovering that the *Speedwell* was leaking, they returned to Plymouth, crammed into the *Mayflower*, and set sail again on September 16, 1620.

Meeting of John Winthrop with local native in around 1630

Two months later the 102 Pilgrims arrived at Cape Cod. Before disembarking, they formulated the "Mayflower Compact," agreeing to govern themselves democratically with "just and equal laws...for the general good of the colony." The Pilgrims named their new home Plymouth and soon made friends with the natives. On April 1, 1621, Governor John Carver and Chief Massasoit signed a peace treaty. They celebrated the first Thanksgiving that year sharing provisions with their native hosts.

FOUNDING OF BOSTON

Charles I assigned land 40 miles (65 km) north of Plymouth colony, near the Charles River, to the Massachusetts Bay Company, a large group of Puritans. In the spring of 1630 over 1,000 Puritans departed in 11 ships bound for Massachusetts. Some settled in Salem and other communities along the Massachusetts Bay. The vast majority,

TIMELINE

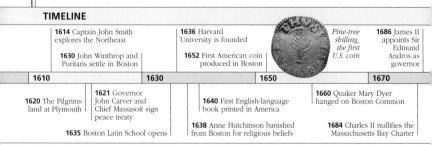

1614 Captain John Smith explores the Northeast

1630 John Winthrop and Puritans settle in Boston

1636 Harvard University is founded

1652 First American coin produced in Boston

Pine-tree shilling, the first U.S. coin

1686 James II appoints Sir Edmund Andros as governor

1610	1630	1650	1670

1620 The Pilgrims land at Plymouth

1621 Governor John Carver and Chief Massasoit sign peace treaty

1635 Boston Latin School opens

1640 First English-language book printed in America

1638 Anne Hutchinson banished from Boston for religious beliefs

1660 Quaker Mary Dyer hanged on Boston Common

1684 Charles II nullifies the Massachusetts Bay Charter

however, followed John Winthrop, their newly appointed governor, to the mouth of the Charles River. Across the river lived a recluse, an Anglican clergyman, William Blackstone. He learned that disease was rampant among the Puritans due to the scarcity of fresh drinking water, and invited them to move their settlement over the river. Winthrop and his followers were quick to accept. They first called this new land Trimountain, but soon renamed it Boston after the town in England they had left behind. In 1635

Mary Dyer with other condemned Quakers, before being hanged in 1660

they established the Boston Latin School, the first public school in the British colonies. A year later the Puritans founded a university, named subsequently after John Harvard, who had bequeathed it his library.

Although the Puritans had come to Massachusetts in pursuit of religious freedom, they often proved intolerant of others. Anne Hutchinson was driven out of Boston in 1638 for not conforming to the Puritan tradition. Many Quakers were also beaten, fined, or banished. The Quaker preacher Mary Dyer was hanged for religious unorthodoxy on June 1, 1660 on Boston Common. In 1692 after several girls in the town of Salem accused three women of witchcraft, mass hysteria broke out throughout Massachusetts, and many innocents were tried, and hanged. No one felt safe until Governor William Phips put an end to the trials in 1693.

SEEDS OF REBELLION

The British had passed the Navigation Acts to encourage the colonists to trade only with them, but when the colonists refused to obey, Charles II withdrew the Massachusetts Bay Charter in 1684, putting the colony under the control of the king. His successor James II appointed Sir Edmund Andros as royal governor. After James II lost power, the colonists arrested their governor and in 1689 established their own government. But in 1691 William and Mary granted a new charter to the Massachusetts Colony, combining the Massachusetts Bay and Plymouth colonies and recognizing a bicameral legislature. Later, the British and French started a long series of battles over New World territory. France finally ceded control of Canada and the American West, but the cost of war had taken its toll on the British, and the colonists were asked to pay their share in taxes. The seeds of rebellion were sown.

View of the commercial port of Boston in about 1730

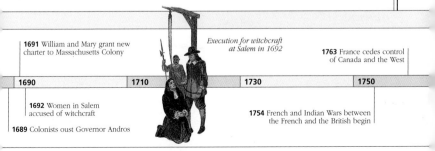

1691 William and Mary grant new charter to Massachusetts Colony

Execution for witchcraft at Salem in 1692

1763 France cedes control of Canada and the West

1690   1710   1730   1750

1692 Women in Salem accused of witchcraft

1754 French and Indian Wars between the French and the British begin

1689 Colonists oust Governor Andros

Revolutionary Boston

It was in Boston, the most important city in the 13 British colonies, that ideas for independence were nurtured and the American Revolution born. The colonists' main quarrel with Britain lay in taxation. The Stamp Act of 1765, and the later Townshend Acts, which placed duties on imports, inflamed colonists because they had no vote. "No taxation without representation" became a common cry. The so-called "Sons of Liberty," led by Samuel Adams, demanded and received the repeal of the Stamp Act. However, attempts to enforce the Townshend Acts led to the Boston Massacre, a tragedy which signaled increasingly poor relations between Britain and its colonies.

Samuel Adams

The Boston Tea Party (1773)
In protest at taxation, Boston patriots boarded three British East India Company ships and threw their cargoes of tea into Boston Harbor (see p75).

THE BOSTON MASSACRE (1770)
At the time of the Townshend Acts, British troops were sent to Boston to protect customs commissioners. Bostonians often scoffed at the soldiers and threw stones. On March 5, 1770 the jeering got out of hand. Shots were fired and five Americans fell.

Old State House (see pp60–61)

Five Americans were killed when British troops shot into the crowd.

The Battle of Bunker Hill (1775)
In June 1775, militiamen from all over New England had traveled to Boston to wrest control of the city from the British. The Americans lost the ensuing battle, the bloodiest of the Revolution.

TIMELINE

British Revenue stamp

1765 British Parliament passes the Stamp Act

1773 Tea Act gives British East India Company monopoly. Boston Tea Party

1765

1770

1767 Townshend Acts place duties on imports

1770 Five Americans killed in Boston Massacre

1766 Repeal of the Stamp Act

Evacuation of Boston 1776
Following the Battle of Bunker Hill, Boston remained under British control. For almost a year American troops lay siege to the city, until in March 1776 George Washington master-minded a strategy that led the British finally to evacuate.

John Hancock
A key participant in the Revolution, Hancock was chosen as a delegate of Massachusetts to attend the first ever Continental Congress, held in 1774.

British soldiers were sent to protect customs commissioners.

Declaration of Independence (1776)
Events surrounding the Battle of Bunker Hill and the evacuation of Boston inspired insurrection throughout the 13 colonies. This led, in July 1776, to the signing of the Declaration of Independence. Freedom from Britain finally came in 1781.

PAUL REVERE'S RIDE

On April 18, 1775 the British planned to march to Lexington to capture Samuel Adams and John Hancock, and then on to Concord to seize arms. To warn of the arrival of British troops, sexton Robert Newman hung lanterns in the tower of the Old North Church (*see p71*) and, so legend has it, Paul Revere undertook his "midnight ride." Revere's ride is immortalized in Longfellow's epic 1863 poem *Tales of a Wayside Inn.* During the ensuing skirmish at Lexington Green, eight American militiamen were killed – the first battle of the American Revolution had been fought.

Warning lights in the Old North Church

ed & Sold by PAUL REVERE BOSTON

1774 Intolerable Acts passed; Boston Harbor is closed

1776 Siege of Boston ends. Declaration of Independence adopted by Continental Congress

1781 General Cornwallis surrenders at Yorktown, Virginia

1775

1780

1775 Midnight ride of Paul Revere

Grand Union, America's first national flag

1783 U.S. and Britain sign Treaty of Paris

1777 U.S. victory at Battle of Saratoga is the turning point of the war

ATHENS OF AMERICA

With the end of the Revolutionary War, Boston's population began to grow and its economy flourish. Its port boomed, and trade, with China in particular, flourished. Some Bostonians made their fortunes at sea; others started profitable textile mills. A number of old Boston families – the Cabots, the Lowells, the Lodges – rose to great prominence boasting of their lineage, their wealth, and their Yankee independence. The United States elected not one but two members of the Adams family (both Boston residents) to the presidency: John Adams (1797–1801) and his son John Quincy Adams (1825–1829). John Adams' wife Abigail, one of the nation's most revered first ladies, made an early call for women's rights when she admonished her husband to "remember the Ladies," for "we ...will not hold ourselves bound by any law in which we have no voice, or representation."

Boston soon earned a reputation as the intellectual capital of the new United States. The Boston Athenaeum *(see p49)*, both a museum and a

Abigail Smith Adams (1744–1818)

library, was first organized in 1807 "for the promotion of literary and scientific learning." Eminent Bostonians *(see pp30–31)* at this time included the essayist Ralph Waldo Emerson, who formed the Transcendental Club, naturalist Henry David Thoreau, novelist Nathaniel Hawthorne, poet Henry Wadsworth Longfellow, whose epic poem made famous the midnight ride of Paul Revere *(see p21)*, James Russell Lowell, the first editor of the *Atlantic Monthly*, and poet, diarist and educational reformer Oliver Wendell Holmes *(see p45)* . The Boston Public Library, the oldest free library in the U.S., was founded in 1852.

Initially most of Boston's European settlers came from England, but from 1846 Boston attracted thousands of immigrants driven out of Ireland by the potato famine. When the Irish first arrived they settled in overcrowded tenements along the city's waterfront and faced discrimination from the city's residents, especially its social elite, the Boston Brahmins *(see p45)*. Signs went up

The Boston Athenaeum, first organized in 1807 but later housed in this building, which was designed in 1846

TIMELINE

1787 Constitutional Convention held in Philadelphia

1789 Inauguration of George Washington as president

1812 War with England

1825 William Ellery Channing founds American Unitarian Association

1800

1820

1786 Daniel Shay's rebellion

1796 John Adams elected as second president

1807 Boston Athenaeum is founded

George Washington (1732–99)

Irish immigrants, who poured into mid 19th-century Boston

and popular stopping-off points were the Second African Meeting House, the home of Lewis Hayden (a former slave), and John J. Smith's barbershop on the corner of Howard and Bulfinch Streets. When the first shots of the Civil War were fired on Fort Sumter on April 12, 1861, President Abraham Lincoln immediately asked volunteers to enlist. The state of Massachusetts answered the call first, sending 1,500 men within four days. As soon as African Americans were admitted to the Union forces, black soldiers started training in Boston. The Boston Brahmin, Colonel Robert Gould Shaw *(see p30)* led these men (the 54th Regiment of the Massachusetts Volunteer Infantry) in an assault on Fort Wagner, South Carolina – Shaw and 62 members of the regiment lost their lives. The battle is still remembered for the role played by African Americans, and a monument *(see p47)* to it on Boston Common was dedicated on May 31, 1897.

around the city with the words "No Irish Need Apply." But despite these obstacles, the Irish rose in stature and by the end of the 19th century would dominate Boston politics and other areas of the city's life.

THE ABOLITION MOVEMENT

Some of America's most vehement anti-slavery sentiment originated in Boston. William Lloyd Garrison *(see p30)* published the first issue of *The Liberator* on January 1, 1831 calling for the unconditional abolition of slavery: "I will not equivocate … I will not excuse … I will not retreat a single inch … and I will be heard." Not all Bostonians sympathized with his cause. To escape from angry mobs he once had to seek safety for the night in a Boston jail. Garrison and other abolitionists (Charles Sumner, Wendell Phillips, Frederick Douglass) gave rousing anti-slavery speeches in Faneuil Hall *(see p63)*, and accounts of their fiery oratory spread across the United States. The city also played an active role in the underground railroad. Fugitive slaves were assured a safe haven,

Attack on Fort Wagner by black soldiers of the 54th Massachusetts

1846 First influx of Irish immigrants into Boston

1852 Boston Public Library founded

1861 First shots at Fort Sumter begin Civil War

1840

1860

1831 First issue of William Lloyd Garrison's abolitionist newspaper, *The Liberator*

Mural in the Boston Public Library

1863 The 54th Massachusetts leads assault on Fort Wagner

1865 General Robert E. Lee surrenders. The Union is preserved. President Abraham Lincoln is assassinated

GROWTH AND DESTRUCTION

The end of the Civil War in 1865 led to a decline in shipping, but the Industrial Revolution, specifically in cotton and wool manufacturing, enabled Boston to thrive again and grow both in size and population. The Back Bay had been filled and some of the neighboring towns already annexed. However, on November 9, 1872, Boston suffered a terrible setback as flames from a fire that started in a dry goods store spread to warehouses downtown, destroying 765 buildings. Newspaper headlines declared a loss of $250 million with "rich men beggared in a day." The city recovered quickly, though, rebuilding and revitalizing textile and shoe manufacturing.

The Great Fire of Boston, November 9, 1872

Public institutions also continued to flourish. The Museum of Fine Arts, Boston *(see pp104–7)* was opened in 1876, and the Boston Symphony Orchestra *(see p160)* founded in 1881. The first subway in the United States, the "T," opened in 1897. In Boston and the surrounding areas educational establishments such as Harvard, Radcliffe, the Massachusetts Institute of Technology (M.I.T.), the New England Conservatory of Music, and Boston University all played their part in making the city a mecca for young students. The renowned collector of art Isabella Stewart Gardner *(see p103)*, a rich, famously outspoken, and well-connected woman, opened her house to the public on New Year's Day, 1903.

THE EARLY 20TH CENTURY

Following World War I, changing political and cultural attitudes across the U.S. increasingly left government clashing violently with the wishes of the people. Life in Boston was no exception. The Boston Police Strike of 1919 marks one of the most dramatic chapters in the U.S. Labor movement. As many as 1,290 policemen filed complaints over low wages, unsanitary stations, and lack of overtime compensation and sought affiliation with the American Federation of Labor (A.F.L.). When the strike started, mobs smashed windows and looted stores. After a skirmish with state militia, in which two were wounded and nine killed, A.F.L. president Samuel Gompers persuaded the police to return to work.

However, this was not just a time of conflict, but also

Harvard University students rowing on the Charles River, 1896

TIMELINE

1872 The Great Fire of Boston

1884 First Irish mayor, Hugh O'Brien, elected

1897 The "T," the U.S.'s first subway, opens.

1905 "Honey Fitz" elected mayor

1919 Boston Police Strike results in riots

1875

1900

1925

1876 Museum of Fine Arts, Boston opened

1881 Boston Symphony Orchestra formed

Museum of Fine Arts, Boston exhibit

1912 Fenway Park opens

1914 James Michael Curley elected mayor for the first time

1903 Isabella Stewart Gardner opens her house to the public one when popular culture came to the fore. One way this manifested itself was in spectator sports, which began to enjoy unparalleled popularity. Fenway Park in Boston, home to the Boston Red Sox, had opened on April 20, 1912. The Boston Red Sox won the World Series four times before 1918. Supposedly cursed by the sale of slugger Babe Ruth to the New York Yankees, they did not win the World Series again until 2004.

Prominent politicians from this time included John F. Kennedy's grandfather, John F. Fitzgerald, or "Honey Fitz," as he was known, who was elected mayor in 1905. The flamboyant James Curley, son of Irish immigrants, who became mayor, congressman, and governor, and spent time in jail for fraud, became a legend in his own lifetime.

John F. Kennedy, perhaps the most famous of all American politicians, born of Boston Irish stock

Babe Ruth (1895–1948) in an ad for chewing gum

POST-WAR POLITICS
The most famous Boston-born politician was John F. Kennedy, the great-grandson of an Irish potato famine immigrant. In 1960 he became the U.S.'s first Catholic, and youngest elected, president. His brother, Robert, served as attorney general and U.S. senator for New York. The Irish, however, were not the only immigrants to enter politics. Michael Dukakis, the son of Greek immigrants, was elected governor in 1974, becoming Democratic presidential candidate in 1988.

The late 20th century saw extensive immigration from the Caribbean, Southeast Asia, Pakistan, and India, adding new talents and cultural traditions to city life.

CITY RENAISSANCE
In the late 20th and early 21st centuries, Boston built a prosperous economy based on finance, medicine, and higher education, revitalizing the city's cultural life and gentrifying historic neighborhoods. In 2004 the Boston Red Sox broke their curse and won baseball's World Series, transforming Boston's ethos from resignation to aspiration. The Big Dig – a 20-year, $15-billion project to bury the I-93 highway – finally ended in 2005, providing new tunnels and bridges.

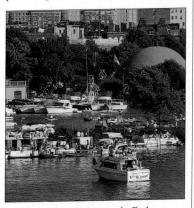

Spending leisure time in boats on the Charles River, evidence that Boston is prospering

1960 John F. Kennedy elected president

1988 Governor Michael Dukakis becomes Democratic presidential candidate

1993 John F. Kennedy Library and Museum (see p102) opens

2006 Deval Patrick elected as first African-American governor of Massachusetts

1975

2000

2025

62 Edward dy elected U.S. Senate

1963 John F. Kennedy assassinated

2004 Red Sox win World Series

Michael Dukakis, Democratic presidential candidate in 1988

2010 Museum of Fine Arts, Boston (see pp104–7) opens Art of the Americas wing

BOSTON AT A GLANCE

Although it is a small, compact city, Boston offers a wealth of attractions that draw visitors from all over the world. Indeed the range of attractions can exceed that of much larger cities in the U.S. The sights in the center and a little way out of Boston are covered in the *Area by Area* section of the book. There are historic neighborhoods, such as Beacon Hill and Back Bay; examples of some of the best Federal architecture in the U.S., such as the Massachusetts State House; and beautiful examples of late 19th-century opulence such as Trinity Church. The treasures of the Museum of Fine Arts and the Harvard Museums are also shown. A selection of Boston's best is featured below.

BOSTON'S TOP TEN ATTRACTIONS

Beacon Hill
See pp42–5

Old State House
See pp60–61

Massachusetts State House
See pp50–51

Museum of Fine Arts *See pp104–7*

New England Aquarium
See pp76–7

John Hancock Tower
See p97

Trinity Church
See pp94–5

Old North Church
See p71

Harvard
See pp110–14

Boston Common
See pp46–7

◁ Trinity Church, reflected in the John Hancock Tower

Boston's Best: Museums

The city of Boston's Athenian self-image is manifested in dozens of museums, galleries, and archives. Wealthy 19th-century patrons stocked art museums that have now become world-class collections, the best example being the Museum of Fine Arts. Likewise, Boston's leadership in scientific inquiry has created first-rate natural history and science collections. Museums such as the John F. Kennedy Library and Museum provide insight into some of the city's most compelling and influential historical figures, while a strong architectural heritage means that some of the museum buildings are also very beautiful.

Museum of Science
A favorite family destination, this museum has more than 550 interactive exhibits, that explain the laws of nature and the science of computers.

Harvard University Museums
These museums house a diverse range of collections: European Art, archaeology, natural history, and Asian and Near Eastern Art. The Sackler Museum (right) displays highlights of the art collection.

Isabella Stewart Gardner Museum
This Venetian-style palazzo stands as Isabella Gardner left it – filled to the brim with fine old masters and modern paintings. Her taste in art was considered by many to be impeccable.

Museum of Fine Arts
One of the largest museums in North America, the MFA is famous for its Greek, Roman, and Egyptian art, and French Impressionist paintings.

Otis House Museum
Designed by Charles Bulfinch (see p53), this house ushered in the Federal style of architecture. It presents a snapshot of life in the early days of the American Republic.

New England Aquarium
This aquarium displays a huge array of creatures from the world's oceans. The researchers at the aquarium are also involved in key international fish and whale conservation programs.

Institute of Contemporary Art
Boston's first new major art museum to open in nearly a century. It occupies a prime spot on the South Boston waterfront.

| 0 meters | 500 |
| 0 yards | 500 |

Nichols House Museum
An elegant Federal-style house on Beacon Hill, this museum offers a glimpse of the domestic life of the 19th-century social elite.

John F. Kennedy Library and Museum
The nation's 35th president is celebrated here – video clips of the first president to fully grasp the power of the media make this a compelling museum.

Eminent Bostonians

Founded as a refuge for religious idealists, Boston has always been obsessed with ideas and learning. Mark Twain once observed that "In New York they ask what a man is worth. In Boston they ask, 'What does he know?'" This insistence on the power of ideas has made Boston a magnet for thinkers and doers, and a hotbed of reform movements and social revolution. Education has always been one of the city's leading industries. Consequently, Boston is disproportionately represented in the honor roll of American intellectual life. Bostonians are generally considered to be liberal minded, and tend to occupy the left flank of American political thought.

Phillis Wheatley (1753–84)

Malcolm X (1925–65), one of Boston's many famous residents

REFORMERS, RABBLE ROUSERS, AND REVOLUTIONARIES

Even while Boston was still in its infancy, Bostonians began to agitate to do things differently. Anne Hutchinson (1591–1643) was exiled for heresy in 1638 (she moved south to found Portsmouth, Rhode Island), while friend and fellow religious radical Mary Dyer died on the Boston Common gallows for Quakerism in 1660 *(see p19)*. Spokesman for the Sons of Liberty and part-time brewer Samuel Adams (1722–1803) incited Boston to revolution in the "Boston Tea Party" *(see p75)*. The city bubbled

Abolitionist William Lloyd Garrison (1805–79)

over with 19th-century reformers, including Dorothea Dix (1802–87), who championed the welfare of the mentally ill, and William Lloyd Garrison (1805–79), publisher of *The Liberator*, who was one of America's most strident voices calling for the abolition of slavery. Malcolm Little (1925–65) spent his adolescence in Boston before converting to Islam in prison and emerging as the charismatic Black Muslim leader Malcolm X. Like Malcolm X, Nguyen Tat Thanh (1890–1969) spent part of his youth in Boston, working for a time in the restaurant of the Omni Parker House Hotel *(see p58)*. Traveling much of the world in his 20s, he was later to assume the name Ho Chi Minh.

BOSTON BRAHMINS

In 1860 Oliver Wendell Holmes (1809–94) dubbed Boston's prosperous merchant class the "Boston Brahmins … a harmless, inoffensive, untitled aristocracy" *(see p45)*. Any suggestion that the Brahmins were unaccomplished, however, could not be farther from the truth. Julia Ward Howe (1819–1910) was a prominent abolitionist and later a crusader for women's rights. She also penned the Unionists' Civil War marching song, "The Battle Hymn of the Republic." Brahmin Colonel Robert Gould Shaw (1837–63) led the all-Black 54th Massachusetts Regiment in the Civil War, and Major Henry Lee Higginson (1834–1919) survived the war to found the Boston Symphony Orchestra in 1881.

Many famous authors were also Brahmins, notably the Lowell clan: James Russell Lowell (1819–91) was the leading literary critic of his day, Amy Lowell (1874–1925) championed "free verse" and founded *Poetry* magazine, and Robert Lowell (1917–77) broke the barriers between formal and informal verse in American poetry. The Brahmins' greatest chronicler was the noted historian Samuel Eliot Morison (1887–1976).

The Brahmins persist through business partnerships, family trusts, and intermarriage, as highlighted in their ditty: "And this is good old Boston, The home of the bean and the cod, Where the Lowells talk to the Cabots, And the Cabots talk only to God."

INVENTORS AND ENTREPRENEURS

Innovation has always been a way of life in Boston. Donald McKay's (1810–80) East Boston clipper ships revolutionized international sea trade in the 1850s. Working in his Cambridge

Edwin Land (1909–91), inventor of Polaroid instant photography

workshop, Elias Howe (1819–67) created the modern sewing machine, radically altering both the clothing trade and the shoe industry. Alexander Graham Bell (1847–1922) had offices in Cambridge and Boston, and later joined the faculty of Boston University. This was part of a trend of academic affiliation that became almost the rule for Boston's inventors. Edwin H. Land (1909–91) experimented with polarized light in his Harvard lab before inventing Polaroid instant photography. The innovators Bolt, Beranek, and Newman also made academic affiliations with the Massachusetts Institute of Technology, and they also sent the world's first electronic mail message in the 1970s.

THINKERS

In addition to showing the world how to do things, Bostonians have always been adept at explaining why. In his many essays and poems, Ralph Waldo Emerson (1803–82) first laid the philosophical groundwork for an American school of transcendental religious thought. Meanwhile, his friend and fellow Harvard graduate Henry David Thoreau (1817–62) wrote many seminal works of natural philosophy. A professor at Harvard, William James (1842–1910) not only taught psychology and physiology, but also promulgated philosophical pragmatism, the concept that the worth of an idea is based on its usefulness. His student, George Santayana (1863–1952) blossomed as the 20th-century's chief philosopher of aesthetics.

More pragmatically, the Harvard economist John Kenneth Galbraith (1908–2006) investigated the sources of societal affluence and advocated social policies to put that affluence to work for the common good.

POLITICAL LEADERS

Boston's most infamous politician was the "rascal king" James Michael Curley (1874–1958), who served many terms as mayor and U.S. Congressman, winning his last election from a jail cell. His life was to serve as the model for the novel *The Last Hurrah*. Boston also gave the country four presidents: John Adams (1735–1826) and his son John Quincy Adams (1767–1848); the tight-lipped ex-governor Calvin Coolidge (1872–1933), who rose to prominence by crushing the Boston police strike in 1919; and John F. Kennedy, infamously assassinated in Dallas in 1963. Kennedy's brothers were also prominent on the national stage: Robert F. Kennedy (1925–1968) served as attorney general and then as senator, when he, too, was assassinated. Edward M. Kennedy (1932–2010) served for 46 years in the U.S. Senate as a leading advocate for social justice. His good friend, Thomas P. "Tip" O'Neill (1912–94), served as U.S. Speaker of the House.

John F. Kennedy campaign button

AUTHORS

America's first published author was Boston's Anne Bradstreet (1612–72). The first published African American author was Phillis Wheatley (1753–84), born in Africa, enslaved, then freed in Boston. Her 1778 volume, *Poems on Various Subjects, Religious and Moral*, echoed Boston authors' moral concerns. Henry Wadsworth Longfellow (1807–82) made his fortune from best-selling verse epics such as *Evangeline* and *Hiawatha*, but made his mark translating Dante. Although associated with nearby Concord, popular novelist Louisa May Alcott (1832–88) also lived on Beacon Hill and was active in Boston reform movements. New York-born Henry James (1843–1916) was educated at Harvard and often returned to Boston from his London home, spending a lifetime contrasting American and European culture. Former U.S. poet laureate Robert Pinsky (born 1940) teaches at Boston University, as does novelist Leslie Epstein (born 1938). The popular Boston-based fictional detective Spenser is the creation of Robert Parker (1932–2010), and when not hanging out with Clint Eastwood, suspense novelist and screenwriter Dennis Lehane (born 1966) broods at Fort Point Channel.

Author Louisa May Alcott (1832–88), part of Boston's reform movement

Boston's Architecture

Buildings followed British styles through the 1790s, when the first American architect of note, Charles Bulfinch, defined the Federal style. In the 19th century, Bostonians evolved a local Victorian style, which first embraced Greek Classicism, then French and Italian styles. Two styles of the late 19th century, Renaissance Revival and Richardsonian Romanesque, remained influential through World War I. In the 20th century, Harvard University and Massachusetts Institute of Technology (M.I.T.) attracted many leading modern and post-modern architects, all of whom left their mark.

Renaissance Revival interior of the Boston Public Library

Freestanding Federal-style Harrison Gray Otis House

FEDERAL

Charles Bulfinch and his protégé Asher Benjamin adapted British Georgian styles to create Boston's first signature architectural style. Typical of this style are freestanding mansions and town houses, with symmetrical brick façades adorned by shuttered windows, and ground-floor windows set in recessed arches. Entrances are often cut from granite slabs, featuring gently fluted columns. The largest and most elegant rooms of Federal homes are usually found on the second floor.

Some of the grander examples of Federal domestic architecture, found mainly on Beacon Hill, feature ornamental ironwork and are often crowned with octagonal cupolas. Chestnut Street on Beacon Hill (see pp42–3) represents the greatest concentration of Federal-style row houses in Boston. Individual examples of the style include the Harrison Gray Otis House (see p52) and the Hepzibah Swan Houses (see p45).

BOSTON GRANITE

The granite outcrops found around Boston Harbor provided stone for the city's waterfront development in the early 19th century. Technological advances had made it possible to cut entire columns from single blocks of granite. Freed from the constraints of soft limestone or sandstone, Alexander Parris and other architects adopted granite as a principal material for markets and warehouses, as can be seen for example at Charlestown Navy Yard (see p115) and Quincy Market (see p64). Although the basic style is an adaptation of Greek Revival, it also includes modern innovations such as iron tension rods and laminated wooden ribs to support copper domes.

Granite Greek Revival façade of Quincy Market

Distinctive, multicolored, square tower of Trinity Church

RENAISSANCE REVIVAL

Charles McKim's 1887 design for the Boston Public Library (see p96), conceived as a "palace of the people," established Renaissance Revival architecture as a favorite American style for monumental public structures. Evenly spaced windows and arches, adorned by inscriptions and sculptural details, define the style. Soaring, barrel vaulted interiors are also featured. Boston's Renaissance Revival structures make extensive use of New England and Italian marbles, carved stucco ceilings, and carved wood in staircases and walls. Many of the Italian artisans who were brought over to execute this work stayed in Boston, forming an elite group within the Italian immigrant community by around 1900.

RICHARDSONIAN ROMANESQUE

America is far too young to boast a true Romanesque style, but Henry Hobson Richardson effectively created one from European inspirations and American stone. By the 1870s, the wealthy city of Boston demanded more elaborate churches than the existing sparsely designed "boxes with a spire." Gothic styles, however, were associated with medieval Catholicism and were unacceptable to the Protestant heirs of the Puritans. Richardson's churches provided a pleasing alternative. Often, the building's main components were massed around a central tower, as can be seen in Boston's most important example of the style, Trinity Church *(see pp94–5)*, as well as in the First Baptist Church *(see p92)*. In sharp contrast to the Boston Granite style, which used many similar materials and sharp angles, Richardson used stones of contrasting colors and rounded off virtually every square edge.

Italianate interior detail of the Victorian Gibson House Museum

upper Newbury Street and Massachusetts Avenue reflect a more mature synthesis: raised granite entrances, slate-shingled mansard roofs, and dormer and bay windows. Nowhere is the transition from early to late Victorian styles so evident than on the walk westward, from the center of Boston, along Commonwealth Avenue *(see p93)*.

ART DECO

Most of Boston's Art Deco buildings are clustered around Post Office Square in the Financial District, with the former Post Office *(see p65)* and the New England Telephone Building *(see p65)* being the finest examples. Essentially tall buildings of light gray granite, they are constructed with vertical strips and slit windows that elongate their forms. Elaborate geometric steps and surface ornament on the

upper stories help relieve their mass. Boston Art Deco tends also to make great use of Greco-Roman geometric friezes and stylized, vegetable-inspired ornament. Some Financial District Art Deco buildings also feature bas-relief murals of historic and heroic themes. Back Bay was once the site of many Art Deco storefronts with stylized Parisian pilasters and grillwork, but only the former quarters of Shreve, Crump & Low Inc. on Boylston Street *(see p96)* remain intact.

Modernist interior of the Kresge Chapel, built in the 1950s

MODERNISM

The willing embrace of Modernism at Boston and Cambridge colleges has graced the Boston area with a wide range of outstanding 20th-century buildings where simplicity of form is favored over ornament, and expressive lines grow out of function. When Bauhaus director Walter Gropius fled the Nazis for the safety of Harvard University, he served as a magnet for some of the mid-century's great designers and architects. The range of styles in Boston's Modernist buildings is diverse: the poetic sculptural grace of Eero Saarinen's Kresge Auditorium and Chapel at M.I.T. *(see p109)*; Le Corbusier's Carpenter Center for the Visual Arts *(see p111)*; and Josep Lluis Sert's International-style Holyoke Center, both near Harvard Yard *(see pp110–11)*.

Romanesque-style front portico of the First Baptist Church

VICTORIAN

Boston's Victorian style largely eschews the pointed Gothic lines of English Victorian in favor of French Academic, French Empire, and various Italianate influences. The variations are displayed in an almost chronological march of styles in the Back Bay and South End *(see pp88–9)*, paralleling the decade-by-decade creation of filled land in those neighborhoods in the second half of the 19th century. Earlier buildings tend to reflect their stylistic influences more accurately; for example, the Italianate Gibson House Museum *(see p92)* on Beacon Street, which would have been among the first wave of Back Bay development. The later town houses of

The Art Deco New England Telephone Building, overlooking Post Office Square

BOSTON THROUGH THE YEAR

Perhaps more than in any other city in the U.S., Boston's cultural life tends to follow the academic calendar, with the "year" beginning when classes commence at its many colleges and universities in September, and winding down a little with the start of the summer recess in May and June. In between is so-called "ice cream" season, when the warm weather causes most activities to shift out of doors, and reading lists favor

Model of a saint, North End Italian Feast Days

fiction over more scholarly texts. Though the cultural life of the city tends to flourish from fall to spring, the summer months do feature many of Boston's major carnivals, festivals, parades, and free outdoor concerts at the Hatch Shell (*see p92*). After the students' return to their studies in the fall, the busy performing arts season begins, with symphony concerts, theater, and ballet continuing into the following spring.

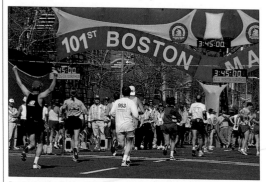

Springtime tulips in full bloom, Boston Public Garden

SPRING

When the weather warms, Boston bursts into bloom. Thousands of tulips explode in the Public Garden, and the magnolia trees of Commonwealth Avenue are sheathed in pink and white. Spring is a season of remembrance, with commemorations of events leading up to the American Revolution. It also marks the start of the season for the Boston Red Sox.

MARCH

Reenactment of Boston Massacre (*early Mar*), Old State House. Marks watershed event that turned Bostonians against their British rulers.
New England Spring Flower Show (*mid-Mar*), various venues. Oldest annual flower exhibition in the United States.
St. Patrick's Day Parade (*mid-Mar*), South Boston.

This annual parade also commemorates the British evacuation of Boston during the Revolutionary War.

APRIL

Baseball (*first week*), Fenway Park. Major league season starts for Boston Red Sox.
Annual Lantern Celebration (*Patriots Day Eve*), Old North Church. Commemorates hanging signal lanterns in the steeple to warn revolutionaries.
Patriots Day Parade (*third Mon*), from City Hall Plaza to Paul Revere Mall, where the start of Paul Revere's Midnight Ride is reenacted.
Boston Marathon (*third Mon*), Hopkinton to Back Bay. America's oldest marathon.

MAY

May Fair (*first Sat*), Harvard Square. International street fair.
Walk for Hunger (*first Sun*), 20-mile (32-km) walk, one of

the oldest and largest pledge walks in the country, raises funds for food banks.
Duckling Day Parade (*second Sun*), Boston Common. Parade retracing the route of the ducklings in Robert McCloskey's classic children's storybook, *Make Way for Ducklings*.
Arts First (*early May*), Cambridge. More than 200 free performances of music, theater, and dance – all on Harvard campus.
Hidden Gardens of Beacon Hill (*third Thu*), Beacon Hill. Garden tours organized.
Lilac Sunday (*third Sun*), Arnold Arboretum. More than 400 lilac bushes are in bloom.
Street Performers Festival (*late May*), Faneuil Hall Marketplace. Street musicians, jugglers, acrobats and other performers.
Boston Pops (*May–Jun*), Symphony Hall. Season features light Classical repertory and American popular music.

Runners at the finish of the annual Boston Marathon, held in April

AVERAGE DAILY HOURS OF SUNSHINE IN BOSTON

Hours

Sunshine Chart
This chart shows the average daily number of hours of sunshine in Boston each month. The city enjoys long and light summer days from June to August, with July being the sunniest month. Fall has more sunshine than spring, but while spring is mild, fall becomes quite chilly. Winter days are shorter, but many are still clear and bright.

SUMMER

When summer's heat finally arrives, Bostonians head outdoors to relax on the grassy banks of the Charles River, along the harbor, and in the city's many parks. The Hatch Shell on the Esplanade becomes the scene of many free open-air concerts. The grandest celebration occurs on the Fourth of July, with one of the country's greatest fireworks displays, following an invariably rousing performance by the Boston Pops Orchestra.

Fourth of July fireworks lighting up the sky over the Charles River

Summer outdoor concert at Hatch Shell, Charles River Esplanade

JUNE

Performing Arts Series at the Hatch Shell *(Wed & Fri–Sun, Jun–Sep)*, Hatch Shell, Esplanade. Free outdoor movies, and pop, rock, and classical concerts.
Scooper Bowl *(early Jun)*, City Hall Plaza. One of the largest ice cream festivals in the U.S.
Boston Pride *(mid-Jun)*. New England's largest gay pride parade and festival caps a week of celebrating diversity.
Bunker Hill Weekend *(weekend before Jun 17)*,

Charlestown. Costumed reenactments, demonstrations, a parade, and guided tours at Bunker Hill Monument.
Dragon Boat Festival *(mid-Jun)*, Charles River. Traditional Asian dragon boat races.
Cambridge River Festival *(mid-Jun)*. Multicultural festival on the banks of the Charles River.

JULY

Italian Feast Days *(Jul–Aug)*, North End. Religious processions with music and food take place almost every weekend.
Boston Harborfest *(week of Jul 4)*. Features children's events, concerts, harbor cruises, and a Chowderfest on City Hall Plaza.
Boston Pops Annual Fourth of July Concert and Fireworks *(Jul 4)*, Esplanade. The largest of the free Boston Pops concerts in July.
Bastille Day *(Fri before Jul 14)*, Back Bay. Annual celebration sponsored by the French Library of Boston.

Annual Festival Betances *(late Jul)*, South End. Annual Puerto Rican festival with music, dance, and food.

AUGUST

August Moon Festival *(mid-Aug)*, Chinatown. Lion dance, martial arts, Chinese opera.
Boston Restaurant Week *(late Aug)*, Boston and Cambridge. More than 80 restaurants offer low fixed-price lunch and dinner menus.
Boston Caribbean Carnival *(third weekend)*, Franklin Park. Extravagant costumes, music, food, and dancing.

July 4th parade, Government Center

AVERAGE MONTHLY TEMPERATURE

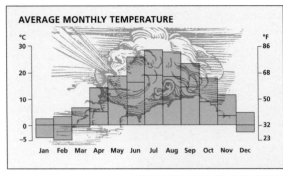

Temperature Chart
This chart shows the average minimum and maximum temperatures for each month in Boston. The highest temperatures of the year are in July and August, when it is hot and humid. Winters are cold, and while they can be clear and bright, they are also often stormy, resulting in wind-chill temperatures well below freezing point.

FALL

After Labor Day, Boston's massive student community returns. This time also sees the start of seasons for the performing arts and for basketball and hockey. The vivid colors of New England's deciduous fall trees attract thousands of people to Boston, on their way to backcountry tours. Mid-November brings cold weather and the beginning of the holiday season.

Famous fiery colors of New England's fall foliage

SEPTEMBER

Feast of Saints Cosma & Damiano *(second weekend)*, East Cambridge. Italian festival with parade.
Cambridge Carnival *(mid-Sep)*. Ethnic cuisine, music, crafts, and a colorful parade to celebrate African and Caribbean cultural heritage.
BeanTown Jazz Festival *(late Sep)*, South End. This event features contemporary jazz, blues, and salsa.
Boston Fashion Week *(late Sep)*, city-wide. A variety of events showcase Boston's

Outdoor musical performance

established couturiers and rising fashionistas.
Boston Open Studios *(Sep–early Dec)*. Art communities in Boston, including Fort Point and the South End, schedule studio tours.

OCTOBER

Boston Symphony Orchestra Season *(Oct–Apr)*. Orchestra performs in historic Symphony Hall.
Basketball *(Oct–Apr)*, TD Garden. NBA (National Basketball Association) season begins for the Boston Celtics.
Hockey *(Oct–Apr)*, TD Garden. NHL (National Hockey League) season begins for the Boston Bruins.
Columbus Day Parade *(early Oct)*, Parade alternates between East Boston (even years) and Downtown.
Boston Ballet Season *(mid-Oct–May)*, Opera House. Professional repertory company gives performances.

Head of the Charles Regatta *(second to last Weekend Oct)*, Cambridge. Rowing event featuring 1,400 boats and 3,000 athletes.
Ellis Memorial Antiques Show *(late Oct–early Nov)*, various locations.
Boston International Antiquarian Book Fair *(late Oct–early Nov)*, Hynes Convention Center. One of oldest and largest in the U.S.
Boston Jewish Film Festival *(late Oct–mid-Nov)*, contemporary films on Jewish themes, lectures, and discussions.

NOVEMBER

Ice Skating on Frog Pond *(mid-Nov–March)*, Boston Common.
Ski and Snowboard Expo *(mid-Nov)*, Bayside Expo. Sports enthusiasts prepare for the winter season.
Veterans Day Parade *(Nov 11)*, Downtown. Marching and high school bands, and veterans' groups honor all those who served in the armed forces.

AVERAGE MONTHLY PRECIPITATION

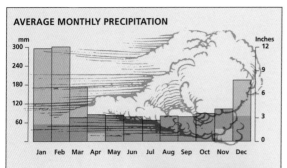

mm												Inches
300												12
240												9
180												6
120												3
60												0

Jan Feb Mar Apr May Jun Jul Aug Sep Oct Nov Dec

Rainfall Chart

This chart shows the average monthly rain and snowfall in Boston. Precipitation levels are fairly constant throughout the year, at around 3–4 inches (8–10 cm) per month. During the winter much of this falls as snow, which stays on the ground until March.

▨ Rainfall (from baseline)

▨ Snow (from baseline)

WINTER

Tree-lighting ceremonies and decorated store windows help make Boston's cityscape magical at Christmas. As the old year ends, the entire city, from downtown to the most remote neighborhoods, erupts with the joy of First Night, a worldwide institution launched in Boston. When the frigid weather arrives in mid-January, Bostonians get geared up to a busy season of performing arts and food and wine expositions.

DECEMBER

CRAFTBOSTON Holiday *(mid-Dec)*, Boston Center for the Arts. Top-quality juried crafts exhibition for artistic gift-buying.
Reenactment of the Boston Tea Party *(mid-Dec)*. Begins at Old South Meeting House and proceeds to Boston Harbor, where this key historical event is replayed.

First Night ice sculpture

First Night *(Dec 31)*. The original city-wide New Year's Eve celebration, now an international phenomenon.

JANUARY

Chinese New Year *(late Jan to Mar depending on lunar calendar)*, Chinatown. Celebration includes parade, dragon dances, and firecrackers.
Boston Wine Expo *(late Jan–early Feb)*, World Trade Center. Two arduous days of international wine tastings and cooking demonstrations.

FEBRUARY

Beanpot Tournament *(mid-Feb)*, TD Garden. Annual college hockey tournament between Boston College, Boston University, Northeastern University, and Harvard University *(see pp110–11)*.
Longfellow Birthday Celebration, *(late Feb)*, Cambridge. Tours of Longfellow House, poetry readings, and wreath-laying at the illustrious poet's grave.
Harvard's Hasty Pudding Club Parades *(variable)*, Cambridge. Outrageous Harvard theatrical club presents Man and Woman of the Year Awards to Hollywood celebrities after cross-dressing parades through Harvard Square.

PUBLIC HOLIDAYS

New Year's Day (Jan 1)
Martin Luther King Day (3rd Mon, Jan)
Presidents Day (mid-Feb)
Evacuation Day (Mar 17) (Boston only)
Patriots Day (3rd Mon, Apr) (Middlesex and Suffolk counties, including Boston and Cambridge)
Memorial Day (end May)
Bunker Hill Day (Jun 17) (Boston only)
Independence Day (Jul 4)
Labor Day (1st Mon, Sep)
Columbus Day (2nd Mon, Oct)
Veterans Day (Nov 11)
Thanksgiving (4th Thu, Nov)
Christmas Day (Dec 25)

Christmas lights on a snowy Boston Common in December

Aerial view of Boston and waterfront ▷

BOSTON
AREA BY AREA

BEACON HILL AND WEST END 40–53

OLD BOSTON AND THE FINANCIAL
DISTRICT 54–65

NORTH END AND THE WATERFRONT 66–77

CHINATOWN AND THE THEATER
DISTRICT 78–87

BACK BAY AND SOUTH END 88–99

FARTHER AFIELD 100–119

THREE GUIDED WALKS 120–127

BEACON HILL AND WEST END

eacon Hill was developed
from pastureland in the
1790s. The south slope,
facing Boston Common,
became the main seat of
Boston wealth and power,
while the north slope and the
land rolling down to the mouth
of the Charles River, known as
the West End, became pop-
ulated by tradesmen, servants, and
free blacks. South-slope Beacon Hill

**Stained glass,
Massachusetts
State House**

retained its cachet into the late
19th century, while the north
slope and West End degen-
erated. Urban renewal in the
1950s and 1960s cleared away
the slums and coherent neighborhood of the West End, while
gentrification of the north slope
made even the most modest
homes on Beacon Hill highly
desirable, and this neighborhood
one of Boston's most picturesque.

SIGHTS AT A GLANCE

Historic Streets and Squares
Beacon Street **6**
Charles Street **1**
Louisburg Square **2**
Mount Vernon Street **3**

Historic Buildings, Churches, and Museums
Boston Athenaeum **10**
Hepzibah Swan Houses **5**
Massachusetts General Hospital **15**
Massachusetts State House pp50–51 **11**
Museum of African American History **12**
Museum of Science and Science Park **16**
Nichols House Museum **4**
Old West Church **14**
Otis House Museum **13**
Park Street Church **8**

Parks and Cemeteries
Boston Common and Public Garden pp46–7 **7**
Old Granary Burying Ground **9**

GETTING THERE
This area is well served by public transportation. Park Street, Boylston, and Arlington "T"
stations are closest to the main sights. The area
is also served by Charles/ M.G.H. and Science
Park. Buses 43 and 55 go to Boston Common.

0 meters   250
0 yards   250

KEY
▨ Street-by-street map pp42–3

Ⓣ "T" station

🛈 Tourist information

◁ **Front view of the Massachusetts State House, seen from Boston Common**

Street-by-Street: Beacon Hill

Lion door knocker, Beacon St.

From the 1790s to the 1870s, the south slope of Beacon Hill was Boston's most sought-after neighborhood – its wealthy elite decamped only when the more exclusive Back Bay *(see pp88–99)* was built. Many of the district's houses were designed by Charles Bulfinch *(see p53)* and his disciples, and the south slope evolved as a textbook example of Federal architecture. Elevation and view were all, and the finest homes are either on Boston Common or perched near the top of the hill. Early developers abided by a gentleman's agreement to set houses back from the street, but the economic depression of 1807–12 resulted in row houses being built right out to the street.

Cobbled street, once typical of Beacon Hill

Louisburg Square
The crowning glory of the Beacon Hill district, this square was developed in the 1830s. Today, it is still Boston's most desirable address ❷

Charles Street Meeting House was built in the early 19th century to house a congregation of Baptists.

KEY

— — — Suggested route

DE LUCA'S MARKET

"FRESHEST BY FAR SINCE 1905"

★ **Charles Street**
This elegant street is the main shopping area for Beacon Hill. Lined with upscale grocers and antique stores, it also has some fine restaurants ❶

PINCKNEY STREET

LOUISBURG SQUARE

MOUNT VERNON STREET

CEDAR STREET

CHARLES STREET

CHESTNUT STREET

Back Bay and South End

STAR SIGHTS

★ Charles Street

★ Nichols House Museum

★ **Nichols House Museum**
This modest museum offers an insight into the life of Beacon Hill resident Rose Nichols, who lived here from 1885 to 1960 ❹

LOCATOR MAP
See Street Finder map 1

| 0 meters | 50 |
| 0 yards | 50 |

Mount Vernon Street
Described in the 19th century as the "most civilized street in America," this is where the developers of Beacon Hill (the Mount Vernon Proprietors) chose to build their own homes ❸

→ **Massachusetts State House**

WALNUT STREET

BRUCE STREET

BEACON STREET

↓ **Boston Common**

Hepzibah Swan Houses
Elegant in their simplicity, these three Bulfinch-designed houses were wedding gifts for the daughters of a wealthy Beacon Hill proprietress ❺

Beacon Street
The finest houses on Beacon Hill were invariably built on Beacon Street. Elegant, Federal-style mansions, some with ornate reliefs, overlook the city's most beautiful green space, Boston Common ❻

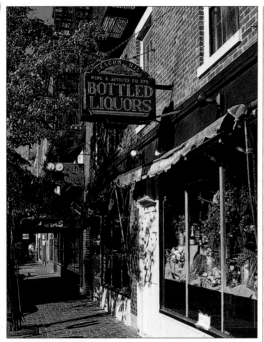

Charles Street, lined with shops catering to the residents of Beacon Hill

Charles Street ❶

Map 1 B4. Ⓣ *Charles/MGH.*

This street originally ran along the bank of the Charles River, although subsequent landfill has removed it from the riverbank by several hundred feet. The main shopping and dining area of the Beacon Hill neighborhood, the curving line of Charles Street hugs the base of Beacon Hill, giving it a quaint, village-like air. Many of the houses remain residential on the upper stories, while street level and cellar levels were converted to commercial uses long ago. Though most of Charles Street dates from the 19th century, widening in the 1920s meant that some of the houses on the west side acquired new façades. The Charles Street Meeting House, designed by Asher Benjamin *(see p32)* in 1807, was built for a Baptist congregation that practiced immersion in the then adjacent river. It is now a commercial building. Two groups of striking Greek Revival row houses are situated at the top of Charles Street, between Revere and Cambridge Streets. Charles Street was one of the birthplaces of the antique trade in the U.S. and now has more than a dozen antique dealers.

Louisburg Square ❷

Map 1 B4. Ⓣ *Charles/MGH, Park Street.*

Home to millionaire politicians, best-selling authors, and corporate moguls, Louisburg Square is arguably Boston's most prestigious address. Developed in the 1830s as a shared private preserve on Beacon Hill, the square's tiny patch of greenery surrounded by a high iron fence sends a clear signal of the square's continued exclusivity. On the last private square in the city, the narrow Greek Revival bow-fronted town houses sell for a premium over comparable homes elsewhere on Beacon Hill. Even the on-street parking spaces are deeded. The traditions of Christmas Eve carol singing and candlelit windows are said to have begun on Louisburg Square. A statue of Christopher Columbus, presented by a wealthy Greek merchant in 1850, stands at its center.

Mount Vernon Street ❸

Map 1 B4. Ⓣ *Charles/MGH, Park Street.*

In the 1890s the novelist Henry James *(see p31)* called Mount Vernon Street "the most civilized street in America," and it still retains that air of urbane culture. Most of the developers of Beacon Hill, who called themselves the Mount Vernon Proprietors, chose to build their private homes along this street. Architect Charles Bulfinch *(see p53)* envisioned Beacon Hill as a district of large freestanding mansions on spacious landscaped grounds, but building costs ultimately dictated much denser development. The sole remaining example of Bulfinch's vision is the second Harrison Gray Otis House, built in 1800 at No. 85. The Greek Revival row houses next door (Nos. 59–83), graciously set back from the street by 30 ft (9 m), were built to replace the single mansion belonging to Otis's chief development partner, Jonathan Mason. The original mansion was torn down after Mason's death in 1836. The three Bulfinch-designed houses at Nos. 55, 57, and 59 Mount Vernon Street were built by Mason for his daughters. No. 55 was ultimately passed on to the Nichols family *(see p45)* in 1885.

Columbus Statue, Louisburg Square

OLIVER WENDELL HOLMES AND THE BOSTON BRAHMINS

In 1860, Oliver Wendell Holmes *(see p30)* wrote that Boston's wealthy merchant class of the time constituted a Brahmin caste, a "harmless, inoffensive, untitled aristocracy" with "their houses by Bulfinch, their monopoly on Beacon Street, their ancestral portraits and Chinese porcelains, humanitarianism, Unitarian faith in the march of the mind, Yankee shrewdness, and New England exclusiveness." So keenly did he skewer the social class that the term has persisted. In casual usage today, a Brahmin is someone with an old family name, whose finances derive largely from trust funds, and whose politics blend conservatism with *noblesse oblige* toward those less fortunate. Boston's Brahmins founded most of the hospitals, performing arts bodies and museums of the greater metropolitan area.

Oliver Wendell Holmes (1809–94)

Drawing room of the Bulfinch-designed Nichols House Museum

Nichols House Museum ❹

55 Mount Vernon St. **Map** 1 B4. **Tel** (617) 227-6993. Ⓣ *Park Street.* ◯ *Apr–Oct: 11am–4pm Tue–Sat; Nov–Mar: 11am–4pm Thu–Sat.* 🗓 💷 🖶 www.nicholshousemuseum.org

The Nichols House Museum was designed by Charles Bulfinch in 1804 and offers a rare glimpse into the tradition-bound lifestyle of Beacon Hill. Modernized in 1830 by the addition of a Greek Revival portico, the house is nevertheless a superb example of Bulfinch's domestic architecture. It also offers an insight into the life of a true Beacon Hill character. Rose Standish Nichols moved into the house aged 13 when her father purchased it in 1885. She left it as a museum in her will in 1960. A woman ahead of her time,

strong-willed and famously hospitable, Nichols was, among other things, a self-styled landscape designer who traveled extensively around the world to write about gardens.

Hepzibah Swan Houses ❺

13, 15 & 17 Chestnut St. **Map** 1 B4. Ⓣ *Park Street.* ◼ *to the public.*

The only woman who was ever a member of the Mount Vernon Proprietors *(see p44)*, Mrs. Swan had these houses built by Bulfinch as wedding presents for her daughters in 1806, 1807 and 1814. Some of the most elegant and distinguished houses on Chestnut Street, they are backed by Bulfinch-designed stables that face onto Mount Vernon Street. The deeds restrict the height of the stables to 13 ft (4 m) so that her daughters would still have a view over Mount Vernon Street. In 1863–65, No. 13 was home to Dr. Samuel Gridley Howe, abolitionist and educational pioneer who, in 1833, founded the first school for the blind in the U.S.

Beacon Street ❻

Map 1 B4. Ⓣ *Park Street.*

Beacon Street is lined with urban mansions facing Boston Common. The 1808 **William Hickling Prescott House** at No. 55, designed by Asher Benjamin, offers tours of rooms decorated in Federal, Victorian, and Colonial Revival styles. The American Meteorological Society occupies No. 45, which was built as Harrison Gray Otis's last and finest house, with 11 bedrooms and an elliptical room behind the front parlor where the walls and doors are curved. The elite Somerset Club stands at Nos. 42–43 Beacon Street. In the 1920s to 1940s, Irish Catholic mayor James Michael Curley would lead election night victory marches to the State House, pausing at the Somerset to taunt the Boston Brahmins within. The Parkman House at No. 33 is now a city-owned meeting center. It was the home of Dr. George Parkman, who was murdered by Harvard professor and fellow socialite Dr. John Webster in 1849. Boston society was torn apart when Webster was sentenced to be hanged.

🏛 William Hickling Prescott House
55 Beacon St. **Tel** (617) 742-3190. ◯ *May–Oct: noon–4pm Wed, Thu, Sat.* 🗓 🚫 🖶

Elegant Federal-style houses on Beacon Street, overlooking Boston Common

Boston Common and Public Garden ❼

Acquired by Boston in 1634 from first settler William Blackstone, the 48-acre (19-ha) Boston Common served for two centuries as common pasture, military drill ground, and gallows site. British troops camped here during the 1775–76 military occupation. As Boston grew in the 19th century, the Boston Common became a center for open-air civic activity and remains so to this day. By contrast, the 24-acre (10-ha) Public Garden is more formal. When the Charles River mudflats were first filled in the 1830s, a succession of landscape plans were plotted for the Public Garden before the city chose the English-style garden scheme of George F. Meacham in 1869. The lagoon was added to the garden two years later.

The Public Garden, a popular green space in the heart of the city

Make Way for Ducklings
Based on the classic children's story by Robert McCloskey, this sculpture is of a duck and her brood of ducklings.

The Ether Monument memorializes the first use of anaesthesia in 1846.

★ George Washington Statue
Cast by Thomas Ball from bronze, with a solid granite base, this is one the finest memorial statues in Boston. It was dedicated in 1869.

CHARLES STREET

Statue of Edward Everett Hale

Lagoon Bridge
This miniature, ornamental bridge over the Public Garden lagoon was designed by William G. Preston in 1869 in a moment of whimsy. The lagoon it "spans" was constructed in 1861.

Statue of Reverend William Ellery Channing

The Swan Boats, originally inspired by Wagner's *Lohengrin,* have been a feature of the Public Garden lake since 1877.

★ Shaw Memorial
This relief immortalizes the Civil War's 54th regiment of Massachusetts Infantry, the first free black regiment in the Union Army, and their white colonel Robert Shaw.

The Soldiers and Sailors Monument, erected in 1877, features prominent Bostonians from the time of the Civil War.

Blackstone Memorial Tablet recalls the purchase of the common in 1634 and is cited as proof that it belongs to the people.

Park Street subway

Brewer Fountain was purchased at the 1867 Paris Expo.

Visitors' Center

Parkman Bandstand
This bandstand was built in 1912 to memorialize George F. Parkman, who bequeathed $5 million for the care of Boston Common and other parks in the city.

Central Burying Ground
This graveyard, which dates from 1756, holds the remains of many British and American casualties from the Battle of Bunker Hill (see p20). The portraitist Gilbert Stuart is also buried here.

The Flagstaff

| 0 meters | 100 |
| 0 yards | 100 |

STAR FEATURES

★ Shaw Memorial

★ George Washington Statue

Park Street Church at the corner of Tremont and Park Streets, near Boston Common

Park Street Church ❽

1 Park St. **Map** 1 C4. **Tel** (617) 523-3383. Ⓣ Park Street. Ⓞ mid-Jun–Aug: 9am–4pm Tue–Fri, 9am–3pm Sat; Sep–mid-Jun: by appointment. Ⓟ Ⓗ **www**.parkstreet.org

Park Street Church's 217-ft (65-m) steeple has punctuated the intersection of Park and Tremont Streets since its dedication in 1810. Designed by English architect Peter Banner, who adapted a design by the earlier English architect Christopher Wren, the church was commissioned by parishioners wanting to establish a Congregational church in the heart of Boston. The church was, and still remains, one of the city's most influential pulpits.

Contrary to popular belief, the sermons of Park Street ministers did not earn the intersection the nickname of "Brimstone Corner." Rather, the name came about during the War of 1812 when the U.S. and Britain were in conflict over British restrictions on trade and freedom of the seas, as well as the U.S.'s ties with Napoleonic France. The U.S. militia, based in Boston, stored its gunpowder in the church basement as safekeeping against bombardment from the British navy, hence the nickname.

Park Street Church later became famous throughout the islands of the Pacific, when in 1819 the church sent a number of Congregational missionaries to carry the Gospel to Pacific islanders from a base in the Hawaiian Islands. In 1829, William Lloyd Garrison (1805–79), a firebrand of the movement to abolish slavery, gave his first abolition speech from the Park Street pulpit, while in 1849 a speech called *The War System of Nations* was addressed to the American Peace Society by Senator Charles Sumner. Much later, in 1893, the anthem *America the Beautiful* by Katharine Lee Bates debuted at a Sunday service. Today the church continues to be involved in religious, political, cultural, and humanitarian activities.

Old Granary Burying Ground ❾

Tremont Street. **Map** 1 C4. Ⓣ Park Street. Ⓞ 9am–5pm daily.

Named after the early colonial grain storage facility that once stood on the adjacent site of Park Street Church, the Granary Burying Ground dates from 1660. Buried here were three important signatories to the Declaration of Independence *(see p21)* – John Hancock, Samuel Adams, and Robert Treat Paine, along with Benjamin Franklin's parents, merchant-philanthropist Peter Faneuil, and some victims of the Boston Massacre.

The orderly array of gravestones, often featured in films and television shows set in Boston, is the result of modern groundskeeping. Few stones, if any, mark the actual burial site of the person memorialized. In fact, John Hancock may not be here at all. On the night he was buried in 1793, grave robbers cut off the hand with which he had signed his name to the Declaration of Independence, and some scholars believe that the rest of the body was later spirited away during 19th-century construction work. Although many heroes of the Revolution are still known to be buried here, Paul Revere, one of Boston's most famous sons, was nearly denied the honor because the cemetery was technically full when he died in 1818. The city made an exception, and he was able to join his comrades in perpetuity.

Old Granary Burying Ground, final resting place for Revolutionary heroes

Stone frieze decoration on the 19th-century, Renaissance Revival-style Athenaeum

Boston Athenaeum ⑩

10½ Beacon St. **Map** 1 C4. **Tel** (617) 227-0270. ⓣ *Park Street.* ☐ *8:30am–5:30pm Mon–Fri (to 8pm Mon & Wed); Sep–May: 9am–4pm Sat.* ☑ www.bostonathenaeum.org

Organized in 1807, the collection of the Boston Athenaeum quickly became one of the country's leading private libraries. Sheep farmer Edward Clarke Cabot won the 1846 design competition to house the library, with plans for a gray sandstone building based on Palladio's Palazzo da Porta Festa in Vicenza, a building Cabot knew from a book in the Athenaeum's collection. The building reopened in fall 2002 after extensive renovations. Among the Athenaeum's major holdings are the personal library that once belonged to George Washington and the theological library supplied by King William III of England to the King's Chapel *(see p58)*. In its early years the Athenaeum was Boston's chief art museum; when the Museum of Fine Arts was proposed, the Athenaeum graciously donated much of its art, including unfinished portraits of George and Martha Washington purchased in 1831 from the widow of the painter Gilbert Stuart. Non-members of the Athenaeum may visit only the first floor of the building, an area that includes the art gallery (with changing exhibitions) and several reading rooms.

Massachusetts State House ⑪

See pp52–3.

Museum of African American History ⑫

46 Joy St. **Map** 1 C3. **Tel** (617) 725-0022. ⓣ *Park Street.* ☐ *10am–4pm Mon–Sat.* ● *public hols.* ☑ ☑ www.afroammuseum.org

Built from town house plans by Asher Benjamin *(see p32)*, using salvaged materials, the African Meeting House was dedicated in 1806 and is the centerpiece of the museum. The U.S.'s oldest black church building, it was the political and religious center of Boston's African American society. Cato Gardner, a native African, raised $1,500 toward the eventual $7,700 to build the church and is honored with an inscription above the entrance. The interior is plain and simple but rang with the oratory of some of the 19th century's most fiery abolitionists: from Sojourner Truth and Frederick Douglass to William Lloyd Garrison *(see p30)*, who founded the New England Anti-Slavery Society in 1832. The meeting house basement was Boston's first school for African American children until the adjacent Abiel Smith School was built in 1831. When segregated education was barred in 1855, however, the Smith School closed. The meeting house became an Hasidic synagogue in the 1890s, as most of Boston's African American community moved to Roxbury and Dorchester. The synagogue closed in the 1960s, and in 1987 the building reopened as the linchpin site on the Black Heritage Trail.

Abiel Smith School, where Boston's free blacks received an education

BLACK HERITAGE TRAIL

Holmes Alley, once an escape route for slaves on the run

In the first U.S. census in 1790, Massachusetts was the only state to record no slaves. During the 19th century, Boston's substantial free African American community lived principally on the north slope of Beacon Hill and in the adjacent West End. The Black Heritage Trail links several key sites, ranging from the African Meeting House to private homes that are not open to visitors. Among them are the 1797 George Middleton House (Nos. 5–7 Pinckney Street), the oldest standing house built by African Americans on Beacon Hill, and the Lewis and Harriet Hayden House (No. 66 Phillips Street). Escaped slaves, the Haydens made their home a haven for runaways in the "Underground Railroad" of safe houses between the South and Canada. The walking tour also leads through mews and alleys, like Holmes Alley at the end of Smith Court, once used by fugitives to flee professional slave catchers.

Free tours of the Black Heritage Trail are led by National Park Service rangers – (617) 742-5415 – from Memorial Day weekend to Labor Day, 10am, noon, and 2pm Monday to Saturday, leaving from the Shaw Memorial. Tours are at 2pm Mon–Sat or by appointment the rest of the year.

Massachusetts State House ⓫

The cornerstone of the Massachusetts State House was laid on July 4, 1795, by Samuel Adams and Paul Revere. Completed on January 11, 1798, the Charles Bulfinch-designed center of state government served as a model for the U.S. Capitol Building in Washington and as an inspiration for many of the state capitols around the country. Later additions were made, but the original building remains the archetype of American government buildings. Its dome, sheathed in copper and gold, serves as the zero mile marker for Massachusetts, making it, as Oliver Wendell Holmes (see p45) remarked, "the hub of the universe."

The State House, from Boston Common

The Great Hall
is the latest addition to the State House. Built in 1990, it is lined with marble and topped by a glass dome, and is used for state functions.

★ House of Representatives
This elegant oval chamber was built for the House of Representatives in 1895. The Sacred Cod, which now hangs over the gallery, came to the State House when it first opened in 1798, and it has since hung over any place where the representatives have met.

Main Staircase
Beautiful stained-glass windows decorate the main staircase. The windows illustrate the many varied state seals of Massachusetts: from its time as a colony through to modern statehood.

STAR SIGHTS

★ Nurses Hall

★ House of Representatives

The wings of the State House, thought by many to sit incongruously with the rest of the structure, were added in 1917.

Hall of Flags

Flags carried into battle by regiments from the state of Massachusetts are housed here. They are displayed beneath a stained-glass skylight depicting seals of the original 13 colonies.

VISITORS' CHECKLIST

Beacon Hill. **Map** 1 C4. **Tel**
(617) 727-3676. Ⓣ Park Street.
🕐 10am–3:30pm Mon–Fri
(reservations recommended). ♿
🖥 www.sec.state.ma.us/trs

Administrative offices can be found on the upper floors of the building.

★ Nurses Hall

This marble hall is lined with murals depicting critical events leading up to the American Revolution. The name derives from the statue of an army nurse here, erected to honor all the nurses who took part in the Civil War.

The dome was sheathed in copper in 1802 to prevent water leakage, and, in 1872, gilded in 23-carat gold.

Entrance

Senate Chamber

Prior to 1895, this was the meeting chamber of the House of Representatives. Situated directly beneath the State House's magnificent dome, the chamber features a beautiful sunburst ceiling, also designed by Charles Bulfinch.

Doric Hall

George Washington is among the historical figures represented here. The center doors of the hall are only ever opened for a state governor at the end of his term or for a visiting head of state.

Flamboyantly decorated dining room of the Otis House Museum

Otis House Museum ⑬

141 Cambridge St. **Map** 1 C3.
Tel (617) 227-3956.
Ⓣ Charles/MGH, Government
Center. ◯ 11am–4:30pm
Wed–Sun. 🎟 💲 🎥
www.historicnewengland.org

Designed by Charles Bulfinch for Harrison Gray Otis, co-developer of Beacon Hill (see pp42–3) and Boston's third mayor, this 1796 town mansion was built to serve the needs of a young man on the way up in Federal Boston. Descended from both British colonial administrators and Boston revolutionary patriots, Otis took a practical view of local government that paved the way for Boston's development as a powerhouse of international trade and finance. Having already made a fortune in the land development of Beacon Hill, Otis commissioned this home as a showpiece, where he could entertain. It was the first of three homes Bulfinch designed for him.

After Otis moved out, the house fell on hard times as the West End neighborhood around it absorbed successive waves of immigration, and tenements replaced single family homes. By the 1830s the Otis house was serving as a ladies' Turkish bath and later became a patent medicine shop before ending up as a boarding house. Historic New England saved the building in 1916 and established its headquarters here. A gallery in the house depicts the time when the building was a boarding house in the 1950s.

Visitors who tour the Otis house, now restored to the way it looked in around 1800, are often surprised by the bright, even gaudy, style of decoration. Although the rooms were initially decorated

Red-brick façade of Asher Benjamin's Old West Church

in the muted Williams-burg Colonial style, subsequent art history detective work revealed that Bostonians had much more flamboyant taste than, for example, the wealthy Virginians. Thus, the house has been restored with touches typical of such upper-class aspirations. The wallpaper in the main entrance has a border of scenes from Pompeii and scores of lithographs showing views of European cities. The colors throughout the rest of the house are bright, and gilt detail flashes from moldings and furniture.

An architectural walking tour of Beacon Hill begins at the Otis House. It runs from May until the end of October.

Old West Church ⑭

131 Cambridge St. **Map** 1 C3.
Tel (617) 227-5088. Ⓣ Charles/
MGH, Bowdoin. ◯ for Sunday
worship. 🔔 11am Sun. 💲 ♿
www.oldwestchurch.org

A wood-frame church built on this site in 1737 was used as a barracks for British soldiers during the occupation of Boston (see pp20–21) in the period just prior to the American Revolution. The British later razed the original church in 1775, since they suspected revolutionary sympathizers of using the steeple to signal Continental Army troops across the Charles River. Many of the church's timbers were used to construct the African Meeting House (see p49). Asher Benjamin (see p32), a protégé of Charles Bulfinch, designed the current red-brick structure, erected in 1806. The swag-ornamented clocks on the sides of the tower are distinctive landmarks, while inside there is a superb Fisk tracker-action pipe organ, This organ is often played in classical organ concerts and in recordings.

Massachusetts General Hospital ⑮

Cambridge & Fruit Sts. **Map** 1 B2.
Tel *(617) 726-8363.* Ⓣ *Charles/MGH.*
◯ *24 hrs daily.* **Bulfinch Pavilion and Ether Dome** ◯ *9am–8pm Mon–Fri.* ♿ ☑ *self-guided tour brochure available at information desk.* **www**.massgeneral.org/vep

The sprawling complex of Massachusetts General Hospital covers the original site of Harvard Medical School, with which it remains affiliated as one of the world's leading teaching and research hospitals. The main hospital building, the George R. White Memorial Building, is a massive Art Deco structure from 1939, largely hidden from Cambridge Street by other buildings. The most interesting structure on the campus is the Bulfinch

Pavilion and Ether Dome, which was Charles Bulfinch's last Boston commission (1818). Alexander Parris, who succeeded Bulfinch as the city's leading architect, was involved in preparing the drawings for this innovative "modern" hospital built of local Chelmsford granite. The operating theater, with seating for observers, is set beneath a skylit dome. In 1846, the use of ether as a surgical general anesthetic was first demonstrated here. A free tour of the hospital is offered at 12:30pm on the third Friday of each month (Jan–Nov, reservations are required).

Charles Bulfinch's Ether Dome, part of the Massachusetts General Hospital

CHARLES BULFINCH

Born in 1763 in Boston, Charles Bulfinch *(see p32)* was among America's first professional architects and one of the most influential. He rose to prominence with his 1795 plan for the Massachusetts State House *(see pp50–51)*, and went on to design many of the neighboring mansions on Beacon Hill. His own forays into real estate development cast him into bankruptcy, but he continued to enjoy the steady patronage of Boston's wealthiest citizens for his elegant yet boldly confident house designs. These patrons also helped him secure many public commissions, including the renovation of St. Stephen's Church in the North End *(see p72)* and the enlargement of Faneuil Hall *(see p63)*. His application of local granite building stone to the Massachusetts General Hospital surgical pavilion laid out principles later followed by Alexander Parris and others as they forged the Boston Granite style of architecture, exemplified by Quincy Market *(see p64)* and Charlestown Navy Yard *(see p115)*. Bulfinch left Boston in 1818 to assume direction of the construction of the U.S. Capitol Building in Washington, DC.

19th-century view of Massachusetts State House from Boston Common

Museum of Science and Science Park ⑯

Science Park. **Map** 1 B2.
Tel *(617) 723-2500.* Ⓣ *Science Park.* ◯ *9am–5pm Mon–Thu & Sat–Sun (Jul–early Sep: 9am–7pm), 9am–9pm Fri.* ● *Thanksgiving, Dec 25.* 🎦 ♿ 🏠 **www**.mos.org

The Museum of Science straddles the Charles River atop the inactive flood control dam that sits at the mouth of the Charles River. The museum itself was built in 1951, but Science Park has taken shape around it since, virtually obscuring the dam structure with theater and planetarium buildings and a massive parking garage.

With more than 550 interactive exhibits covering natural history, medicine, astronomy, and the wonders of the physical sciences, the Science Museum is oriented to families with children. In 1999 the museum absorbed the holdings of Boston's Computer Museum, one of the first of its kind in the world.

The Mugar Omni Theater contains a five-story domed screen with multi-dimensional sound system with wrap-around sound, and shows mostly educational films, usually with a natural science theme. The Charles Hayden Planetarium offers daily shows about stars, planets, and other celestial phenomena.

An extensive array of educational toys can be bought from the museum's shop, while the food court has a number of concessions catering to children's tastes.

OLD BOSTON AND THE FINANCIAL DISTRICT

British Lion, Old State House

This is an area of Boston where old and new sit one on top of the other. Some of its sights, situated in the older part of the district closest to Boston Common, predate the American Revolution *(see pp20–21)*. Much of what can be seen today, though, was built more recently. The north of the district is home to Boston's late 20th-century, modernist-style City Hall and Government Center, while to the east is the city's bustling Financial District. This once formed part of Boston's harbor waterfront, a district built on mercantile wealth. Today, the wharves and warehouses have been replaced by skyscrapers belonging to banks, insurance companies, and high-tech industries.

SIGHTS AT A GLANCE

Historic Streets and Squares
Blackstone Block ❿
Post Office Square ⓮

Historic Buildings and Churches
Boston City Hall ❽
Center Plaza ❼
Custom House ⓭
Faneuil Hall ⓫
Government Center ❾
King's Chapel and Burying Ground ❷
New England Telephone Building ⓯
Old City Hall ❸
Old Corner Bookstore ❹
Old South Meeting House ❺
Old State House pp60–61 ❻
Omni Parker House ❶
Quincy Market ⓬

0 meters 300
0 yards 300

KEY

▢ Street-by-street map *pp56–7*

Ⓣ "T" station

ℹ Tourist information

GETTING THERE

This area is well served by public transportation. Bowdoin, Government Center, State, and Haymarket "T" stations are located at the heart of the district. The area is also served by buses 6, 7, 92, 93, 352, 353, 354, and 355.

◁ **Custom House, Boston's original skyscraper and one of the most distinctive buildings on the city skyline**

Street-by-Street: Colonial Boston

An important part of Boston's Freedom Trail
(*see pp124–7*) runs through this historic
core of the city, the site of which predates
American Independence. Naturally, the area
is now dominated by 19th- and 20th-century
development, but glimpses of a colonial past
are prevalent here and there in the Old State
House, King's Chapel and its adjacent burying
ground, and the Old South Meeting House.
Newer buildings of interest include the Omni
Parker House, as well as the towering
skyscrapers of Boston's financial district,
located on the northwest edges of this area.

**Irish Famine memorial,
Washington Street**

Government
Center

★ King's Chapel
and Burying Ground

*A church has stood
here since 1688,
though the current
building dates from
1749. The adjacent
cemetery is the resting
place of some of the
most important figures
in U.S. history* ❷

SCHOOL STREET

PROVINCE STREET

Omni Parker House
*This hotel (see p133) first opened
its doors in 1855, then underwent many renovations. Famed
for its opulence, in the 19th
century the hotel also gained a
reputation as a meeting place for
Boston intellectuals. The current
building was erected in 1927* ❶

| 0 meters | 50 |
| 0 yards | 50 |

STAR SIGHTS

★ Old South
Meeting House

★ Old State House

★ King's Chapel and
Burying Ground

Old City Hall
*This building served
as Boston's City Hall from
1865 to 1969. Today it
houses a steak house* ❸

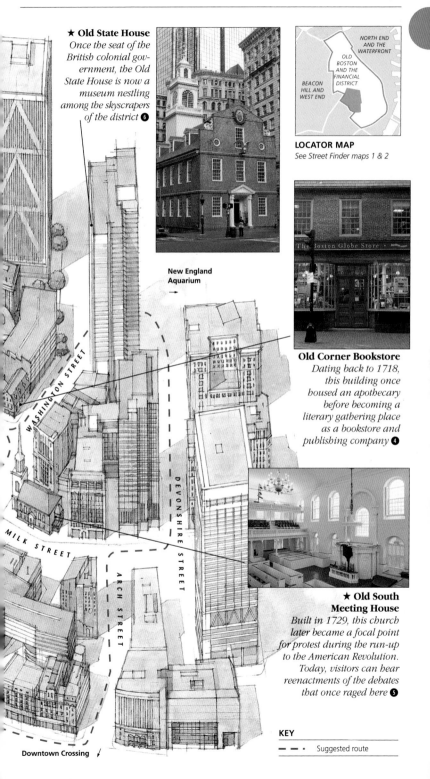

★ **Old State House**
Once the seat of the British colonial government, the Old State House is now a museum nestling among the skyscrapers of the district ❻

LOCATOR MAP
See Street Finder maps 1 & 2

NORTH END AND THE WATERFRONT

OLD BOSTON AND THE FINANCIAL DISTRICT

BEACON HILL AND WEST END

New England Aquarium →

WASHINGTON STREET

DEVONSHIRE STREET

MILK STREET

ARCH STREET

Old Corner Bookstore
Dating back to 1718, this building once housed an apothecary before becoming a literary gathering place as a bookstore and publishing company ❹

★ **Old South Meeting House**
Built in 1729, this church later became a focal point for protest during the run-up to the American Revolution. Today, visitors can hear reenactments of the debates that once raged here ❺

Downtown Crossing ↙

KEY

– – – · Suggested route

Omni Parker House ❶

60 School St. **Map** 1 C4.
Tel (617) 227-8600. Ⓣ Park
Street, State, Government Center.
www.omnihotels.com

Harvey D. Parker, raised on a farm in Maine, became so successful as the proprietor of his Boston restaurant that he achieved his ambition of expanding the property into a first-class, grand hotel. His Parker House opened in 1855, with a façade clad in white marble, standing five stories high, and featuring the first passenger elevator ever seen in Boston. It underwent several, rapid transformations during its early years, with additions made to the main structure in the 1860s and a 10-story, French chateau-style annex completed later that century. The building saw many successive transformations, and its latest 14-story incarnation has stood across from King's Chapel on School Street since 1927.

This hotel attained an instant reputation for luxurious accommodations and fine, even lavish, dining, typified by 11-course menus prepared by a French chef.

Among Parker House's many claims to fame are its Boston Cream Pie, which was first created here, and the word "scrod," a uniquely Bostonian term for the day's freshest seafood, still in common usage. Two former Parker House employees later became recognized for quite different careers. Vietnamese revolutionary leader Ho Chi Minh worked in the hotel's kitchens around 1915, while black activist Malcolm X was a busboy in Parker's Restaurant in the 1940s.

Simply decorated, pure white interior of King's Chapel on Tremont Street

King's Chapel and Burying Ground ❷

58 Tremont St. **Map** 1 C4.
Tel (617) 523-1749. Ⓣ Park Street,
State, Government Center. ▢
late May–mid-Sep: 10am–4pm Mon,
Thu, Fri, Sat, 10am–11:15am &
1:30pm–4pm Tue & Wed, 1:30pm–
4pm Sun; mid-Sep–late May: call for
opening hours. Hours subject to
change during ongoing restoration.
Music Recitals 12:15pm Tue.
✚ 11am Sun, 12:15pm Wed.
www.kings-chapel.org

British crown officials were among those who attended Anglican services at the first chapel on this site, which was built in 1688. When New England's governor decided a larger church was needed, the present granite edifice – begun in 1749 – was constructed around the original wooden chapel, which was dismantled and heaved out the windows of its replacement. After the Revolution, the congregation's religious allegiance switched from Anglican to Unitarian. The sanctuary's raised pulpit – dating from 1717 and shaped like a wine glass – is one of the oldest in the U.S. High ceilings, open arches, and clear glass windows enhance the sense of spaciousness and light. The bell inside the King's Chapel is the largest ever cast by Paul Revere (see p21).

The adjacent cemetery is the oldest in Boston.

PARKER HOUSE GUESTS

Boston's reputation as the "Athens of America" was widely acknowledged when members of a distinguished social club began meeting for lengthy dinners and lively intellectual exchanges in 1857. Their get-togethers took place on the last Saturday of every month at Harvey Parker's fancy hotel. Regular participants included New England's literary elite (see pp30–31): Henry Wadsworth Longfellow, Ralph Waldo Emerson, Nathaniel Hawthorne, and Henry David Thoreau, to name a few. Charles

John Wilkes Booth, infamous Parker House guest

Dickens participated while staying at the Parker House during his American speaking tours, and used his sitting-room mirror to rehearse the public readings he gave at Tremont Temple next door. The mirror now hangs on a mezzanine wall. In 1865, actor John Wilkes Booth, in town to see his brother, a fellow thespian, stayed at the hotel and took target practice at a nearby shooting gallery. Ten days later, at Ford's Theatre in Washington, he pulled a pistol and shot Abraham Lincoln.

Old City Hall ❸

45 School St. **Map** 2 D4.
Ⓣ *Park Street, State, Government Center.*

A fine example of French Second Empire architectural gaudiness, this was Boston's City Hall from 1865 to 1969 – it was superseded by the rakishly modern New City Hall structure at nearby Government Center *(see p62)*. The renovated 19th-century building now features a steak house.

Previous occupants have included such flamboyant mayors as Honey "Fitz" Fitzgerald *(see p25)* and James Michael Curley. Statues here memorialize Josiah Quincy, Boston's second mayor and after whom Quincy Market is named, as well as Benjamin Franklin, who was born on nearby Milk Street.

19th-century French-style façade of Boston's Old City Hall

Old Corner Bookstore ❹

1 School St. **Map** 2 D4. Ⓣ *Park Street, State, Government Center.*

A dormered gambrel roof crowns this brick landmark, which opened as Thomas Crease's apothecary shop in 1718 and was reestablished as the Old Corner Bookstore in 1829. Moving in 16 years later, the Ticknor & Fields publishing company became a gathering place for a notable roster of authors:

Emerson, Hawthorne, Longfellow, Thoreau, early feminist writer Margaret Fuller, and *Uncle Tom's Cabin* novelist Harriet Beecher Stowe. The firm is often credited with carving out the first distinctively American literature. The earliest editions of the erudite *Atlantic Monthly* periodical were also printed here under editor James Russell Lowell, before he handed the reins over to William Dean Howells. Julia Ward Howe's rousing tribute to American Civil War bravado, *The Battle Hymn of the Republic*, first appeared in the *Atlantic*'s February 1862 issue. Although no publishing activities take place here, the Old Corner Bookstore remains a touchstone of American literary history.

The Old Corner Bookstore, considered by some to be the cradle of American literature

Old South Meeting House ❺

310 Washington St. **Map** 2 D4.
***Tel** (617) 482-6439.* Ⓣ *Park Street, State, Government Center.* ☐ *Apr–Oct: 9:30am–5pm daily; Nov–Mar: 10am–4pm daily.* 🖼 🚫 🏧 👤 📷
www.oldsouthmeetinghouse.org

Built in 1729 for Puritan religious services, this edifice, with a tall octagonal steeple, had colonial Boston's biggest capacity for town meetings – a fact capitalized upon by a group of rebellious rabble-rousers calling themselves the Sons of Liberty *(see p20)*. Their outbursts against British taxation and other royal annoyances drew increasingly large and vociferous crowds to the pews and upstairs galleries.

During a candlelit protest rally on December 16 1773, fiery speechmaker Samuel Adams flashed the signal that led to the Boston Tea Party *(see p75)* down at Griffin's Wharf several hours later. The British retaliated by turning Old South into an officers' tavern and stable for General John Burgoyne's 17th Lighthorse Regiment of Dragoons. In 1877, the budding Historic Preservation Movement saved the building from destruction and created a museum. Displays, exhibits, and a multimedia presentation entitled *Voices of Protest* relive those raucous days as well as more recent occurrences well into the 20th century. The Meeting House offers a series of lectures covering a wide range of New England topics and also holds chamber music concerts and other musical performances.

There is a shop downstairs containing a broad selection of merchandise, which includes the ubiquitous tins of "Boston Tea Party" tea.

Directly across Washington Street, sculptor Robert Shure's memorial to the 1845–49 Irish Potato Famine was added to the small plaza here in 1998.

Old South Meeting House, in stark contrast to the modern city

Old State House ❻

Dwarfed by the towers of the Financial District, this was the seat of British colonial government between 1713 and 1776. The royal lion and unicorn still decorate each corner of the eastern façade. After independence, the Massachusetts legislature took possession of the building, and it has had many uses since, including produce market, merchants' exchange, Masonic lodge, and Boston City Hall. Its wine cellars now function as a downtown subway station. The Old State House houses two floors of Bostonian Society memorabilia and a sound and light show about the Boston Massacre *(see p20)*.

Old State House amid the sky-scrapers of the Financial District

A gold sculpture of an eagle, symbol of America, can be seen on the west façade.

West Façade
A Latin inscription, relating to the first Massachusetts Bay colony, runs around the outside of this crest. The relief in the center depicts a local Native American.

Entrance

Keayne Hall
This is named after Robert Keayne who, in 1658, gave £300 to the city so that the Town House, predating the Old State House, could be built. Exhibits in the room depict events from the Revolution.

★ Central Staircase
A fine example of 18th-century workmanship, the central spiral staircase has two beautifully crafted wooden handrails. It is one of the few such staircases still in existence in the U.S.

SITE OF THE BOSTON MASSACRE

A circle of cobblestones below the balcony on the eastern façade of the Old State House marks the site of the Boston Massacre *(see pp20–21)*. After the Boston Tea Party *(see p75)*, this was one of the most inflammatory events leading up to the American Revolution.

Cobbled circle: site of the Boston Massacre On March 5, 1770, an unruly mob of colonists taunted British guardsmen with insults, rocks, and snowballs. The soldiers opened fire, killing five colonists. A number of articles relating to the Boston Massacre are exhibited inside the Old State House, including a musket found near the site and a coroner's report detailing the incident.

VISITORS' CHECKLIST

Washington & State Sts. **Map** 2 D4. **Tel** (617) 720-1713. ⓣ *State.* ◷ *9am–5pm daily (to 4pm Jan, 6pm Jul–Aug).* ● *Jan 1, Thanksgiving, Dec 25.* ⬚ ⬚ ⬚ ⬚

The tower is a classic example of Colonial style. In 18th-century paintings and engravings it can be seen clearly above the Boston skyline.

British Unicorn and Lion
A royal symbol of Britain, the original lion and unicorn were pulled down when news of the Declaration of Independence reached Boston in 1776.

★ **East Façade**
This façade has seen many changes. An earlier clock from the 1820s was removed in 1957 and replaced with an 18th-century replica of the sundial that once hung here. The clock has now been reinstated.

Council Chamber
Once the chambers for the royal governors, and from 1780 chambers for the first governor of Massachusetts (John Hancock), this room has seen many key events. Among them were numerous impassioned speeches made by Boston patriots.

The Declaration of Independence was read from this balcony in 1776. In the 1830s, when the building was City Hall, the balcony was enlarged to two tiers.

STAR SIGHTS

★ East Façade

★ Central Staircase

Center Plaza **❼**

Cambridge St. **Map** 1 C3.
Ⓣ *Government Center.*

Downtown's old, irregular street pattern has given rise to some unusual buildings, including the Center Plaza, which was designed in the mid-1960s by Welton Beckett & Associates. It was designed specifically to follow the long curve of the existing Cambridge Street, and the low-slung office complex is often referred to as a "skyscraper laid sideways." Shops and restaurants run at street level along Center Plaza's sidewalk arcade, on the Government Center side, while the plaza behind incorporates some much older city center buildings.

Curved, Modernist structure of Center Plaza, on Cambridge Street

Boston City Hall **❽**

City Hall Plaza. **Map** 2 D3.
Tel *(617) 635-4000.* Ⓣ *Government Center.* ◯ *9am–5pm Mon–Fri.* ♿
www.ci.boston.ma.us

The firm of architects Kallmann, McKinnell & Knowles won a nationwide design competition for their striking city hall, a seemingly top-heavy, cantilevered, Modernist building. Completed in 1968, the concrete-and-brick City Hall combines the offices and services of municipal government, with ample space for holiday-season concerts, school band and glee-club performances, and community art exhibits. An outdoor stage on City Hall's north side is often the venue for evening rock and pop concerts during the summer months.

Old-fashioned flower stall on the sidewalk outside Center Plaza

Government Center **❾**

Cambridge, Court, New Sudbury & Congress Sts. **Map** 2 D3.
Ⓣ *Government Center.*

This city center development was built on the site of what was once Scollay Square, demolished as part of the fad for local urban renewal that began in the early 1960s. Some viewed the development as controversial; others did not lament what was essentially a disreputable cluster of saloons, burlesque theaters, tattoo parlors, and scruffy hotels. The overall master plan for Government Center was inspired by the alfresco vitality and spaciousness of Italian piazzas. Architects I.M. Pei & Partners re-created some of this feeling by surrounding Boston's new City Hall with a vast terraced plaza covering 56 acres (23 ha), paved with 1,800,000 bricks. Its spaciousness makes it an ideal venue for events such as skateboard contests, political and sports rallies, food fairs, patriotic military marches, and concerts. The Cambridge Street side accommodates a farmers' market on Mondays and Wednesdays from around the middle of May to the middle of November.

A remnant of old Boston hangs from the Sears Block at City Hall Plaza's Court Street perimeter. This gilded, 227-gallon *Steaming Tea Kettle* was made for the Oriental Tea Company by a firm of coppersmiths in 1873. Near New Sudbury Street, the John F. Kennedy Federal Office Building features two pieces of abstract art: Dmitry Hadzi's 15-ft (4.5-m) high *Thermopylae* sculpture, and Robert Motherwell's *New England Elegy*, a mural recalling the tragic assassination of President Kennedy in Dallas in 1963. A memorial standing in front of the building marks the site of Alexander Graham Bell's first significant breakthrough toward his invention of the "electrical speech machine" in 1876 *(see p65)*.

Boston City Hall and Government Center, one of Boston's main focal points

Blackstone Block ⑩

Union, Hanover, North & Blackstone Sts. **Map** 2 D3. Ⓣ *Government Center, Haymarket.*

Cobblestones pave Boston's only surviving web of 17th-century lanes and alleyways, a remnant of what was once the oldest neighborhood in Boston, with historical associations dating back to the colonial period. The district's most famous son, Benjamin Franklin, grew up near Union and Hanover Streets, where his father owned a candleworks. Prior to the landfill programs that expanded the city, the block was close to the water's edge, a fact suggested by the names of the streets in this small district: Marsh Lane, Creek Square, and Salt Lane.

The oldest surviving building in the Blackstone Block dates from 1714 – the Duke of Chartres, later to be crowned France's King Louis Philippe, was a guest here in 1798 and gave French lessons to support himself while waiting for funds. Since 1826 the building has housed the Union Oyster House *(see p143)*, renowned for its original mahogany raw oyster bar, its political clientele, including Congressman John F. Kennedy, and of course its oysters.

The Millennium Bostonian Hotel can also be found here, wedged among the Blackstone Block's twisting street pattern, while on afternoons on Fridays and all day on Saturdays vendors sell fruit, vegetables, and fish from stands along Blackstone, Hanover, and North Streets. Across Union Street is the New England Holocaust Memorial, dedicated in 1995 to the Jewish victims of World War II. Designed as a sculpture that the public can walk through, to do so is a surreal, justly disquieting experience.

Liberty and Union, Now and Forever by George Healy, Faneuil Hall

Faneuil Hall ⑪

Dock Sq. **Map** 2 D3. *Tel* No phone. Ⓣ *Government Center, Haymarket, State.* **Great Hall** ◷ *9am–5pm daily (may close for special events).* ♿ 🎥 🎧 **www.**nps.gov/bost

A gift to Boston from the wealthy merchant Peter Faneuil in 1742, this Georgian, brick landmark has always functioned simultaneously as a public market and town meeting place. Master tinsmith Shem Drowne modeled the building's grasshopper weathervane after the one on top of the Royal Exchange in the City of London, England. Revolutionary gatherings packed the hall, and as early as 1763 Samuel Adams used the hall as a platform to suggest that the American colonies

should unite against British oppression and fight to establish their independence *(see pp20–21)*; hence the building's nickname "Cradle of Liberty" and the bold posture of the statue of Sam Adams at the front of the building.

Toward the end of the 18th century it became apparent that the existing Faneuil Hall could no longer house the capacity crowds that it regularly attracted. The commission to expand the building was undertaken by Charles Bulfinch *(see p53)*, who completed the work from 1805 to 1806. The building then remained unchanged until 1898, when it was expanded still farther according to long-standing Bulfinch stipulations. Faneuil Hall was restored in the 1970s as part of the wider redevelopment of Quincy Market *(see p64)*.

Sam Adams statue, in front of Faneuil Hall

Among the paintings upstairs in the Neoclassical Great Hall is George Healy's enormous canvas, *Liberty and Union, Now and Forever*, showing Massachusetts Senator Daniel Webster in full oratorical passion. The uppermost floor contains the headquarters and armory of the Ancient and Honorable Artillery Company, chartered in 1638 for defense of the Massachusetts Bay Colony and an occupant of Faneuil Hall since 1746. Displays include weapons, commendations, and medals.

The Union Oyster House, one of Boston's most famous restaurants, Blackstone Block

Gallery of the Greek Revival main dome in Quincy Market's central hall

Quincy Market ⑫

Between Chatham & Clinton Sts.
Map 2 D3. **Tel** (617) 523-1300. ⓣ
Government Center, State. ◻ *10am–*
10pm Mon–Sat, noon–6pm Sun. ⓰
www.faneuilhallmarketplace.com

This immensely popular shopping and dining complex attracts in the region of 14 million people every year, and was developed from the buildings of the former Faneuil Hall produce and meat market, or Quincy Market. These buildings had fallen into disrepair before they underwent a widely acclaimed restoration by the architects Benjamin Thompson & Associates in the 1970s. The imposing centerpiece, a granite Greek Revival structure *(see p32)* dating from 1825, was planned as an extension to the first Faneuil Hall Markets, which had become overstretched by Boston's rapid development. Originally called the New Faneuil Hall Market, the building came to be known as Quincy Market after the mayor, Josiah Quincy, whose original vision was responsible for the new market's creation. The façade's four Doric columns were, at the time of construction, the largest single pieces of granite ever to be quarried in the U.S. The 535-ft (163-m) long colonnaded hall is now filled with fast food stalls and a comedy nightclub, located in the spectacular Rotunda. Completing the ensemble are twin North and South Market buildings – these individual warehouses have been refurbished to accommodate boutiques, restaurants, pubs, stores, and upstairs offices.

Custom House ⑬

3 McKinley Square. **Map** 2 E3.
Tel (617) 310-6300. ⓣ *Aquarium.*
Museum ◻ 8am–9pm daily.
Tower ◻ 2pm Sat–Thu. ⓰
www.marriott.com

Before landfill altered downtown topography, early Boston's Custom House perched at the water's edge. A temple-like Greek Revival structure with fluted Doric columns, the granite building had a skylit dome upon completion in 1847. Since 1915, however, it has supported an anachronistic tower rising 495 ft (150 m), which means that for the best part of the 20th century, the Custom House was Boston's only bona fide skyscraper. Four sculpted eagles and a four-sided illuminated clock add decorative flourishes. The public has free access to a small museum of maritime history in the 19th-century rotunda. It displays objects on loan from the Peabody Museum in Salem, including maritime paintings, nautical instruments, items that depict Boston's trade with China, and several pieces of decorative art. The observatory, which offers panoramic views, is also open to the public. The rest of the building, occupied by a Marriott hotel and timeshare apartments, is not open to the public.

Glass fountain on the Pearl Street side of Post Office Square

Post Office Square ⑭

Between Congress & Pearl Sts.
Map 2 D4. ⓣ *State, Aquarium.*

This beautifully landscaped park, a small island of green situated amid the soaring skyscrapers of the financial district, replaced an ugly concrete garage that once stood here – it was demolished and rebuilt as an underground parking facility in 1990. Vines climb a 143-ft (44-m) long trellis along one side of the park, and a fountain made of green glass cascades on the square's Pearl Street side. On Angell Memorial Plaza across the road, a fountain dating from 1912 commemorates George Thorndike Angell, founder of the Massachusetts' Society

Greek Revival Custom House tower, one of Boston's most striking sights

ALEXANDER GRAHAM BELL (1847–1922)

A native of Edinburgh, Scotland, and son of a deaf mother, Bell moved to Boston in 1871 to embark on a career of teaching speech to the deaf. It led to his appointment, two years later, as professor of vocal physiology at Boston University. In a rented fifth-floor garret assisted by young repair mechanic and model maker Thomas Watson, Bell worked in his spare time on an apparatus for transmitting sound by electrical current. Initial success came on June 3, 1875, when the barely intelligible utterings of a human voice (his own) traveled over a laboratory wire. History was made on March 17, 1876, when Bell, while experimenting on voice transmission, upset a battery, spilling acid on his clothing. He called to another room: "Mr. Watson, come here. I want you." With each of those seven words reaching Watson clearly and distinctly, the "electrical speech machine" was invented. In August that year, Bell proved its practical value by sending messages over Canadian telegraph wires. By 1878, he had set up the first public telephone exchange in New Haven, Connecticut. Six years later, long-distance calls were being made between Boston and New York City.

Distinctive, Art Deco-style New England Telephone Building

New England Telephone Building ⓯

185 Franklin St. **Map** 2 D4. **Tel** *(617) 743-9340.* Ⓣ *State, Aquarium.* **Museum** ◯ *call for hours.* ♿

for the Prevention of Cruelty to Animals. Some of the most important buildings overlooking the square and plaza include the New England Telephone Building and the John W. McCormack courthouse building, which formerly housed downtown's main post office. Other important buildings include the Langham Boston hotel *(see p133)* – this classic Renaissance Revival showpiece was completed in 1922 and was originally the Federal Reserve Bank – and One Post Office Square, which offers great views over Boston Harbor and Downtown. These views can be seen from the atrium at the top of the building, which, not strictly open to the public, may be accessible through polite inquiry. A focal point for the whole district, the grassy space of the square comes into its own during the warmer months of the year, when office workers can be seen sprawling across its well-kept lawns – a great place for visitors to rest their weary feet and watch Bostonians take a few minutes out.

Dating from 1947 and overlooking the south side of Post Office Square, this Art Deco building is still in use today. Dean Cornwell's monumental 160-ft (49-m) long *Telephone Men and Women at Work* mural – populated by 197 life-size figures – has encircled the lobby since 1951 and is a truly remarkable work of art. Public access to the lobby can be limited, be sure to phone ahead.

The small museum at street level features an accurate restoration of Alexander Graham Bell's Court Street laboratory *(see p31)*, complete with his tools, books, actual workbench, and one of his garret window-frames overlooking a diorama of Scollay Square. The exhibit was constructed from parts of Bell's original workshop. It was opened on June 3, 1959, coincidentally the 84th anniversary of the invention of the telephone. The world's first commercial telephone and first telephone switchboard, both dating from May 1877, are also displayed in the museum.

Telephone Men and Women at Work, New England Telephone Building

NORTH END AND THE WATERFRONT

This was Boston's first neighborhood, and one that has been key to the city's fortunes. Fringed by numerous wharves, the area prospered initially through shipping and shipbuilding, with much of America's early trade passing through its warehouses. The more recent importance of finance and high-tech industries, however, has seen the waterfront evolve; its

Statue in Old North Church garden

old warehouses transformed into luxury apartment blocks and offices. Away from the waterfront, the narrow streets of the North End have historically been home to European immigrants, drawn by the availability of work. The area today is populated largely by those of Italian descent, whose many cafés, delis, and restaurants make it one of the city's most distinct communities.

SIGHTS AT A GLANCE

Historic Sites and Churches
Clough House ❷
Copp's Hill Burying Ground ❶
Old North Church p71 ❸
Paul Revere House ❻
Paul Revere Mall ❹
St. Stephen's Church ❺

Waterfront Sights
Boston Tea Party Ships
& Museum ⓬
Children's Museum ⓭
Christopher Columbus
Park ❼
Institute of
Contemporary Art ⓫
Long Wharf ❽
*New England Aquarium
pp76–7* ❾
Rowes Wharf ❿

0 meters 450
0 yards 450

KEY

▦ Street-by-street map *pp68–9*

Ⓣ "T" station

🚌 Bus station

GETTING THERE
This area is well served by public transportation. Aquarium "T" station is located toward the south of the area, near Long Wharf. The area is also served by buses 6, 92, 93, and 111.

◁ **Institute of Contemporary Art, with the Financial District in the background**

Street-by-Street: North End

Old North Church clock

The main arteries of this area are Hanover and Salem Streets. Topped by the Old North Church, Salem Street is indicative of this area's historical connections – indeed the Old North Church is one of Boston's premier Revolutionary sights. In general the area consists of narrow streets and alleys, with four- and five-story tenements, many of which are now expensive condominiums. Hanover Street, like much of the area, has a distinctly Italian feel, while just south of here is North Square, site of the famous Paul Revere House *(see p73)*.

Clough House
Period furnishings can be seen in this house by Ebenezer Clough, who also helped build the Old North Church ❷

Copp's Hill Burying Ground
During the American Revolution, the British used this low hilltop to fire cannon at American positions across Boston Harbor. Created in 1659 it is the city's second oldest graveyard ❶

★ Old North Church
Built in 1723 and famous for the part it played in Paul Revere's midnight ride (see p21), this is Boston's oldest religious building. On festive occasions, the North End still rings with the sound of its bells ❸

KEY

– – – Suggested route

STAR SIGHTS

★ Old North Church

★ Paul Revere House

★ Paul Revere Mall

Charlestown

Government Center

0 meters   50

0 yards   50

★ Paul Revere Mall
Linking the Old North Church to Hanover Street, this tree-lined mall dates only from 1933. Its antique feel is enhanced by a statue of Paul Revere, which was modeled in 1885 ❹

LOCATOR MAP
See Street Finder map 2

St. Stephen's Church
North End's Italian theme continues in this church, though only by chance. Long before the first Italians arrived, Charles Bulfinch (see p53) incorporated Italian Renaissance features and a bell tower into his refit of an earlier church building ❺

Hanover Street is the most Italian of all Boston's streets, brought to life by Italian restaurants and cafés, as well as the day-to-day activities of its ethnic community.

↘ **The waterfront**

★ Paul Revere House
This is the house where Paul Revere began his midnight ride (see p21). Revere's home from 1770 to 1800, it is now a museum ❻

UNITY STREET

LESTON STREET

REET

HANOVER STREET

CLARK STREET

FLEET STREET

MOON STREET

GARDEN COURT

Slate tombstones of Boston's early settlers, Copp's Hill Burying Ground

Copp's Hill Burying Ground ❶

Entrances at Charter & Hull Sts. **Map** 2 D2. Ⓣ *Government Center, North Station.* Ⓞ *9am–5pm daily.*

Existing since 1659, this is Boston's second-oldest cemetery after the one by King's Chapel *(see p58)*. Nicknamed "Corpse Hill," the real name of the hill occupied by the cemetery derives from a local man by the name of William Copp. He owned a farm on its southeastern slope from 1643, and much of the cemetery's land was purchased from him. His children can be found buried here. Other more famous

people interred here include Robert Newman, the sexton who hung Paul Revere's signal lanterns in the belfry of Old North Church *(see p71)*, and Edmund Hartt, builder of the *U.S.S. Constitution (see p115)*. Increase, Cotton, and Samuel Mather, three generations of a family of highly influential colonial period Puritan ministers, are also buried here. Hundreds of Boston's Colonial-era black slaves and freedmen are also buried here, including Prince Hall, a free black man who founded the African Freemasonry Order in Massachusetts.

During the British occupation of Boston, the site was used by British commanders who had an artillery position here. They would later exploit the prominent hilltop location during the Revolution, when they directed cannon fire from here across Boston harbor toward American positions in Charlestown. King George III's troops were said to have used the slate headstones for target practice, and pockmarks from their musket balls are still visible on some of them.

Copp's Hill Terrace, directly across Charter Street, is a prime observation point for

Decorative column, Copp's Hill

Quiet, leafy street, typical of the area around Copp's Hill

views over to Charlestown and Bunker Hill. It is also the site where, in 1919, a 2.3-million-gallon molasses tank exploded, creating a huge, syrupy tidal wave that killed 21 people.

Clough House ❷

21 Unity St. **Map** 2 E2. **Tel** *(617) 523-6676.* Ⓣ *Haymarket, Aquarium.* Ⓞ *Jun: Wed (call for opening hours).*

Ebenezer Clough was a master mason and one of the Sons of Liberty who participated in the Boston Tea Party *(see p75)*. One of two masons who helped to build the neighboring Old North Church *(see p71)*, he was also the head of a syndicate that laid out Unity Street in 1710 and built a series of six town houses here. The only building to survive is the one at No. 21 Unity Street, which was built in 1712, and was the house in which Ebenezer Clough himself lived. In a bad state of decay for many years, and in danger of demolition, the house was only saved when the Reverend P. Kellet, vicar of Christ Church, launched a fund-raising campaign in 1962. A rather austere three-story building, it is typical of much of Boston's colonial architecture. Now fully restored to its former condition, the house has finely executed window and door lintels, decorated with raised brick panels over the first-floor windows and simple, carved-brick detailing over the door. The Heritage Room on the second floor features typical period furnishings and household accessories.

Clough House once stood alongside an identical brick residence, which was acquired by Benjamin Franklin in 1748. He bought the house for his two widowed sisters but never lived here himself. It was demolished in the 1930s to make way for the Paul Revere Mall *(see p72)*.

Old North Church™ ❸

Christ Episcopal Church is the official name of this, Boston's oldest surviving religious edifice, which dates from 1723. It was built of brick in the Georgian style similar to that of St. Andrew's-by-the-Wardrobe in Blackfriars, London, designed by Sir Christopher Wren. The church was made famous on April 18, 1775, when sexton Robert Newman, aiding Paul Revere *(see p21)*, hung a pair of signal lanterns in the belfry. These were to warn the patriots in Charlestown of the westward departure of British troops, on their way to engage the revolutionaries.

★ **Box Pews**
The unusual, high-sided box pews in the church were designed to enclose footwarmers, which were filled with hot coals or bricks during wintry weather.

Tower
The tower of the Old North Church contains the first set of church bells in North America cast in 1745.

Chandeliers
The distinctive chandeliers were brought from England in January 1724 for the first Christmas season.

Entrance

STAR SIGHTS

★ Bust of George Washington

★ Box Pews

★ **Bust of George Washington**
This marble bust of the first U.S. president, modeled on an earlier one by Christian Gullager, was presented to the church in 1815.

Paul Revere Mall ❹

Hanover St. **Map** 2 E2.
Ⓣ *Haymarket, Aquarium.* ♿

This brick-paved plaza gives
the crowded neighborhood of
the North End a precious
stretch of open space
between Hanover and Unity
Streets. A well-utilized
municipal resource, the Mall
is always full of local people:
children, teenagers, young
mothers, and older residents
chatting in Italian and playing
cards or checkers. Laid out in
1933, and originally called the
Prado, its focal point is Cyrus
Dallin's equestrian statue of
local hero Paul Revere, which
was originally modeled in
1885. However, it was only
sculpted and
placed here in
1940. Bronze bas-
relief plaques on
the mall's side
walls commem-
orate a number
of North End
residents who
have played
an important

**Equestrian statue by Cyrus
Dallin, Paul Revere Mall**

role in the history of Boston.
Benches, a fountain, and twin
rows of linden trees complete
the space, which has a
distinctly European feel.

St. Stephen's Church ❺

401 Hanover St. **Map** 2 E2.
Tel *(617) 523-1230.* Ⓣ *Haymarket,
Aquarium.* ◻ *8:30am–4:30pm
Mon–Sat.* ✝ *11am Sun, 4:30pm
Sat, 7:30am Tue–Fri.*

Opened in 1714 as a
humble Congregationalist
meeting house, St. Stephen's
Church was extensively
enlarged and embellished by
the architect Charles Bulfinch
(see p53) in 1802–04.
Bulfinch incorporated
a range of harmonious
Italian Renaissance
motifs in his re-
design, adding a
number of decor-
ative pediments
and pedestals,
tall arched
windows,
as well as

**St. Stephen's Church, with its
Renaissance-style bell tower**

an ornate bell tower that is
topped by a gilded cap. One
year after that project's completion, the first-ever bell
cast by the famous revolutionary and master metalworker,
Paul Revere *(see p21)*, was
hung in the belfry.
 The church's present name
dates from 1862, when it
became Roman Catholic to
accommodate the North End's
increasing numbers of Irish
immigrants. When Hanover
Street was widened in 1869,
the entire structure was
moved back 16 ft (5 m) and,
a year later, it was raised 6 ft
(2 m) to accommodate a
basement chapel. Damaged
by fires in 1897 and 1929,
and redecorated each time,
the church was restored to
its Bulfinch design in 1965.
 The church's interior features
include a gracefully curved
ceiling, original white-painted
pine columns, and a pair of
pewter chandeliers, which are
copies of those hanging in the
Doric Hall of the Massachusetts
State House. The church's
pews were donated in honor
of the numerous Irish, Italian,
and Portuguese parishioners
who live in the neighborhood,
while the Italian mahogany
Stations of the Cross are part
of the 1965 refit. St. Stephen's
is listed on the National
Register of Historic Places.

THE GREAT BRINKS ROBBERY

Masterminded by Tony Pino, this infamous event took
place on the night of January 17, 1950 on North End's
Commercial Street. Disguised as Brinks guards, seven of
Pino's men made off with $2,775,395.12 in payroll money –
including cash totaling $1,218,211.29 – from the head-
quarters of the Brinks Armored Car Company. Nationwide
headlines trumpeted the robbery as the biggest heist in U.S.
history. Even though all members of the Brinks gang were
eventually caught and imprisoned, only $60,000 of the loot
has been recovered more than half a century after the event.

Members of the infamous Brinks gang, in police custody

Paul Revere House **6**

19 North Sq. **Map** 2 E2. **Tel** (617)
523-2338. Ⓣ Haymarket, Aquarium.
▢ mid-Apr–Oct: 9:30am–5:15pm
daily; Nov–mid-Apr: 9:30am–4:15pm
daily (Pierce-Hichborn House call for
tour hours). ◖ Jan–Mar: Mon. ▨
Ⓐ ▨ Ⓝ www.paulreverehouse.org

The city's oldest surviving
clapboard frame house is
historically significant, for it
was here in 1775 that Paul
Revere began his legendary
horseback ride to warn his
compatriots in Lexington of
the impending arrival of
British troops (see
p21). This historic
event was later
immortalized in
a boldly patriotic,
epic poem by
Henry Wadsworth
Longfellow (see
p108). It begins
"Listen, my chil-
dren, and you shall
hear of the midnight
ride of Paul Revere."

**Colonial banknotes,
exhibited in the Paul
Revere House**

 Revere, a Huguenot descen-
dent, was by trade a versatile
gold- and silversmith, copper
engraver, and maker of
church bells, cannons, and
false teeth. He and his second
wife Rachel, mother of eight
of his 16 children, owned the

house from 1770 to 1800.
Small leaded casement
windows, an overhanging
upper story, and nail-studded
front door all contribute to
make it a fine example of
17th-century Early American
architecture. In the courtyard
along one side of the house is
a large bronze bell, cast by
Paul Revere for a church in
1804 – Revere made nearly
200 church bells. Three rooms
in the house contain period
artifacts, including original
pieces of family furniture,
items made in Revere's
workshop, and colonial banknotes. The house, which
by the mid-19th
century had be-
come a decrepit
tenement fronted
by stores, was
saved from demo-
lition by preserva-
tionists' efforts led
by a great-grandson
of Revere.
 Next door, the
early 18th-century
Pierce-Hichborn
House is the earliest brick
town house remaining in
New England. It features
Georgian English motifs such
as shallow arches over the
doors and windows, and twin
chimneys. Admission is via
the Paul Revere House.

**Paul Revere House kitchen, as
it was in the 17th century**

Christopher
Columbus Park **7**

Atlantic Avenue, between Long &
Commercial Wharves.
Map 2 E3. Ⓣ Aquarium.

Extensive urban renewal
along the Inner Harbor
resulted in the completion of
this handsome park in 1976.
It covers 4.5 acres (2 ha) with
wisteria clinging to a 340-ft
(104-m) long arched trellis,
and is a superlative spot for
views of the waterfront and
the Financial District. The com-
memorative Rose Fitzgerald
Kennedy Garden was added
to the park's layout in 1987.

View toward the Custom House and the Financial District, across Christopher Columbus Park

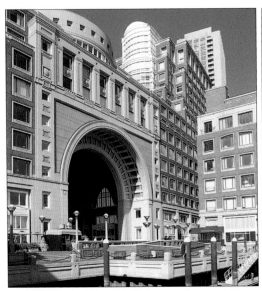

Rowes Wharf development, typical of Boston's waterfront regeneration

Institute of Contemporary Art ⓫

Northern Avenue. **Map** 2 F5.
Tel (617) 478-3100. Ⓣ Courthouse.
◻ 10am–5pm Tue, Wed, Sat, Sun,
10am–9pm Thu, Fri. 🏛 ♿

In 2006 the Institute of Contemporary Art moved to a dramatic wood, steel, and glass landmark building on Fan Pier. Light-flooded galleries, a performance space open to harbor views, and a cutting-edge media center mean that the ICA can extend its seven-decade history of innovation well into the 21st century. Its exhibitions typically break the mold of convention and it is building its first permanent collection of avant-garde work.

Long Wharf ❽

Atlantic Avenue. **Map** 2 E3.
Ⓣ Aquarium.

The nation's oldest continuously operated wharf was built in 1710 to accommodate the boom in early maritime commerce. The following century was to be Boston's international maritime heyday; it was the busiest port in North America and one of the most important in the colonies, surpassed only by London and Bristol in the amount of cargo that it handled. Once extending 2000 ft (610 m) into Boston harbor, and lined with shops and warehouses, Long Wharf provided secure mooring for the largest ships of the time.

Today, Long Wharf is used by boat services to Provincetown, Charlestown Navy Yard, and the Harbor Islands. The attractive esplanade at the end also offers good views across the city's waterfront. Running along the waterfront, Harbor Walk connects Long Wharf with other adjacent wharves, such as Union, Lewis, and Commercial wharves. Dating from the early 1800s, most are now converted to fashionable harborside apartments and condominiums.

New England Aquarium ❾

See pp76–7.

Rowes Wharf ❿

Atlantic Avenue. **Map** 2 E4.
Ⓣ Aquarium.

Completed in 1987, this fine example of waterfront revitalization replaced the two-part India wharf dating from the 1760s. Built of Bostonian red brick and designed by Skidmore, Owings & Merrill, the complex houses the luxury Boston Harbor Hotel (see p133), condominiums, offices, and a marina. A large archway links the city to the harbor.

Boston Tea Party Ships & Museum ⓬

Congress St. Bridge. **Map** 2 E5. **Tel**
(617) 338-1773. Ⓣ South Station.
● at least until summer 2012. 🏛
www.historictours.com/boston

Griffin's Wharf, where the Boston Tea Party took place on December 16, 1773 (see p75), was buried beneath landfill many years ago. Since 2009, replicas of three British East India Company ships involved in the Tea Party have anchored in Fort Point Channel. Today, modern-day patriots toss imitation bales of tea overboard, recreating one of the acts of American defiance that

View down Long Wharf toward the waterfront and Custom House

prompted Britain to close Boston Harbor in 1773 and put the Massachusetts Bay Colony under martial law.

On an adjacent pier, ship models, Tea Party memorabilia, and other educational exhibits are displayed in a museum.

Playing on the mini-construction site at Boston's Children's Museum

Children's Museum ⓮

300 Congress St. **Map** 2 E5. *Tel* (617) 426-6500. Ⓣ *South Station.* ◯ *10am–5pm daily (to 9pm Fri).* 📷 ⬥ **www**.boston childrensmuseum.org

Overlooking Fort Point Channel, a pair of rejuvenated 19th-century wool warehouses contain one of the country's best children's museums, which underwent an extensive expansion in 2007. There are many interesting exhibits, and youngsters are able to participate in games and learning activities, and hoist themselves up a climbing structure in the New Balance Center.

The Art Studio provides a hands-on recycling area with barrels of materials that children can use in self-instructive creative projects, while the KidPower exhibition is designed to encourage active, healthy lifestyles. An international flavor is injected into the proceedings by a visit to the silk merchant's house, which has been transplanted from the city of Kyoto in Japan (Boston's sister city).

A towering milk bottle from a local dairy stands outside in front of the museum building and is used as an ice-cream stand in summer. An outdoor park features mazes, giant boulders, and spaces for outdoor performances.

THE BOSTON TEA PARTY

In 1767, when Britain decided to tax its American colonies, there was outrage. Boycotts were placed on British goods, and protesters took to the streets. One such protest in 1773 culminated in the Boston Massacre *(see p20).*

Despite a subsequent reduction in taxation, tax on tea remained. Parliament then granted the British East India Company sole rights to sell tea in the colonies, which caused prices to rise further. In November 1773, ships arrived in Boston Harbor loaded with tea, and merchants, who refused to buy the tea, came under pressure from Thomas Hutchinson, the Monarchist governor. On the night of December 16, however, around 7,000 rebels, gathered by Samuel Adams, marched to the wharf declaring "Tonight Boston Harbor is a teapot!" Fifty men, dressed as Mohawks, boarded the ships and dumped their cargoes into the water.

Britain reacted strongly, closing the port and putting Massachusetts under martial law. This retribution unified patriots across America, and the "Boston Tea Party," as the protest was soon known, became the spark that ignited the Revolutionary War.

Thomas Hutchinson *Governor of Boston and staunch monarchist, Thomas Hutchinson tried to force the rebels to comply with British colonial law.*

Many of the rebels were dressed as Mohawks.

342 bales of tea were thrown into the sea.

A crowd of about 7,000 watched the events from the quayside.

The Boston Tea Party, depicted in a 19th-century engraving

New England Aquarium ❾

The waterfront's prime attraction dominates
Central Wharf. Designed by a consortium of
architects in 1969, the aquarium's core encloses
a vast four-story ocean tank, which contains a
wide array of marine animals. A curving
walkway runs around the outside of the tank
from top to bottom and provides viewpoints
of the interior of the tank from different levels.
Also resident are colonies of penguins, playful
harbor and fur seals, anacondas, rays, and
mesmerizing seadragons. An IMAX® Theatre
rounds out the facility.

Edge of the Sea Tidepool
*A fiberglass shore recreates a
world where the land meets the
sea. It is home to animals such as
horseshoe crabs and sea urchins.*

★ **Penguin Pool**
*One of the main attactions
of the aquarium, the
penguin pool runs
around the base of the
giant tank. It contains
African, rockhopper,
and little blue penguins.*

★ **Whale Watch**
*A naturalist aboard the
aquarium boat explains
marine ecology on trips
to Stellwagen Bank,
75 minutes away.
You can see whales,
sea birds, and other
marine life.*

**Main
entrance**

**Ticket
booth**

Harbor Seals
*An outdoor tank covered by a steel
canopy, is home to a lively colony
of harbor seals.*

Marine Mammal Center

Northern fur seals frolic in this open-air exhibit where the aquarium meets the harbor. Shallow pools and large decks allow visitors to interact and learn about marine mammals up close.

VISITORS' CHECKLIST

Central Wharf.
Map 2 E3.
Tel (617) 973-5200.
🚇 *Aquarium.*
🕐 Sep–Jun: 9am–5pm
Mon–Fri, 9am–6pm Sat & Sun;
Jul–Aug: 9am–6pm Sun–Thu,
9am–7pm Fri & Sat. 🎫 ♿ 🎧
🖥 📷 www.neaq.org

★ Giant Ocean Tank

This tank contains 200,000 gallons (900,000 liters) of salt water and houses a Caribbean coral reef. The creatures that inhabit it include sharks, sea turtles, barracudas, and moray eels.

STAR SIGHTS

★ Penguin Pool

★ Whale Watch

★ Giant Ocean Tank

Gift Shop

Harbor View Café

↓ **IMAX® Theatre**

Tropical Gallery

This exhibit provides an account of the many types of environment manifested in reefs: starting with a darkened exhibit of deep-water reef fishes and ending with a brightly lit, Pacific coral reef.

CHINATOWN AND THE THEATER DISTRICT

Located south of Boston Common (see pp46–7) and west of the Financial District, this part of town has a noticeably gritty, more down-to-earth ambience. The area around Washington Street, with Downtown Crossing at its center (see pp80–81), is the city's main shopping district. South of here is Chinatown, one of the most populous in the United States – only the Chinatowns

Gilt cherub, the Colonial Theater

in San Francisco and New York are larger. West of Chinatown is the Theater District, featuring touring Broadway shows and local productions. The former "Combat Zone," located at the lower end of Washington Street, between Chinatown and Boston Common, has rebounded as an extension of the Theater District following the restoration of two historic theaters.

SIGHTS AT A GLANCE

Historic Streets, Buildings, and Churches
Bay Village ⑩
Brattle Book Shop ④
Chinatown ⑧
Downtown Crossing ②
Ladder District ③
Jacob Wirth ⑨
Massachusetts State Transportation Building ⑥
St. Paul's Cathedral ①

Theaters
Colonial Theatre ⑦
Opera House ⑤
Shubert Theatre ⑪
Wang Theatre ⑫

KEY

▓ Street-by-street map pp80–81

Ⓣ "T" station

GETTING THERE

This area is well served by public transportation. Park Street, Downtown Crossing, and Chinatown "T" stations are located centrally in the district, while New England Medical Center and Arlington serve outlying sights. The area is also served by buses 3, 9, 11, 43, 49, 55, 300, 301, 304, and 305.

0 meters 200
0 yards 200

◁ Colorful August Moon Festival, held in Boston's Chinatown

Street-by-Street: Around Washington Street

Decoration, Downtown Crossing

Running northeast from the Theater District, Washington Street lies at the heart of Boston's longtime main shopping area. Its focal point, Downtown Crossing, lies at its intersection with Winter and Summer Streets. Saturday afternoons, in particular, offer visitors a glimpse of Boston's sophisticated, and often multi-ethnic population, as they go about their shopping. Macy's is the main department store, though Washington Street and the streets off it offer a range of outlets such as bookstores, camera stores, and jewelers. Just to the south, the Theater District and Chinatown are only a few minutes away on foot. Note that incidences of petty crime sometimes occur in this crowded area.

Sidewalk café on Summer Street

Boston Common

St. Paul's Cathedral
Dating from around 1820, this was one of the first Greek Revival granite buildings to go up in Boston. Today it is still used to broadcast Sunday morning religious programs ❶

WINTER

TEMPLE PLACE

WEST STREET

★ Brattle Book Shop
At first glance, there is not a lot to recommend a second look at this Boston literary landmark. Inside, however, are more than 250,000 rare books and magazines, a treat for any lover of the printed word ❹

Theater District and Chinatown

AVE

★ Opera House
This building was opened as a theater in 1928. Closed in 1991, it was completely restored and reopened in 2004, making it the focus of a newly revitalized lower Washington Street ❺

Ladder District
Stretching along the east side of Boston Common, the trendy Ladder District includes Winter Street, Temple Place, West Street, and Washington Street.

LOCATOR MAP
See Street Finder maps 1 & 2

BEACON HILL AND WEST END

CHINATOWN AND THE THEATER DISTRICT

↗ **Old South Meeting House**

Downtown Crossing
This intersection buzzes with activity, but, despite being the site of Macy's department store, the area can seem a little tawdry. Nevertheless, it is a great place to soak up the atmosphere of Downtown Boston ②

| 0 meters | 50 |
| 0 yards | 50 |

KEY

— — — Suggested route

Macy's is one of the most famous stores in the U.S. – the most well-known store is in New York.

Lafayette Center

STAR SIGHTS

★ Opera House

★ Brattle Bookshop

FAYETTE

↙ **Boston Tea Party Ship**

Washington Street
The main street of this district, Washington Street has many stores. New developments and theater restorations make it increasingly upscale.

Classical chancel and box pews of the interior of St. Paul's Cathedral, typically austere in style

St. Paul's Cathedral ❶

138 Tremont St. **Map** 4 E1.
Tel *(617) 482-5800.* Ⓣ *Park Street.*
🚪 *8am, 10am & 12:30pm Sun;*
1pm Mon, 12:15pm Tue & Fri. ♿
www.stpaulboston.org

Consecrated in 1820, Boston's second example of Greek Revival architecture was designed by Alexander Parris, five years before the completion of his Quincy Market hall *(see p64)*, which also has the outward appear-ance of a Greek temple. The first Greek Revival Church in Boston came about with Charles Bulfinch's design for the fa-çade of the original New South Church, which was subse-quently demolished.

The stone work on St. Paul's Cathe-dral is by Solomon Willard, who gave the church a por-tico of six unfluted stone columns with Ionic capitals. The building's pediment was initially intend-ed to feature a frieze depicting St. Paul preaching before King Agrippa, but this was never constructed due to consider-ations of the cost involved.

The interior of the church, dominated by a classical chan-cel, curved apse, and box pews, is spacious and austere, typical of a style found in New England churches.

In 1908 the church became the cathedral of Massachusetts' Episcopal diocese, the largest in the U.S. The United States' longest-running religious radio program has been broadcast from the cathedral each Sunday since the 1920s.

Downtown Crossing ❷

Washington, Winter & Summer Sts.
Map 4 F1. Ⓣ *Downtown Crossing.*

As an antidote to heavy traffic congestion, this shopping-district crossroads was laid out as a pedestrian zone between 1975 and 1978. The area is anchored by the Beaux Arts building, which was formerly Filene's, and Modernist Macy's. Smaller retail outlets, some in restored buildings with terracotta and cast-iron façades, are plentiful in the streets radiating from Downtown Crossing and Washington Street. Lively push-cart vendors and sparkling diamonds in the jeweler's district can also be found here. South of Downtown Crossing, the area recaptures an earlier era when it was part of Boston's original Theater Row.

Ladder District ❸

Connecting streets and rear alleys between Washington & Tremont Sts.
Map 4 E1–F2. Ⓣ *Downtown Crossing & Chinatown.*

Once a rather rundown part of Downtown, the web of small streets connecting Washington and Tremont Streets, along the east side of Boston Common, came into its own at the start of the new millennium. Soaring buildings were erected on vacant parking lots and old architectural treasures on the dark streets were refurbished and brought back to life. Today they house restaurants, bars, and nightclubs.

Along with upmarket condos came the Ritz-Carlton Boston Common hotel *(see p134)*, housed in a building that stretches the length of Avery Street. This building played a central role in the renaissance of what used to be a no man's land between the Theater District and Downtown Crossing. In addition to the luxury hotel, a cutting-edge restaurant, and a fashionable gym, the Sports

Beaux Arts façade of former Filene's department store, Downtown Crossing

Club/LA, the structure also houses the Loews Boston Common *(see p161)*. Boston's first premier cinema has 19 screens, stadium seating, an upmarket bar, and multiple dining concessions.

The nightclubs and restaurants of the Ladder District are often indistinguishable, although if a long line is standing outside, the establishment probably serves more liquor than food. Club names also tend to change frequently as owners tweak the themes to attract different crowds. Many maps do not show all the small streets in the district, such as Pi Alley, so it is best to take a leisurely stroll and discover the area for yourself.

Vintage magazines displayed at the Brattle Book Shop

Brattle Book Shop ❹

9 West St. **Map** 4 E1.
Tel (617) 542-0210.
Ⓣ Park Street, Downtown Crossing. Ⓞ 9am–5:30pm Mon–Sat. ♿
www.brattlebookshop.com

Founded in 1825 and located at various sites around Boston since, this bibliophiles' treasure house is packed with more than 250,000 used, rare, and out-of-print books. Proprietor Kenneth Gloss also stocks back issues of periodicals, *Life, Look,* and *Collier's* magazines among them, along with antiquarian ephemera such as maps, prints, postcards, greeting cards, and autographed manuscripts. In front of and alongside the three-story building, passersby browse through bins and carts full of discounted bargain books priced in the range of $1 to $5.

Spanish Baroque, terracotta ornamentation on the façade of the Opera House

Opera House ❺

539 Washington St. **Map** 4 E1.
Tel (617) 931-2787. Ⓣ Downtown Crossing, Chinatown, Boylston. ♿
www.broadwayacrossamerica.com

The building that is now the Opera House has been known by many names. Built on the site of the original Boston Theater, and designed by Thomas Lamb, it opened in 1928 as the B. F. Keith Memorial Theater, named after the late 19th-century showman who added the term "vaudeville" to show business vocabulary. It was renamed the Savoy Theater in the 1940s and served as home for the Opera Company of Boston from the late 1950s until 1991. The venue became internationally recognized for Sarah Caldwell's daringly innovative productions.

With its white Spanish Baroque, terracotta façade, high ceilings, and three-tier horseshoe balconies, the theater represents the apogee of early 20th century hall design. A $38 million renovation completed in 2004 restored the theater's original opulence with gilded surfaces and exquisite ceiling murals, while installing modern climate control, technical systems, and seating. Primarily used for large touring Broadway musicals, the Opera House is again the jewel of lower Washington Street.

LIBERTY TREE

At the corner of Washington Street and Boylston Street, a low relief of a tree marks the exact site of the famous Liberty Tree, where the Sons of Liberty would meet during the prelude to the American Revolution. The tree's fame first became widespread when it became a focal point for opposition to the Stamp Act *(see p20)*. The British stamp master, Andrew Oliver, was hung in effigy from its branches, an incident that caused people from all over the region to gather around it. The tree was also a meeting place in the days running up to the Boston Tea Party *(see p75)*. In August 1775, during the early part of the Revolution when Boston was still occupied by the British, a mob of Redcoats vented their anger on the tree and chopped it down.

Bostonians protest the Stamp Act of 1765, around the Liberty Tree

Massachusetts State Transportation Building 6

8–10 Park Plaza, Stuart & Charles Sts. **Map** 4 E2. ⓣ *Boylston.*
Atrium restaurants ◯ *11am–8pm Mon–Fri, noon–6pm Sat.* ♿

The main feature of the Massachusetts State Transportation Building, constructed in 1983, is its seven-story-high, skylit City Place atrium, which is directly accessible to the public. Covering most of a sizeable city block, this red-brick and glass cantilevered building has won several prestigious design awards. It incorporates offices and public-service facilities, maintained by the state's transportation administrators, around a central mall of wide-ranging shops and restaurants.

Lunchtime concerts, pop or light-classical music, are frequently scheduled in the central mall, while gallery showings are often held on the upper levels overlooking the atrium. Other facilities in the building include a bank, newsstand, and several fast-food eateries.

The City Place atrium in the Massachusetts State Transportation Building

Gilt ornamentation from the lavishly decorated interior of the Colonial Theater

Colonial Theatre 7

106 Boylston St. **Map** 4 E2.
Tel *(617) 426-9366.* ⓣ *Boylston.*
◯ *phone to check.* ♿
www.broadwayacrossamerica.com

Clarence H. Blackall designed 14 Boston theaters during his architectural career, among them the Colonial, which is the city's oldest theater to have been in continuous operation under the same name. A two-story loggia sits atop Blackall's structure, which is otherwise quite plain. The interior, on the other hand, is an impressively opulent show-piece by H.B. Pennell: his Rococo lobby boasts gilded trim, chandeliers, and lofty arched ceilings. The 1,658-seat auditorium is decorated with allegorical figures, frescoes, and friezes.

The theater opened on December 20, 1900 with a suitably extravagant performance of the melodrama *Ben Hur*, featuring a cast of 350 and an on-stage chariot race involving a dozen horses pulling Roman chariots on treadmills. Today the theater is best remembered for premiering lavish shows. In particular it was the venue for productions by directors such as Irving Berlin, Sigmund Romberg, and Rodgers and Hammerstein, and is where Ziegfeld premiered his Follies (*see p87*).

Chinatown 8

Bounded by Kingston, Kneeland, Washington & Essex Sts. **Map** 4 E2. ⓣ *Chinatown.*

This area is the third largest Chinatown in the U.S. after those in San Francisco and New York. It covers blocks of filled land that had been the South Cove tidal backwater until the early 19th century. Pagoda-topped telephone booths, as well as a three-story gateway guarded by four marble lions, set the neighborhood's Asian tone.

The first 200 Chinese to settle in New England came by ship from San Francisco in 1870. Mostly unskilled, they were recruited to break a labor strike at a shoe factory in Massachusetts, but were jobless by 1874. At this time, some drifted to Boston, at first pitching their tents on Oliver Place, which they renamed

Colorful, contemporary city mural in Chinatown

Ping On Alley – "the Street of Peace and Security." In the 1880s another wave of Chinese immigration from California was prompted by an economic boom that led to job openings in construction, on the railroad, and the laying of telephone lines. Boston's Chinese colony was fully established by the turn of the 19th century, and with it came the ubiquitous garment and textile industries.

Political turmoil in China immediately following World War II, and more recent arrivals from Vietnam, Laos, Korea, Thailand, and Cambodia, have swelled Chinatown's population, which now stands at around 8,000. Restaurants, bakeries, food markets, curio shops, and dispensers of Chinese medicine are especially numerous along the main thoroughfare of Beach Street, as well as on Tyler, Oxford, and Harrison Streets.

Typical store and restaurant façades in Boston's Chinatown

Jacob Wirth ❾

31–37 Stuart St. **Map** 4 E2. **Tel** (617) 338-8586. Ⓣ Boylston, Chinatown. ◖ 11:30am–8pm Sun & Mon (to 10pm Tue–Thu, to midnight Fri, to 11pm Sat). & www.jacobwirth.com

Occupying a 19th-century row house, Jacob Wirth (see p145) has been in business since 1868. It is Boston's second oldest restaurant after the Union Oyster House (see p143). Restaurateur Jacob Wirth had the majestic mahogany restaurant bar shipped in small pieces from Russia. The old-fashioned beer-hall, with its globe lighting, ceiling fans, dark paneling, bare wood floors, and brass railings, has barely changed since it first opened. Sausage-and-sauerkraut menu staples, combined with draft beers and Rhine wines, make this the only authentic German restaurant in a city that is far more famous for its Irish and Italian heritage. Friday night piano sing-alongs are very popular.

Bay Village ❿

Bounded by Tremont, Arlington & South Charles Sts. **Map** 4 D2. Ⓣ New England Medical Center, Boylston.

Originally an expanse of mud flats, the Bay Village area was drained in the early 1800s and initially became habitable with the construction of a dam in 1825. Many carpenters, cabinetmakers, artisans, and house painters involved in the construction of Beacon Hill's pricier town houses built their own modest but well-crafted residences here. As a result there are many similarities between the two neighborhoods, including plenty of red brick, arched doorways, window boxes and shutters, courtyards, tidy gardens, and antique gas lamps. Fayette Street was laid out in 1824 to coincide with the triumphant U.S. visit of the Marquis de Lafayette, the French general who allied himself with George Washington for some of the campaigns of the Revolutionary War.

Bay Street, located just off Fayette Street, features a single dwelling and is generally regarded as the city's

Bay Village doorway, similar to those of Beacon Hill

shortest street. In 1809, poet and short-story writer Edgar Allen Poe was born in a boarding house on Carver Street, where his thespian parents were staying while in Boston on tour with a traveling theatrical company.

In the 1920s, at the height of the Prohibition era, clandestine speakeasies gave Bay Village its still-prevalent bohemian ambience. More recently, the neighborhood has become a center for Boston's gay community.

Bay Village's Piedmont Street is noteworthy for two very different reasons. The W. S. Haynes Company at No. 12 has been hand-crafting flutes and piccolos since 1888, and has acquired a worldwide reputation for its instruments among soloists and symphony orchestra performers alike.

The street's other claim to fame is less auspicious. The Coconut Grove nightclub fire of 1942, when 491 of the club's patrons died, remains one of the United States' highest fire death tolls. This devastating occurrence resulted in infamy for the area but, ultimately, to more stringent fire-safety codes throughout the United States.

The vast Grand Lobby of the Wang Theatre

Shubert Theatre ⓫

265 Tremont St. **Map** 4 E2.
Tel (617) 482-9393. Ⓣ Boylston,
New England Medical Center.
◯ phone for details. ♿
www.citicenter.org

The 1,650-seat Shubert
Theater rivals the Colonial
Theater (see p84) for its
long history of staging
major pre-Broadway musical
productions. Designed by
the architects Charles Bond

**Palladian-style window over the
entrance to the Shubert Theater**

and Thomas James, the
theater first opened its doors
in 1910, and during its
heyday many famous stars
walked the boards here.
Among them were Sarah
Bernhardt, W.C. Fields,
Cary Grant, Mae
West, Humphrey
Bogart, Ingrid
Bergman, Henry
Ford, and Rex
Harrison.
    The Shubert Theater
is listed on the National
Register of Historic
Places, and features
a white, Neoclassical façade
with a pair of Ionic columns
flanking a monumental,
Palladian-style window that
sits over the entrance. The
entrance also boasts an ornate, wrought-iron canopy.
    The theater closed for a
number of years but in 1997
it reopened to premiere
the pre-Broadway hit *Rent*.
Local companies also stage
performances here.
    A plaque to the side of
the main entrance recounts
the history of the theater.

**Ornate, gilt
decoration at
the Wang**

Wang Theatre ⓬

270 Tremont St. **Map** 4 E2.
Tel (617) 482-9393. Ⓣ Boylston,
New England Medical Center.
◯ phone for details. ♿
www.citicenter.org

Opened in 1925 as the
Metropolitan Theater and
later named the Music Hall,
New England's most ornate
variety theater was inspired
by the Paris Opera House,
and was originally intended
to be a movie theater. Like
the nearby Colonial Theater,
the Metropolitan was de-
signed by Clarence Blackall.
When it was first built the
auditorium had over 4,000
seats, which made it one
of the largest in the world.
It was so big that at its
opening, which over
20,000 people attended,
one Hollywood magnate
described it as a theater
of "mountainous splendour,
a movie palace of fabulous
grandeur and stupendous
stage presentations." Another
observer described it as a
"cathedral of the movies."
    The theater was restored
and renamed in 1983.
The five-story Grand
Lobby and seven-story
auditorium are designed
in a magnificent and ornate
Renaissance Revival style:
gold-plated chandeliers,
bronze detailing,
stained glass,
florid ceiling
murals, rose
jasper pillars,
and marble-framed
doorways. There are
also three sumptuous
lobbies, which visitors
must pass through
before finally arriving at the
awesome Grand Lobby.
    Today, the theater hosts
a wide variety of events,
including Broadway road
shows, touring national
and international dance
and opera productions,
celebrity concert appearances,
and motion-picture revivals. It
is also a popular performance
venue for local dance and
theater companies. Both
the Wang and Shubert
theaters are operated by
Citi Performing Arts Center.

The History of Boston's Theater District

Boston's first theater opened in 1793 on Federal Street. Fifty years later Boston had become a major tryout town and boasted a number of lavish theaters. The U.S. premiere of Handel's *Messiah* opened in 1839, the U.S. premiere of Gilbert and Sullivan's *H.M.S. Pinafore* in 1877, and the world premiere of Tchaikovsky's *First Piano Concerto* in 1875. In

South Pacific, Rodgers and Hammerstein

the late 19th century theaters came under fire from the censorious Watch and Ward Society. In the 20th century, dramas such as Tennessee Williams' *A Streetcar Named Desire* and Eugene O'Neill's *Long Day's Journey into Night* debuted here. Premieres included *Ziegfeld Follies*, Gershwin's *Porgy and Bess*, and musicals by Rodgers and Hammerstein.

Theatergoers *in 19th-century Boston came primarily from the city's social elite, who were often patrons of the arts. In this way Boston's theaters flourished.*

The planned new theater remained in use until 1835. It became the Academy of Music from 1835 to 1846.

Old theater

Athena

Cupids

The Federal Street Theater, *designed by Charles Bulfinch, burned down in 1798. The old and new theaters are depicted in this allegorical painting, possibly a set design, which also shows characters from Greek mythology. Other Bulfinch buildings are also shown.*

Tennessee Williams' A Streetcar Named Desire *premiered at Boston's Wilbur Theater. It starred a young Marlon Brando and Jessica Tandy.*

Ziegfeld Follies, *produced in the 1920s, had eight pre-Broadway "tryouts" at the Colonial Theater (see p84).*

The Rodgers and Hammerstein *musical* Oklahoma! *premiered in Boston as a production entitled* Away We Go! *It was refined in Boston before hitting Broadway.*

BACK BAY AND SOUTH END

Until the 19th century Boston was situated on a narrow peninsula surrounded by tidal marshes. Projects to fill Back Bay began in the 1850s and were made possible by new inventions such as the steam shovel. The Back Bay was filled by 1880 and developers

Sargent mural, Boston Public Library

soon moved in. Planned along French lines, with elegant boulevards, Back Bay is now one of Boston's most exclusive neighborhoods. The more bohemian South End, laid out on an English model of town houses clustered around squares, is home to many artists and Boston's gay community.

SIGHTS AT A GLANCE

Historic Streets and Squares
Boylston Street **8**
Commonwealth Avenue **4**
Copley Place **14**
Copley Square **7**
The Esplanade **1**
Newbury Street **5**
Union Park **16**

Historic Buildings, Churches, and Museums
Boston Center for the Arts **15**

Boston Public Library **9**
Christian Science Center **13**
First Baptist Church **3**
Gibson House Museum **2**
Berklee Performance Center **11**
John Hancock Tower **10**
Prudential Center **12**
Trinity Church
pp94–5 **6**

KEY

	Street-by-street map *pp90–91*
Ⓣ	"T" station
🚆	Railroad station
🚌	Bus station
🛈	Tourist information

GETTING THERE

The area has good public transportation. Arlington, Copley, and Hynes. "T" stations serve the Back Bay. Back Bay/ South End and Prudential "T stations serve the South End. Buses 1, 8, 9, 10, 39, 43, 49, 55, and 302, and the Silver Line Mass Transit serve the area.

| 0 meters | 450 |
| 0 yards | 450 |

◁ **View of Back Bay's characteristic row houses, from the top of the Prudential Center Skywalk observatory**

Street-by-Street: Back Bay

This fashionable district unfolds westward from the Public Garden *(see pp46–7)* in a grid that departs radically from the twisting streets found elsewhere in Boston. Commonwealth Avenue, with its grand 19th-century mansions and parkland, and Newbury and Boylston Streets are its main arteries. Newbury Street is a magnet for all of Boston wanting to indulge in some upscale shopping, whereas the more somber Boylston Street bustles with office workers. Copley Square anchors the entire area and is the site of Henry Hobson Richardson's magnificent Trinity Church *(see pp94–5)* and the 60-story John Hancock Tower *(see p97)*, the tallest building in New England.

Weekly summer and fall farmers' market, Copley Square

Copley Square

This square was a marsh until 1870. It took on its present form only in the late 20th century as buildings around its edges were completed. A farmers' market, concerts, and folk-dancing feature regularly **❼**

Boylston Street

The site of the Prudential Center (see p98) and the Boston Public Library (see p96), Boylston Street is also the location of the fabulous New Old South Church (see p96) **❽**

★ Boston Public Library

One of the first free public libraries in the world, this building was designed by Charles McKim. Inside are murals by John Singer Sargent **❾**

Fenway Park ←

COMMONWEALTH AVENU

NEWB

DARTMOUTH STREET

BOYLSTON STREET

South End

First Baptist Church
By Henry Hobson Richardson (see p92), this church is a fine example of his Romanesque Revival style ❸

Beacon Hill

COMMONWEALTH AVENUE

CLARENDON STREET

TREET

Public Garden

BEACON HILL AND WEST END

BACK BAY AND SOUTH END

LOCATOR MAP
See Street Finder map 3

Commonwealth Avenue
Envisioned as Boston's Champs-Elysées, this avenue boasts beautiful town houses and a tree-lined central mall ❹

★ **Newbury Street**
High fashion outlets, galleries, and restaurants characterize this street – Boston's most fashionable, and a great place for people-watching ❺

KEY

– – – Suggested route

★ **Trinity Church**
Acknowledged as Henry Hobson Richardson's Romanesque Revival masterpiece, this is one of the most important churches in the U.S. ❻

STAR SIGHTS

★ Newbury Street

★ Trinity Church

★ Boston Public Library

0 meters   50
0 yards   50

The Esplanade ❶

Map 1 A4. Ⓣ *Charles/MGH.*
🚪 *24 hrs daily.* 🅰

Running along the Boston side of the Charles River, between Longfellow Bridge and Dartmouth Street, are the parkland, lagoons, and islands known collectively as the Esplanade. The park is used extensively for in-line skating, cycling, and strolling and it is also the access point for boating on the river, including gondola rides. It is also the site of the city's leading outdoor concert venue.

In 1929, Arthur Fiedler, then the young conductor of the Boston Pops Orchestra, chose the Esplanade for a summer concert series that became a tradition. The Hatch Memorial Shell was constructed in 1939, and its stage is widely used by musical ensembles and other groups throughout the summer. Fourth of July concerts by the Boston Pops, which are followed by fireworks, can attract upward of 500,000 spectators *(see p35).*

Fountains at the Esplanade, next to the Charles River

Gibson House Museum ❷

137 Beacon St. **Map** 1 A4.
Tel (617) 267-6338. Ⓣ *Arlington.*
🚪 *obligatory tours at 1pm, 2pm, 3pm Wed–Sun.* 📷 🚫 📹
www.thegibsonhouse.org

Among the first houses built in the Back Bay, the Gibson House preserves its original Victorian decor and furnishings throughout all six stories. The 1860 brownstone and red-brick structure was

The original Victorian-style library of the Gibson House Museum

designed in the popular Italian Renaissance Revival style for the widow Catherine Hammond Gibson, who was one of the few women to own property in this part of the city. Her grandson Charles Hammond Gibson, Jr., a noted eccentric, poet, travel writer, horticulturalist, and bon vivant, arranged for the house to become a museum after his death in 1954. As a prelude to this, Gibson began to rope off the furniture in the 1930s, instead inviting his guests to sit on the stairs to drink martinis made with his own bathtub gin.

One of the most modern houses of its day, the Gibson House boasted such technical advancements as gas lighting, indoor plumbing in the basement, and coal-fired central heating. Visitors can see a full dinner setting in the dining room or admire the whimsical Turkish pet pavilion. But it is Gibson's preservation of the 1860s decor (with some modifications in 1888) that makes the museum a true time capsule of Victorian life in Boston.

Detail of Bartholdi's frieze atop the distinctive square tower of the First Baptist Church

First Baptist Church ❸

110 Commonwealth Ave.
Map 3 C2. *Tel (617) 267-3148.*
Ⓣ *Arlington.* 🚪 *for Sunday worship.* ✝ *11am Sun.* 🚫 🅰

The Romanesque-style First Baptist Church on the corner of Commonwealth Avenue and Clarendon Street was Henry Hobson Richardson's *(see p32)* first major architectural commission and became an instant landmark when it was finished in 1872. Viewed from Commonwealth Avenue, it is one of the most distinctive buildings of the city skyline.

Richardson considered the nearly freestanding bell tower, which he modeled roughly on Italian campaniles, to be the church's most innovative structure. The square tower is topped with a decorative frieze and arches protected by an overhanging roof. The frieze was modeled in Paris by Bartholdi, the sculptor who created the Statue of Liberty, and was carved in place by Italian artisans after the stones were set. The faces in the frieze, which depict the sacraments, are likenesses of prominent Bostonians of that time, among them Henry Wadsworth Longfellow and Ralph Waldo Emerson *(see p31).* The trumpeting angels at the corners of the tower gave the building its nickname, "Church of the Holy Bean Blowers."

Four years after the church was completed, the Unitarian congregation dissolved because it was unable to bear the expense of the building. The church stood vacant until 1881, when the First Baptist congregation from the South End took it over.

Commonwealth Avenue ④

Map 3 B2. ⓣ *Arlington, Copley, Hynes Convention Center/ICA.*

Back Bay was Boston's first fully planned neighborhood, and architect Arthur Gilman made Commonwealth Avenue, modeled on the elegant boulevards of Paris, the centerpiece of the design. At 200 ft (61 m) wide, with a 10 ft (3 m) setback from the sidewalks to encourage small gardens in front of the buildings, Commonwealth became an arena for America's leading domestic architects in the second half of the 19th century. A walk from the Public Garden to Massachusetts Avenue is like flicking through a catalog of architectural styles.

Few of the grand buildings on either side of the avenue are open to the public, but

strollers on the central mall of the avenue encounter a number of historic figures in the form of bronze statues. Some have only tangential relationships to the city, like Alexander Hamilton, the first secretary of the U.S. Treasury. The end of the mall features an heroic bronze of Leif Erikson, erected as a historically unsupported flight of fancy that the Norse explorer landed at Boston. The patrician statue of abolitionist William Garrison is said to capture exactly the man's air of moral superiority. The best-loved memorial depicts sailor and historian Samuel Eliot Morison dangling his feet from a rock.

William Garrison statue on Commonwealth Avenue

Newbury Street ⑤

Map 3 C2. ⓣ *Arlington, Copley, Hynes Convention Center/ICA.*

Newbury Street is a Boston synonym for "stylish." The Taj Boston, formerly the Ritz-Carlton Hotel, at Arlington Street sets an elegant tone for the street that continues with a mix of prestigious and often

well-hidden art galleries, stylish boutiques, and some of the city's most *au courant* restaurants.

Churches provide vestiges of a more decorous era. The Church of the Covenant at No. 67 Newbury contains the world's largest collection of Louis Comfort Tiffany stained-glass windows and an elaborate Tiffany lantern.

A chorus and orchestra perform a Bach cantata each Sunday at Emmanuel Church on the corner of Newbury and Berkeley Streets.

Most of Newbury Street was constructed as town-house residences, but the desirability of these spaces for retail operations has pushed residents to the upper floors, while ground and under-ground levels are devoted to chic boutiques and eateries. Modern-day aspiring celebrities may be spotted at the sidewalk tables of Newbury's "hottest" restaurants, such as Sonsie *(see p147).*

🔒 **Church of the Covenant**
67 Newbury St. **Tel** (617) 266-7480. ⏱ *10:30am Sun for church service.* 🚫 ♿ 🎥 ⌂
www.churchofthecovenant.org

Stylish Newbury Street, with its elegant shops, galleries, and restaurants, the epitome of Boston style

Trinity Church ❻

Routinely voted one of America's 10 finest buildings, this masterpiece by Henry Hobson Richardson dates from 1877. Trinity Church was founded in 1733 near Downtown Crossing, but the congregation moved the church to this site in 1871. The church is a granite and sandstone Romanesque structure standing on wooden piles driven through mud into bedrock, surmounted with granite pyramids. John LaFarge designed the interior, while some of the windows are designed by Edward Burne-Jones and executed by William Morris.

The bell tower was inspired by the Renaissance cathedral at Salamanca, central Spain.

Bas-relief in Chancel
On the wall of the chancel, behind the altar, are a series of gold bas-reliefs. This one shows St. Paul before King Agrippas.

★ **North Transept Windows**
Designed by Edward Burne-Jones and executed by William Morris, the three stained-glass windows above the choir relate the story of Christmas.

Parish House

The pulpit is covered with carved scenes from the life of Christ, as well as por-traits of great preachers through the ages.

Chancel
Designed by Charles Maginnis, the present-day chancel was not dedicated until 1938. The seven windows by Clayton & Bell, of London, show the life of Christ.

David's Charge to Solomon
*Located in the baptistry, to
the right of the chancel, this
beautiful window is also the
result of a partnership between
Edward Burne-Jones and
William Morris. The story
shown is one of the few in the
church from the Old Testament.*

John LaFarge's lancet windows
show Christ in the act of blessing.
They were designed at the request
of Phillips Brooks – he wanted
LaFarge to create an inspirational
design for the west nave,
which he could look at
while preaching.

★ **West Portico**
*Richardson disliked the original flat
façade of Trinity Church, and so
modeled the deeply sculpted west
portico after St. Trophime in Arles,
France. It was added after his death.*

**Carving of Phillips
Brooks and Christ**

PHILLIPS BROOKS

Born in Boston in 1835
and educated at Harvard,
Brooks was a towering
charismatic figure. Rector
of Trinity Church from
1869, he gained a reputa-
tion for powerful sermons.
From 1872 Brooks worked
closely with Henry
Hobson Richardson on
the design of the new
Trinity Church – at least
five sculpted likenesses
of him can be seen in
and around the building.

STAR SIGHTS

★ West Portico

★ North Transept
   Windows

**Main
entrance**

The New Old South Church, which looks across Copley Square

Copley Square **7**

Map 3 C2. Ⓣ *Copley.*

Named after John Singleton Copley, the great Boston painter born nearby in 1737, Copley Square is a hive of civic activity surrounded by some of Boston's most striking architecture. Summer activities include weekly farmers' markets, concerts, and even folk-dancing.

The inviting green plaza took years to develop; when Copley was born it was just a marshy riverbank, which remained unfilled until 1870. Construction of the John Hancock Tower in 1975 anchored the southeastern side of Copley Square, and Copley Place (see *p99)* completed the square on the southwestern corner in 1984. Today's Copley Square, a wide open space of trees, grass, and fountains, took shape in the heart of the city in the 1990s, after various plans to utilize this hitherto wasted space were tendered.

A large plaque honoring the Boston Marathon, which ends at the Boston Public Library, was set in the sidewalk in 1996 to coincide with the 100th race. As well as pushcart vendors, the plaza has a booth for discounted theater, music, and dance tickets.

Boylston Street **8**

Map 3 C2. Ⓣ *Boylston, Arlington, Copley, Hynes Convention Center/ICA.*

The corners of Boylston and Berkeley streets represent Boston architecture at its most diverse. The stately French Academic-style structure on the west side was erected for the Museum of Natural History, a forerunner of the Museum of Science (see *p53)*. The east side spouts a Robert A.M. Stern tower and a Philip Johnson office building that resembles a table radio. Boston's finest jeweler, Shreve, Crump & Low, occupied the Art Deco building at the corner of Arlington Street until relocating to 440 Boylston Street in 2005.

Some notable office buildings stand on Boylston Street. The lobby of the New England building at No. 501 features large historical murals and dioramas depicting the process of filling Back Bay during the late 19th century. The towers of the Prudential Center (see *p98)* dominate the skyline on upper Boylston Street. Adjoining the Prudential is the Hynes Convention

Center. It was enlarged in 1988 to accommodate the city's burgeoning convention business and added upscale public dining.

The Italian Gothic-style **New Old South Church**, at the corner of Dartmouth and Boylston Streets, was built in 1874–5 by the congregation that had met previously at the Old South Meeting House (see *p59)*.

🔒 **New Old South Church**
645 Boylston St. **Map** 3 C2.
Tel (617) 536-1970. 🕐 9am–7pm Mon–Fri, 10am–4pm Sat, 9am–4pm Sun. 🕐 9am, 11am Sun, 6pm Thu. 🐾 ♿ 🎦 📷 www.oldsouth.org

Boston Public Library **9**

Copley Square. **Map** 3 C2. ***Tel*** (617) 536-5400. Ⓣ *Copley.* **General Library** 🕐 9am–9pm Mon–Thu, 9am–5pm Fri–Sat, 1–5pm Sun. 🌑 public hols; Jun–Sep: Sun. 📷 2:30pm Mon, 6pm Tue & Thu, 11am Fri & Sat, 2pm Sun. ♿ 📷 www.bpl.org

Founded in 1848, the Boston Public Library was America's first metropolitan library for the public. It quickly outgrew its original building, hence the construction of the Italian *palazzo*-style Copley Square building in 1887–95, with "Free to All" emblazoned above the entrance. The architect Charles McKim drew on the highly skilled force of mostly Italian construction workers and artisans who had come to Boston to build mansions in the Back Bay and South End. Sculptor Daniel Chester French fashioned the huge bronze doors that represent Music and Poetry, Knowledge and Wisdom, and Truth and Romance. French painter Puvis de Chavannes executed the murals that wind up the staircase and along the second-floor corridor. Edward Abbey's

The vast Bates Hall in the Boston Public Library, noted for its high barrel-vaulted ceiling

Pre-Raphaelite murals of the Quest for the Holy Grail line the book request room, and John Singer Sargent's murals of Judaism and Christianity cover a third-floor gallery.

The McKim building, largely restored for its 1995 centennial, is a marvel of wood and marble. Bates Hall, on the second floor, is particularly noted for the soaring barrel-vaulted ceiling. A café and restaurant offer breakfast, lunch, and afternoon tea.

The library's circulating collection is housed in the 1971 Boylston Street addition, a modernist structure by architect Philip Johnson.

John Hancock Tower ⑩

200 Clarendon St. **Map** 3 C2. Ⓣ Copley. ⬤ to the public.

The tallest building in New England, the 740-ft (226-m) rhomboid that is the John Hancock Tower cuts into Copley Square with its slimmest edge, its mirrored façade reflecting the surroundings and sky. The innovative design has created a 60-story office building that shares the square with its neighbors, the Romanesque Trinity Church and the Italian Renaissance Revival Copley Plaza Hotel, without dwarfing them. When the tower was under construction, 65 windows, each weighing 500lb (1,100 kg), came crashing to the ground. All 10,344 panes were replaced at a cost of almost $7 million before the building could be occupied in 1975.

Designed by Henry Cobb of I.M. Pei & Partners, the magnificent building inspired Massachusetts author John Updike to observe: "All art, all beauty, is reflection." From one angle viewers can see the reflections of Trinity Church and the original (1947) Hancock Building, topped by a weather beacon.

The observatory on the 60th floor of the tower closed for safety reasons following the tragic events in September 2001 at the World Trade Center in New York.

View over Back Bay and the Charles River

Berklee Performance Center ⑪

136 Massachusetts Ave. **Map** 3 A3. **Tel** (617) 266-7455. Ⓣ Hynes. **www**.berkleebpc.com

Acquired by the Berklee College of Music in 1972, the Berklee Performance Center has since undergone extensive renovations to transform it into one of the city's entertainment and cultural highlights.

The largest independent music college in the world, Berklee was founded in 1945 and has produced a number of stars in jazz, rock, and pop music. Included in the list of well-known talents are the likes of producer and arranger Quincy Jones, the singer and songwriter Melissa Etheridge, and jazz saxophonist and composer Branford Marsalis. The school's students and distinguished faculty enliven the Boston music scene, performing primarily at the on-site Berklee Performance Center. The center boasts extraordinary acoustics and a state-of-the art light and sound system. It frequently hosts a wide range of events, including legendary music recitals, operas, plays, and comedy nights. Mainstream and emerging artists perform here and there are also faculty and student concerts. There is a full program of special events, including film screenings and business conferences, available. The center's website gives up-to-date and informative listings of all upcoming events.

Musicians playing at the state-of-the-art Berklee Performance Center

Prudential Center ⑫

800 Boylston St. **Map** 3 B3. **Tel** (617) 859-0648. Ⓣ Prudential, Hynes Convention Center/ICA. **Skywalk** ◻ Mar–Oct: 10am–10pm daily; Nov–Feb: 10am–8pm daily. ● Thanksgiving, Dec 25. 🎫 ♿ 🎁

When it was erected in 1965, the Prudential Tower was the first skyscraper in the Back Bay, rising 52 floors. Office buildings and a shopping center now girdle its base, and the "Pru" is linked through indoor walkways with the Hynes Convention Center and the Sheraton Back Bay Hotel in one unified complex. An enclosed walkway even links its shops to the more

Inside the beautiful, stained-glass Mapparium, Christian Science Center

Prudential Tower viewed across the Christian Science reflecting pool

glamorous Copley Place across busy Huntington Avenue. Apart from the shops and food courts, the principal attraction of the "Pru" is the Skywalk on the 50th floor. The Skywalk is the only 360-degree aerial observatory in Boston, and its location near the top of Boylston Street hill provides striking views of the Emerald Necklace (see p103) as well as downtown and the waterfront. Signs on the windows assist in identifying the landmarks below. A similar view, which visitors do not need to pay for, is available at the Top of the Hub restaurant on the 52nd floor. Some of the bar windows here face west, so those having a drink can enjoy spectacular sunset views over Boston.

Christian Science Center ⑬

175 Huntington Ave. **Map** 3 B3. Ⓣ Symphony. **Mother Church Tel** (617) 450-2000. ◻ noon–4pm Thu–Sat. 🎫 11am Sun. **Library Tel** (617) 450-7000. ◻ 10am–4pm Tue–Sun (last entry to Mapparium 3:40pm). 🎫 ✝ 10am & 7pm Sun, noon & 7:30pm Wed (no evening service Jul–Aug). ♿ 🎫 www.marybakereddylibrary.org

The world headquarters of the First Church of Christ, Scientist, occupies 14 acres on the corner of Huntington and Massachusetts Avenues. Known also as the Christian Science Church, this religious body was formed in 1879 by Mary Baker Eddy. The granite, Romanesque-style Mother Church dates from 1894, but it serves only as a chapel at the rear of a grander basilica, which was built in 1906 to seat 5,000 worshipers. The basilica houses the western hemisphere's largest pipe organ, manufactured in Boston by the Aeolian-Skinner Company. Between 1968 and 1973 the Christian Science complex expanded to its present design, which includes an elegant office tower, a reflecting pool, and a monumental plaza.

The Mary Baker Eddy Library for the Betterment of Humanity, on the Massachusetts Ave side of the complex, emphasizes Eddy's inspiration rather than church doctrine. Visitors can peer through a glass wall into the newsroom of the Christian Science Monitor. The most

---

MARY BAKER EDDY

Born in Concord, New Hampshire in 1821, Mary Baker was plagued with poor health for much of her early life. Fearing death after a severe fall in 1866, she sought comfort in her Bible, where she found an account of how Jesus had healed a palsied man. Her own miraculous recovery led her to the principle of Christian Science, a doctrine which emphasizes spiritual regeneration and healing through prayer alone. In 1875 she published her ideas in Science and Health with Key to the Scriptures, the textbook of Christian Science, and gathered students around her, including Asa Gilbert Eddy, whom she married in 1877. Two years later she organized the First Church of Christ, Scientist, in Boston, from which Christian Science churches spread across the world. Mrs. Eddy remained the active leader of the Christian Science movement until her death in 1910. She is buried at Mount Auburn Cemetery in Cambridge.

popular exhibit is the Mapparium, where visitors literally walk through the globe viewing the planet from the inside. The different colors represent the world's political boundaries of 1935.

Copley Place ⑭

Huntington Ave & Dartmouth St. **Map** 3 C3. *Tel* (617) 369-5000. ⓣ *Back Bay/South End, Copley.* ◯ *10am–9pm Mon–Sat, 11am–6pm Sun.* ♿

Copley Place is a creature of late 20th-century urban development, with hotels, an upscale shopping center, and restaurants. Offices and luxury apartments are also part of the development, which rises on land created above the Massachusetts Turnpike. Copley Place bears little relation to Copley Square, but the shopping mall was a success from the day it opened in 1984 and still ranks as Boston's most luxurious indoor shopping mall. Its stores include the jeweler Tiffany's and the status-conscious department store Neiman-Marcus (*see p153*).

Boston Center for the Arts ⑮

539 Tremont St. **Map** 4 D3. *Tel* (617) 426-5000. ⓣ *Back Bay/South End.* **Cyclorama** ◯ *call for hours.* **Mills Gallery** ◯ *noon–5pm Wed & Sun, noon–9pm Thu–Sat.* ◉ *public hols.* 🎟 *for performances.* 🚫 ♿ **www.**bcaonline.org

The centerpiece of a resurgent South End, the BCA complex includes four stages, an art gallery, and artists' studios as well as the Boston Ballet Building, home to the company's educational programs, rehearsal space, and administrative offices.
    The Tremont Estates Building at the corner of Tremont Street, an organ factory in the years after the Civil War, now houses artists' studios, rehearsal space, and an art gallery.
    The largest of the BCA buildings is the circular, domed Cyclorama, which

Caption: **Bow-fronted, red-brick houses, typical of South End's Union Park**

opened in 1884 to exhibit the 50-ft (15-m) by 400-ft (121-m) painting *The Battle of Gettysburg* by the French artist Paul Philippoteaux. The painting was removed in 1889 and is now displayed at Gettysburg National Historic Park. The Cyclorama now serves as a performance and exhibition space.
    The Stanford Calderwood Pavilion, with a 360-seat and a 200-seat theater, opened in 2004 as the first new theater built in Boston in 75 years.
    The Mills Gallery houses exhibitions focusing on emerging contemporary artists, with the emphasis on multimedia installations and shows with confrontational, often provocative, themes.

Red-brick façade of the Boston Center for the Arts, site of theaters and exhibition spaces

Union Park ⑯

Tremont & Shawmut Sts. **Map** 4 D4. ⓣ *Back Bay/South End.* ♿

Union Park is the green gem of the South End, built from 1857 to 1859 when the neighborhood was still fashionable. South End property values crashed in the Panic of 1873, and the entire district, Union Park included, became tenement housing for immigrants arriving from eastern Europe and the Middle East. The South End remains broadly mixed by ethnicity, race, and sexual orientation. The handsome town houses along Union Park led the South End's economic resurgence in the 1970s, once it has become, once again, a coveted address. A pair of fountains, an iron fence, and large shade trees present a truly parklike setting for the beautifully restored brick row houses. The 19th-century ornamental ironwork on and around these houses is particularly prized by architecture buffs. Union Park is strictly residential, although there are a few small shops, and restaurants which have become very popular for Saturday and Sunday brunch.

FARTHER AFIELD

Statue of William Prescott, Bunker Hill Monument

The late 19th and 20th centuries saw Boston expand out of the central colonial and Victorian city into the surrounding area. The old marshlands of the Fenway now house two of Boston's most important art museums, the Museum of Fine Arts and the Isabella Stewart Gardner Museum. Southeast of the city center, Columbia Point was developed in the mid-20th century and is home to the John F. Kennedy Library and Museum. West of central Boston, across the Charles River, lies Cambridge, sometimes referred to as the "People's Democratic Republic of Cambridge," a reference to the politics of Harvard and the Massachusetts Institute of Technology, its two major colleges. Harvard Square is a lively area of bookstores, cafés, and street entertainers. Charlestown is the site of the Bunker Hill Monument and the Charlestown Navy Yard, where the U.S.'s most famous warship, the U.S.S. *Constitution*, is moored. Farther northwest lie historic Concord and Lexington, where the first major battles of the Revolutionary War took place in 1775.

SIGHTS AT A GLANCE

Towns
Cambridge ❼
Charlestown ❽
Concord ❾
Lexington ❿

Museums and Historic Sites
Isabella Stewart Gardner Museum ❺

John F. Kennedy Library and Museum ❶
John F. Kennedy National Historic Site ❹
Museum of Fine Arts, Boston pp104–7 ❻

Gardens and Zoos
Arnold Arboretum ❸
Franklin Park Zoo ❷

KEY

▦	Main sightseeing area
▢	Urban area
✈	Airport
🚉	Railroad station
═	Highway
▬	Major road
═	Minor road
—	Railroad

5 km = 3 miles

◁ **Central courtyard of the *palazzo*-style Isabella Stewart Gardner Museum**

John F. Kennedy Library and Museum ❶

Columbia Point, Dorchester.
Tel (617) 514-1600. Ⓣ JFK/U Mass.
☐ 9am–5pm daily. ◕ Jan 1,
Thanksgiving, Dec 25. 🖼 ⌖ ⌖ ⌖
www.jfklibrary.org

The soaring white concrete and glass building housing the John F. Kennedy Library stands sentinel on Columbia Point near the mouth of the Boston Harbor. This striking white and black modern building by the architect I. M. Pei is equally dramatic from the interior, with a 50-ft (15-m) wall of glass looking out over the sea. Exhibitions extensively chronicle the 1,000 days of the Kennedy presidency with an immediacy uncommon in many other historical museums. Kennedy was among the first politicians to grasp the power of media. The museum takes full advantage of film and video footage to use the president's own words and image to tell his story: his campaign for the Democratic Party nomination, landmark television debates with Republican opponent Richard M. Nixon (who later became infamous for the Watergate Scandal), and his many addresses to the nation.

Several rooms recreate key chambers of the White House during the Kennedy administration, including the Oval Office, and gripping film clips capture the anxiety of nuclear brinksmanship during the Cuban missile crisis as well as the inspirational spirit of the space program and the founding of the Peace Corps. Exhibits on Robert F. Kennedy's role as Attorney General touch on both his deft handling of race relations and his key advisory role to his brother. The combination of artifacts, displays, and television footage evoke both the euphoria of "Camelot" and the numb horror of the assassination.

Lowland gorilla with her baby in the simulated natural environment of Franklin Park Zoo

Franklin Park Zoo ❷

1 Franklin Park Rd. **Tel** (617) 541-5466. Ⓣ Forest Hills. 🚌 16 from Forest Hills subway. ☐ Apr–Sep: 10am–5pm Mon–Fri, 10am–6pm Sat–Sun; Oct–Mar: 10am–4pm daily. ◕ Jan 1, Thanksgiving, Dec 25. 🖼 ⌖ **www**.zoonewengland.com

The zoo, originally planned as a small menagerie, has expanded dramatically over the past century and long ago discarded caged enclosures in favor of simulated natural environments. Lowland gorillas roam a forest edge with caves for privacy, lions lounge around a rocky kingdom while zebras, ostriches, and giraffes are free to graze on open grassland. Bird's World, a structure dating from the zoo's 1913 opening, features a free-flight cage with dozens of species of birds. A special enclosed exhibit simulates night conditions for nocturnal birds. Youngsters can interact with farm animals in a small petting zoo.

Arnold Arboretum ❸

125 Arborway, Jamaica Plain.
Tel (617) 524-1718. Ⓣ Forest Hills.
🚌 39. ☐ sunrise–sunset daily.
Visitors Center ☐ 9am–4pm
Mon–Fri, 10am–4pm Sat, noon–4pm Sun. ◕ public hols. ⌖
www.arboretum.harvard.edu

Founded by Harvard University in 1872 as a living catalog of all the indigenous and exotic trees and shrubs adaptable to New England's climate, the Arboretum is planted with

Dramatic, modern structure of the John F. Kennedy Library and Museum

more than 15,000 labeled specimens. It is the oldest arboretum in the U.S. and a key resource for botanical and horticultural research. The Arboretum also serves as a park where people jog, stroll, read, and paint.

The park's busiest time is on the third Sunday in May – Lilac Sunday – when tens of thousands come to revel in the sight and fragrance of the lilac collection, one of the largest in the world. The range of the Arboretum's collections guarantees flowers from late March into November, beginning with cornelian cherry and forsythia. Blooms shift in late May to azalea, magnolia, and wisteria, then to mountain laurel and roses in June. Sweet autumn clematis bursts forth in September, and native witch hazel blooms in October and November. The Arboretum also has fine fall foliage in September and October.

A large scale model of the Arboretum can be seen in the Visitors' Information Center just inside the main gate.

John F. Kennedy National Historic Site ❹

83 Beals St, Brookline. **Tel** (617) 566-7937. ⓣ Coolidge Corner. ◯ late May–Sep: 10am–4:30pm Wed–Sun. ● Thanksgiving. ▨ ✄ ⬤ ✄ ⬤ **www**.nps.gov/jofi

The first home of the late president's parents, this Brookline house saw the birth of four of nine Kennedy children, including J.F.K. on May 29, 1917. Although the Kennedys moved to a larger house in 1921, the Beals Street residence held special memories for the family, who repurchased the house in 1966 and furnished it with their belongings circa 1917 as a memorial to John F. Kennedy. The guided tour includes a taped interview with J.F.K.'s mother Rose. A walking tour takes in other neighborhood sites relevant to the Kennedy family's early years.

Central courtyard of the *palazzo*-style Isabella Stewart Gardner Museum

Isabella Stewart Gardner Museum ❺

280 The Fenway. **Tel** (617) 566-1401. ⓣ MFA. ◯ 11am–5pm Tue–Sun. ● Jan 1, Thanksgiving, Dec 25. ▨ ✄ ♫ call for concert schedule. **www**.gardnermuseum.org

The only thing more surprising than a Venetian *palazzo* on The Fenway is the collection of more than 2,500 works of art inside. Advised by scholar Bernard Berenson, the strong-willed Isabella Stewart Gardner turned her wealth to collecting art in the late 19th century, acquiring a notable collection of Old Masters and Italian Renaissance pieces. Titian's *Rape of Europa*, for example, is considered his best painting in a U.S. museum. The eccentric "Mrs. Jack" had an eye for her contemporaries as well. She purchased the first Matisse to enter an American collection and was an ardent patron of James McNeill Whistler and John Singer Sargent. The paintings, sculptures, and tapestries are displayed on three levels around a stunning skylit courtyard. Mrs. Gardner's will stipulates the collection should remain assembled in the manner she originally intended. However, today, blank spaces can be seen where thieves stole 13 priceless works in 1990. Amongst the stolen art was a rare Rembrandt, *Storm on the Sea of Galilee*, then conservatively valued at $200 million. An annex, designed by Renzo Piano, is due to open in 2012 and will house the visitors' center and entrance.

THE EMERALD NECKLACE

Best known as designer of New York's Central Park, Frederick Law Olmsted based himself in Boston, where he created parks to solve environmental problems and provide a green refuge for inhabitants of the 19th-century industrial city. The Emerald Necklace includes the green spaces of Boston Common and the Public Garden (see pp46–7) and Commonwealth Avenue (see p93). To create a ring of parks, Olmsted added the Back Bay Fens

Jamaica Pond, part of Boston's fine parklands

(site of beautiful rose gardens and gateway to the Museum of Fine Arts and the Isabella Stewart Gardner Museum), the rustic Riverway, Jamaica Pond (sailing and picnicking), Arnold Arboretum, and Franklin Park (a golf course, zoo, and cross-country ski trails). The 5-mile (8-km) swath of parkland makes an excellent bicycle tour or ambitious walk.

The Museum of Fine Arts, Boston ❻

This is the largest art museum in New England and one of the five largest in the United States. Its collection includes around 450,000 items, ranging from Egyptian artifacts to paintings by John Singer Sargent. The original 1909 Beaux Arts-style MFA building was augmented in 1981 by the addition of the Linde Family wing, designed by I.M. Pei. The Art of the Americas wing opened in 2010 and was designed by architect Norman Foster. The wing has 53 galleries and displays over 5,000 works of art.

American Silver
The revolutionary Paul Revere (see p21) was also a noted silversmith and produced many beautiful objects, such as this ornate teapot.

★ **Japanese Temple Room**
This room was created in 1909 to provide a space in which to contemplate Buddhist art. The MFA has one of the finest Japanese collections outside Japan.

★ **Egyptian Mummies**
Among the museum's Egyptian and Nubian art is this tomb group of Nes-mut-aat-neru (767–656 BC) of Thebes.

Fenway Entrance

Calderwood Courtyard

Sha
Cou

Huntingdon Entrance

★ **Copley Portraits**
John Singleton Copley (1738–1815) painted the celebrities of his day, hence this portrait of a dandyish John Hancock (see p21).

Lower Ground

Head of Aphrodite
This rare example of Ancient Greek sculpture dates from about 330–300 BC.

Level 3

Level 2

Level 1

VISITORS' CHECKLIST

Avenue of the Arts,
465 Huntington Ave.
Tel *(617) 267-9300.* Ⓣ *MFA.*
⬚ *10am–4:45pm Mon–Tue,*
10am–9:45pm Wed–Fri, 10am–
4:45 Sat & Sun. ⬤ *most public*
hols. 📷 ♿ 🎫 🎧
Lectures, concerts, and films.
🍴 🏪 📷 *www.mfa.org*

Sargent Murals
John Singer Sargent spent the last years of his life creating artwork for the MFA. Originally commissioned to produce three paintings, Sargent instead constructed these elaborate murals, which were unveiled in 1921 and can still be seen today. He went on to create the works of art in the adjacent colonnade until his death in 1925.

★ Impressionist Paintings
Boston collectors were among the first to appreciate French Impressionism. Dance at Bougival (1883) by Renoir is typical of the MFA collection.

GALLERY GUIDE
The Linde Family wing (west side) displays Contemporary art and houses a restaurant and the museum store. European, Classical, Far Eastern, and Egyptian art and artifacts occupy the original MFA building. Arts from North, Central, and South America are displayed over four levels of the Art of the Americas wing. Works on display are subject to change.

STAR EXHIBITS

★ Japanese Temple
   Room

★ Egyptian Mummies

★ Copley Portraits

★ Impressionist
   Paintings

KEY

- ⬚ Art of Europe
- ⬚ Contemporary Art
- ⬚ Art of Asia, Oceania, and Africa
- ⬚ Art of the Ancient World
- ⬚ Art of the Americas
- ⬚ Special/Temporary exhibitions
- ⬚ Non-exhibition space

Exploring the Museum of Fine Arts, Boston

11th-century, silver Korean ewer

In addition to the major collections noted below, the Museum of Fine Arts has important holdings in the arts of Africa, Oceania, and the ancient Americas. The museum also houses collections of works on paper, contemporary art, and musical instruments. Several galleries are devoted to temporary thematic exhibitions. Other features of the museum include a seminar room, lecture hall, and well-stocked bookstore. There are regular talks, artist demonstrations, and events at the museum; check the website for the latest information.

EUROPEAN PAINTINGS, DECORATIVE ARTS, AND SCULPTURE

This collection of European paintings and sculpture ranges from the 7th to the late 20th century. It showcases numerous masterpieces by English, Dutch, French, Italian, and Spanish artists, including various portraits by the 17th-century Dutch painter Rembrandt. The collection of works from 1550 to 1700 is impressive both for the quality of art and for its size, which includes Francisco de Zurbarán, El Greco, Paolo Veronese, Titian, and Peter Paul Rubens.

Boston's 19th-century collectors enriched the MFA with wonderful French painting: the museum features several paintings by Pierre François Millet (the MFA has, in fact, the largest collection of his work in the world) as well as by other well-known 19th-century French artists, such as Edouard Manet, Pierre-Auguste Renoir, and Edgar Degas. Among this collection are the hugely popular and infamous *Waterlilies* (1905) by Claude Monet and *Dance at Bougival* (1883) by Renoir. The MFA's Monet holdings are among the world's largest, and there is also a good collection of paintings by the Dutch artist Vincent

Boston Harbor by the Luminist painter Fitz Hugh Lane (1804–65)

ART OF THE AMERICAS COLLECTION

The MFA's Art of the Americas wing features work from the birth of the United States through to the third quarter of the 20th century. The collection includes masterpieces of both ancient and contemporary Native American art. Designed by the English architect Norman Foster, the wing showcases approximately 5,000 works produced in North, Central, and South America.

The Colonial period in U.S. art is well represented, with more than 60 portraits by John Singleton Copley, perhaps America's most talented 18th-century painter, as well as works by Charles Wilson Peale. Other works on display are 19th-century landscapes, including harbor scenes by Fitz Hugh Lane, an early Luminist painter; lush society portraits by John Singer Sargent; and

paintings by other late 19th-century artists who constituted the "Boston School." Other notable highlights include seascapes by Winslow Homer and the muscular figure portraiture of Thomas Eakins. The MFA also exhibits works by 20th-century masters such as Stuart Davis, Jackson Pollock, Georgia O'Keeffe, and Arthur Dove.

The museum's holdings of American silver are superb. In addition to works by John Coney, there are two cases containing tea services and other pieces by Paul Revere *(see p73)*. The MFA also traces the development of the Boston style of 18th-century furniture through a definitive collection of desks, high chests, and tall clocks. Its famed period rooms display decorative arts in a historical context.

La Berceuse by the Dutch painter Vincent van Gogh (1853–90)

Part of the Processional Way of Ancient Babylonia (6th century BC)

galleries of the museum are intended to thematically highlight the influence of Greek arts on both Etruscan and Roman art. The Etruscan collection has several carved sarcophagi, gold jewelry, bronze mirrors, and colorful terracottas, while the Roman collection features grave markers, portrait busts, and a series of wall panel paintings unearthed in Pompeii on an MFA expedition in 1900–01.

van Gogh. Early 20th-century European art is also exhibited.

The MFA is well known for its extensive collection of European decorative arts. Tableware, ceramics, and glass clustered by period from the early 17th to early 20th centuries are some examples of the works exhibited. Painstakingly transferred medieval stained-glass windows, beautifully illuminated bibles, and delicate French tapestries are displayed alongside works by Old Masters.

Some of the museum's most prized decorative arts include the opulent displays of 18th-century French silver housed in the Louis XVI-style gallery, and some of the world's most extensive holdings of Chinese export porcelain.

ANCIENT EGYPTIAN, NUBIAN, AND NEAR EASTERN ART

The MFA's collection of Egyptian and Nubian materials is unparalleled outside of Africa, and derives primarily from MFA-Harvard University excavations along the Nile, which began in 1905. One of the highlights is a 1998 installation showing Egyptian Funerary Arts, which uses the MFA's superb collection of mummies from nearly three millennia to illustrate the technical and art historical aspects of Egyptian burial practices. Also on display are some exceptional Babylonian, Assyrian, and Sumerian reliefs. Works from ancient Nubia, the cultural region around the Nile stretching

roughly between the modern African cities of Aswan and Khartoum, encompass gold and silver artifacts, ceramics, and jewels.

Other highlights from the Egyptian and Nubian collections include two monumental sculptures of Nubian kings from the Great Temple of Amen at Napata (620–586 BC and 600–580 BC). A few of the galleries are set up to re-create Nubian burial chambers, which allows cuneiform wall carvings to be displayed in something akin to an original setting; a superb example is the offering chapel of Sekhem-ankh-Ptah from Sakkara (2450–2350 BC).

CLASSICAL ART

The MFA boasts one of America's top collections of Greek ceramics. In particular the red- and black-figured vases dating from the 6th and 5th centuries BC are exceptional. The Classical

ASIAN ART

The Asian collection is one of the most extensive that can be found under one roof. A range of works from India, the Near East and Central Asian art are exhibited.

Tang Dynasty Chinese Horse (8th century)

Among the highlights are Indian sculpture and changing exhibitions of Islamic miniature paintings and Indian narrative paintings. Elsewhere, works from Korea feature some Buddhist paintings and sculptures, jewelry, and ornaments.

The museum also boasts calligraphy, ceramics, and stone sculptures from China and the largest collection of Japanese prints outside Japan. Extensive holdings and limited display space mean that specific exhibitions change often, but the MFA's exhibitions of Japanese and Chinese scroll and screen paintings are, nevertheless, unmatched in the West. The strength of the MFA's Japanese art collection is largely due to the efforts of collectors such as Ernest Fenollosa and William Bigelow Sturgis. In the 19th century they encouraged the Japanese to maintain their traditions, and salvaged Buddhist temple art when the Japanese imperial government had withdrawn subsidies from these institutions. This collection is considered to contain some of the finest examples of Asian temple art in the world.

Roman fresco, excavated from a Pompeian villa (1st century AD)

Cambridge **⑦**

Part of the greater Boston metropolitan area, Cambridge is, nonetheless, a town in its own right, and has the mood and feel of such. Principally a college town, it is dominated by Harvard University and other college campuses. It also boasts a number of important historic sights, such as Christ Church and Cambridge Common, which have associations back to the American Revolution. Harvard Square is the area's main entertainment and shopping district.

Site of the Washington Elm, on Cambridge Common

🏛 Longfellow National Historic Site

105 Brattle St. **Tel** (617) 876-4491.
◯ Jun–Oct: 10am–4:30pm Wed–Sun. ◑ Nov–May.
🖼 🚫 ♿ 📷 **www**.nps.gov/long
This house on Brattle Street, like many around it, was built by Colonial-era merchants loyal to the British Crown during the Revolution. It was seized by American revolutionaries and served as George Washington's headquarters during the Siege of Boston.

The poet Henry Wadsworth Longfellow boarded here in 1837, was given the house as a wedding present in 1843, and lived here until his death in 1888. He wrote his most famous poems here, including *Tales of a Wayside Inn and The Song of Hiawatha*. Longfellow's status as literary dean of Boston meant that Nathaniel Hawthorne and Charles Sumner, among others, were regular visitors.

🏛 Harvard Square

📱 (617) 491-3434. ♿
www.harvardsquare.com
Even Bostonians think of Harvard Square as a stand-in for Cambridge – the square was the original site of Cambridge from around 1630. Dominating the square is the Harvard Cooperative Society ("the Coop"), a Harvard institution, that sells inexpensive clothes, posters, and books.

Harvard's large student population is very much in evidence here, adding color to the character of the square. Many trendy boutiques, inexpensive restaurants, and numerous cafés cater to their needs. Street performers abound, especially on the weekends, and the square has long been a place where pop trends begin. Club Passim *(see p162)*, for example, has incubated many successful singer-songwriters since Joan Baez first debuted here in 1959.

Street musician, Harvard Square

🏛 Cambridge Common

Set aside as common pasture and military drill ground in 1631, Cambridge Common has served as a center for religious, social, and political activity ever since. George Washington took command of the Continental Army here on July 3, 1775, beneath the Washington Elm, now marked by a stone. The common served as the army's encampment from 1775 to 1776. Today the ball fields and playgrounds are popular with families. In 1997 the first monument in the U.S. to the victims of the Irish Famine was unveiled on the common.

🔒 Christ Church

Garden St. **Tel** (617) 876-0200.
◯ 8am–6pm Sun–Fri, 8am–3pm Sat.
✝ 7:45am, 10:15am Sun; 12:10pm Wed. 🚫 ♿ **www**.cccambridge.org
With its square bell tower and plain, gray shingled edifice, Christ Church is a restrained example of an Anglican church. Designed in 1761 by Peter Harrison, the architect of Boston's King's Chapel *(see p58)*, Christ Church came in for rough treatment as a barracks for Continental Army troops in 1775 – British loyalists had almost all fled Cambridge by this time. The army even melted down the organ pipes to cast musket balls. The church was restored on New Year's Eve, 1775, when George Washington and his wife Martha were among the worshipers. Anti-Anglican sentiment remained strong in Cambridge, and Christ Church did not have its own rector again until the 19th century.

Simple interior of Christ Church, designed prior to the Revolution in 1761

♯ Radcliffe Institute for Advanced Study

Brattle St. **Tel** *(617) 495-8601.* &
www.radcliffe.edu

Radcliffe College was founded in 1879 as the Collegiate Institution for Women, when 27 women began to study by private arrangement with Harvard professors. By 1943, members of Harvard's faculty no longer taught separate undergraduate courses to the women of Radcliffe, and in 1999 Radcliffe ceased its official existence as an independent college. It is now an institute for advanced study promoting scholarship of women's culture. The first Radcliffe building was the 1806 Federal-style mansion, Fay House, on the northern corner of what became Radcliffe Yard. Schlesinger Library, on the west side of the yard, is considered a significant example of

Stained glass, Radcliffe Institute

Colonial Revival architecture. The library's most famous holdings are an extensive collection of cookbooks and reference works on gastronomy.

♯ M.I.T.

77 Massachusetts Ave. **Tel** *(617) 253-4795.* **M.I.T. Museum** ◻ *10am–5pm daily.* 🖼 **Hart Nautical Gallery** ◻ *10am–5pm daily.* **List Visual Arts Center** ◻ *noon–6pm Tue–Sun (to 8pm Thu).* 🗷 & 🗷 www.mit.edu

Chartered in 1861 to teach students "exactly and thoroughly the fundamental principles of positive science with application to the industrial arts," the Massachusetts Institute of Technology has evolved into one of the world's leading universities in engineering and the sciences. Several architectural masterpieces dot M.I.T.'s 135-acre (55-ha) campus along the Charles River. Finnish

VISITORS' CHECKLIST

ⓣ *Harvard.* 🚌 *1, 69.* ℹ
Harvard Square Information Booth *(617) 497-1630,*
Cambridge Office of Tourism
(800) 862-5678, (617) 441-2884.
📅 *Sun.* 🎪 *River Festival (early June.)* www.harvard.edu **or** www.cambridge–usa.org

Modernism is represented by Alvar Aalto's seminal Baker House dormitory (1949). Eero Saarinen's compressed arches make Kresge Auditorium (1955) seem poised for flight. The spare lines of Kresge Chapel (1955) embody ascetic faith. The Wiesner building houses the **List Visual Arts Center**, noted for its avant-garde art.

The **Hart Nautical Gallery** in the Rogers Building focuses on marine engineering, with models of ships and exhibits of the latest advances in underwater research. The **M.I.T. Museum** blends art and science, with exhibits such as Harold Edgerton's ground-breaking stroboscopic flash photographs, and the latest holographic art.

CAMBRIDGE TOWN CENTER

Cambridge Common ①
Christ Church ②
Harvard Square ③
Harvard University Museums
  (see pp112–13) ④
Harvard Yard
  (see pp110–11) ⑤
Longfellow National Historic Site ⑥
Radcliffe Institute for Advanced Study ⑦

0 meters 400
0 yards 400

Key to Symbols *see back flap*

Harvard Yard

In 1636 Boston's well-educated Puritan leaders founded a college in Newtowne. Two years later cleric John Harvard died and bequeathed half his estate and all his books to the fledgling college. The colony's leaders bestowed his name on the school and rechristened the surrounding community Cambridge after the English city where they had been educated. The oldest university in the U.S., Harvard is now one of the world's most prestigious centers of learning. The university has expanded to encompass more than 400 buildings, but Harvard Yard is still at its heart.

Holden Chapel
Built in 1742, the chapel was the scene of revolutionary speeches and was later used as a demonstration hall for human dissections.

Hollis Hall was used as barracks by George Washington's troops during the American Revolution.

Massachusetts Hall, built in 1720, is Harvard's oldest building.

★ **Old Harvard Yard**
This leafy yard dates from the founding of the college in 1636. Freshman dormitories dot the yard, and throughout the year it is a focal point for students.

Harvard University Information Center ✓

★ **John Harvard Statue**
This statue celebrates Harvard's most famous benefactor. Almost a place of pilgrimage, graduates and visitors invariably pose for photographs here.

University Hall, designed by Charles Bulfinch, was built in 1816.

★ **Widener Library**
This library memorializes Harry Elkins Widener who died on the Titanic in 1912. With more than 3 million volumes, it is the third largest library in the U.S.

★ **Memorial Church**
This church was built in 1931 and copies earlier styles. For example, the steeple is modeled on that of the Old North Church (see p71) in Boston's North End.

VISITORS' CHECKLIST

Massachusetts Ave. ⓣ *Harvard.*
◯ *24 hrs.* ◉ *2nd Thu in Jun (Commencement).* ♿ 🔊
🎞 *Mon–Sat (call for details.)*
Harvard Information Center
Tel (617) 495-1573.
Harvard Box Office
Tel (617) 496-2222.
Harvard Film Archive *Tel (617) 495 4700.* **www.**harvard.edu

Memorial Hall, a Ruskin Gothic building, memorializes Harvard's Union casualties from the Civil War.

Sackler and Peabody Museums, and Harvard Museum of Natural History (see pp114–15)

Sever Hall
One of the most distinctive of Harvard's Halls, this Romanesque style-building was designed by Henry Hobson Richardson (see p32).

Fogg Art and Busch-Reisinger Museums (see pp112–13)

Tercentenary Theater

STAR SIGHTS

★ Old Harvard Yard

★ John Harvard Statue

★ Widener Library

★ Memorial Church

0 meters   50

0 yards   50

Carpenter Center for Visual Arts
Opened in 1963, the Carpenter Center is the only building in the U.S. designed by the avant-garde Swiss architect Le Corbusier.

The Harvard University Museums

Harvard's museums were originally conceived to revolutionize the process of education; students were to be taught by allowing them access to artifacts from around the world. Today, this tradition continues, with the museums housing some of the world's finest university collections: art from Europe and America in the Fogg Art and Busch-Reisinger Museums; archaeological finds in the Peabody Museum; Asian, Islamic and Indian art in the Sackler Museum, and a vast collection of artifacts in the Harvard Museum of Natural History.

Main entrance to the Fogg Art and Busch-Reisinger Museums

Fogg Art and Busch-Reisinger Museums

32 Quincy St. **Tel** (617) 495-9400.
for renovation until 2013.
www.artmuseums.harvard.edu

The Fogg Art and Busch-Reisinger museums are closed for renovation until 2013. Select items are currently on display at the Sackler Museum (see p114.) The Fogg Art Museum was created in 1891 when Harvard began to build its own art collection in order to teach art history more effectively. Both the Fogg and the Busch-Reisinger, which was grafted onto the Fogg in 1991, have select collections of art from Europe and America.

The collections, which focus on Western art from the late Middle Ages to the present, are organized around a central courtyard modeled on a 16th-century church in Montepulciano, Italy. The ground-floor corridors surrounding the courtyard feature 12th-century capitals from Moutiers St-Jean in Burgundy, France.

Two small galleries near the entrance, and the two-story Warburg Hall, display the Fogg's collections that prefigure the Italian Renaissance. The massive altarpieces and suspended crucifix in the Warburg are particularly impressive.

The ground floor galleries on the left side of the entrance are devoted to 17th-century Dutch, Flemish, French, and Italian paintings, including four studies for Francesco Trevisiani's *Massacre of the Innocents*, a masterpiece destroyed in Dresden during World War II. Another room details Gian Lorenzo Bernini's use of clay models for his large-scale marbles and bronzes.

The museum's second level features the emergence of landscape as a subject in French 19th-century painting.

Galleries along the front of the building change exhibitions frequently, often focusing on drawings and graphic arts. The highlight of the second level is the Maurice Wertheim collection of Impressionist and Post-Inpressionist art, most of it collected in the late 1930s.

With a number of important paintings by Renoir, Manet, and Degas, the Wertheim gallery is the Fogg's most popular.

Surprises lurk in an adjacent gallery of art made in France 1885-1960, often by expatriate artists. Edvard Munch's 1891 painting of *Rue de Rivoli*, for example, is both bright and impressionistic, in contrast with his bleak Expressionism.

The museum also houses rotating displays from its collection of 19th- and 20th-century African art.

Werner Otto Hall, which contains the Busch-Reisinger Museum, is entered through the second level of the Fogg. The museum's collections focus on Germanic art and

Bernini Model (1674–75) *Gian Lorenzo Bernini crafted this clay model of a kneeling angel to guide the artisans casting his larger bronze.*

First floor

Main entrance

GUIDE TO THE FOGG ART AND BUSCH-REISINGER MUSEUMS

Western art from the Middle Ages to the present is on the first floor of the Fogg Art Museum. French and American art from the 19th and 20th centuries and 20th-century American art are on the second floor. The Busch-Reisinger Museum focuses on Germanic art.

Light-Space Modulator (1923–30) by the Hungarian Moholy-Nagy

design from after 1880, with an emphasis on German Expressionism. Harvard was a safe haven for many Bauhaus artists, architects, and designers who fled Nazi Germany, and both Walter Gropius and Lyonel Feininger chose the Busch-Reisinger as the depository of their personal papers and drawings.

Periodic exhibitions explore aspects of the work and philosophy of the Bauhaus movement. Although small, the museum owns major paintings and sculptures by 20th-century masters such as Max Beckmann, Wassily Kandinsky, Moholy-Nagy, Paul Klee, Oskar Kokoschka, Emil Nolde, and Franz Marc.

Calderwood Courtyard of the Fogg Art Museum

Skating (1877)
This portrait, by Edouard Manet, shows elegantly attired Parisians at a skating rink. It is from the Fogg's renowned collection of French Impressionist paintings.

Entrance to Busch-Reisinger Museum

To study room

Second floor

KEY

- ☐ Fogg Art Museum
- ☐ Hammer Galleries (within the Fogg Art Museum)
- ☐ Busch-Reisinger Museum
- ☐ Non-exhibition space

Christ on the Cross (1446)
Painted by Fra Angelico, this Crucifixion scene is typical of the Italian Renaissance style.

Peabody Museum of Archaeology and Ethnology

11 Divinity Ave. **Tel** (617) 496-1027.
⬤ 9am–5pm daily. ⬤ Jan 1, Jul 4,
Thanksgiving, Dec 24, 25. 🖼 🚹 🎫
www.peabody.harvard.edu

The Peabody Museum of Archaeology and Ethnology was founded in 1866 as the first museum in the Americas devoted solely to anthropology. The many collections, which include several million artifacts and more than 500,000 photographic images, come from all around the world. The Peabody's pioneering investigations began with excavations of Mayan sites in Central America, research on the precontact Anasazi people of the American Southwest, and on the cultural history of the later Pueblo tribes of the same region. Joint expeditions sponsored by the Peabody Museum and the Museum of Fine Arts (see pp104–7) also uncovered some of the richest finds of dynastic and predynastic Egypt. Later research embraced the cultures of the islands of the South Pacific.

The Native American tribes of the Northern Plains are interpreted largely through an exhibition detailing the 1804–6 expedition, from the east to the west coast, by Lewis and Clark, who collected innumerable artifacts on the way. Other outstanding exhibits include totem carvings by Pacific Northwest tribes and a wide range of historic and contemporary Navajo weavings. The third floor is devoted to Central American anthropology, with casts of some of the ruins uncovered at Copán in Honduras and Chichen Itza in Mexico. The fourth floor concentrates on Polynesia, Micronesia, and other islands of the Pacific.

Native American totem pole, Peabody Museum

Harvard Museum of Natural History

26 Oxford St. **Tel** (617) 495-3045. ⬤
9am–5pm daily. ⬤ Jul 4, Thanksgiving, Dec 24, 25. 🖼 🚹 🎫
www.hmnh.harvard.edu

The Harvard Museum of Natural History is actually three museums rolled into one, with collections from the Mineralogical and Geological Museum, the Museum of Comparative Zoology, and the Botanical Museum.

The mineralogical galleries include some of Harvard University's oldest specimen collections. Virtually every New England mineral, rock, and gem type is represented, including rough and cut gemstones and one of the world's premier meteorite collections.

The zoological galleries owe their inception to the great 19th-century biologist Louis Agassiz and include his personal arachnid collection. The collection of taxidermied bird, mammal, and reptile specimens is comprehensive, and there is also a collection of dinosaur skeletons.

The collections in the botanical galleries include the Ware Collection of Blaschka Glass Models of Plants, popularly known as the "glass flowers." Between 1887 and 1936, father and son artisans Leopold and Rudolph Blaschka created these 3,000 exacting models of 850 plant species. Each species is illustrated with a scientifically accurate lifesize model and magnified parts.

Sackler Museum

485 Broadway, Cambridge.
Tel (617) 495-9400.
⬤ 10am–5pm Mon–Sat, 1–5pm
Sun. ⬤ public hols. 🖼 🚹 🎫
www.artmuseums.harvard.edu

Named after a famous philanthropist, physician, and art collector, the Arthur M. Sackler Museum is normally

Triceratops skull in the Harvard Museum of Natural History

home to Harvard's collection of ancient, Asian, Islamic, and later Indian art. During renovations to the Fogg and Busch-Reisinger Museums, lasting through 2013, the Sackler will display select items from the collections of all three museums. Be sure to pick up a gallery map and flyers on the configuration of current exhibitions.

Opened in 1985, the Sackler is housed in a modern building designed by James Stirling and is itself a bold artistic statement, while the starkly modern interior galleries provide optimal display space. The 30-ft (10-m) entrance lobby features a 1997 wall painting by Conceptual artist Sol Lewitt, whose trademark colorful geometric shapes appear to float in space.

The best way to tour the Sackler is to start on the fourth floor and work back to the lobby. The head of the stairwell ends at gallery 10 at the back of the building, which during normal times is devoted to changing exhibitions highlighting ancient Greek art.

The second-floor galleries are equally spacious, but less suffused with natural light. The first-floor gallery, which is behind the ticket booth, is notably smaller than those on the other floors.

Southeast Asian Buddha head, Sackler Museum

Charlestown ⑧

Situated on the north bank of the Charles River, directly opposite the North End, Charlestown exudes history. The site of the infamous Battle of Bunker Hill, when American troops suffered huge losses in their fight for independence, today the district forms a major part of Boston's Freedom Trail *(see pp124–7)*.

Granite obelisk of the Bunker Hill Monument, erected in 1843

♙ Bunker Hill Monument

Monument Square. **Tel** (617) 242-5641. ◯ 9am–5pm daily (Jul & Aug: to 6pm; last climb: 4:30pm). ◑ Jan 1, Thanksgiving, Dec 25. **www**.nps.gov/bost

In the Revolution's first pitched battle between British and colonial troops, the British won but failed to escape from Boston. Following the June 17, 1775 battle, American irregulars were joined by other militia to keep British forces penned up until George Washington forced their evacuation by sea the following March. A Tuscan-style pillar was erected in 1794 in honor of Dr. Joseph Warren, a Boston revolutionary leader who died in the battle, but Charlestown citizens felt something grander was in order. Accordingly, they began raising funds for the Bunker Hill Monument in 1823, laid the cornerstone in 1825, and dedicated the 221-ft (67-m) granite obelisk in 1843. The building has no elevator, but 294 steps lead to the top and give spectacular views of Boston harbor. Exhibitions recount the significance and drama of the bloody battle.

♙ John Harvard Mall

Ten families founded Charlestown in 1629, a year before the rest of Boston was settled. They built their homes and a palisaded fort on Town Hill, a spot now marked by John Harvard Mall. A small monument within the enclosed park pays homage to John Harvard, the young cleric who ministered to the settlers *(see p110)*.

When John Winthrop arrived with three shiploads of Puritan refugees in 1630 *(see p18)*, they settled nearby in the marshes at the base of Town Hill, now City Square.

♙ Charlestown Navy Yard

Tel (617) 242-5601. ◯ 9am–5pm daily (Jul & Aug: to 6pm). ◑ ◉

Established in 1800 as one of the country's first

Municipal art in City Square

military shipyards, for 174 years Charlestown Navy Yard played a key role in supporting the U.S. Atlantic fleet, as the Navy moved from wooden sailing ships to steel giants. The men and women working at the yard built more than 200 warships and carried out maintenance repairs on thousands of others. The yard was designed by Alexander Parris, architect of Quincy Market *(see p64)*, and was one of the first examples of industrial architecture in Boston.

On decommissioning, 30 acres of the Navy Yard were transferred to the National Park Service, and rangers now give tours of the facility on a daily basis, including the Chain Forge (where die-lock anchor chain was first made), the Rope Walk, and Dry Dock 1 (one of the first dry docks in the U.S.). A Visitor Center is located at Building 5.

VISITORS' CHECKLIST

🚇 Community College.
🚌 93. 🚢 from Long Wharf.
📅 Wed. 🎉 June 24.

♙ U.S.S. Constitution

Charlestown Navy Yard. **Tel** (617) 242-5671. ◯ Apr–Oct: 10am–4pm Tue–Sun; Nov–Mar: 10am–4pm Thu–Sun. ◑ ◉ **www**.ussconstitution.navy.mil

The oldest commissioned warship afloat, the U.S.S. *Constitution* saw action in the Mediterranean protecting American shipping from the Barbary pirates. In the War of 1812, she won fame and her nickname of "Old Ironsides" when cannonballs bounced off her in a battle with the British ship *Guerriere*. In the course of her active service, she won 42 battles, lost none, captured 20 vessels, and was never boarded by an enemy.

She underwent a thorough overhaul in time for her 1997 bicentennial, enabling her to carry her own canvas into the wind for the first time in a century. On July 4 each year, she is taken out into the harbor for a turn-around that reverses her position at the pier to ensure equal weathering on both sides. A small museum documents her history.

U.S.S. *Constitution*, built in 1797, moored in Charlestown Navy Yard

Concord 9

First settled in 1635, Concord is linked with neighboring Lexington in the battles of April 19, 1775. Colonials favoring separation from Great Britain hid munitions here and British troops, seeking these supplies, marched on the town, passing first through Lexington *(see p119)*. The resulting battles in Concord, along with the Lexington skirmish, are considered the first of the American Revolution. Half a century later, with the gathering of American writers including essayist Ralph Waldo Emerson, Concord blossomed as the literary heart of the US. The homes of many writers of the era are now preserved as museums.

widely considered to have set off the war, as the Colonials drove three British companies from the bridge and chased them back to their occupation barracks in Boston.

Across the bridge is the famous **Minute Man** statue, crafted by Concord native Daniel Chester French (1850–1931). A short trail leads from the bridge to the North Bridge Visitor Center. A re-enactment of the battle takes place every year in April.

North Bridge in Minute Man National Historical Park

Monument Square

At Concord's center is Monument Square. The square was the focus of a battle between British troops and Colonists on what has become known as Patriots Day. Having seized the gun cache of rebel forces, British soldiers began burning them. Nearby Colonial forces saw the smoke and, believing the British were torching the town, rushed to Concord's defense.

Minute Man National Historical Park – North Bridge Visitor Center

174 Liberty St. *Tel (978) 318-7810.* ☐ Apr–Oct: 9am–5pm daily; Nov: 9am–4pm daily. ● Thanksgiving, Dec–Mar. ♿ **www**.nps.gov/mima

Although British troops met little resistance on Lexington Battle Green and managed to prevail in Concord center, they fared less well in the countryside. Colonial militia and citizen-soldiers (Minute Men) successfully hid their cannon and powder stashes from a contingent of British soldiers by burying the munitions in newly plowed fields. They then confronted British troops who were patrolling North Bridge. The so-called "shot heard round the world," memorialized in Emerson's "Concord Hymn" (1837), is

Minute Man statue in Concord

Emerson House

28 Cambridge Tpk. *Tel (978) 369-2236.* ☐ mid-Apr–late Oct: 10am–4:30pm Thu–Sat, 1–4:30pm Sun. ♿ **www**.emersonhouse.rwe.org

Following his graduation from Harvard, Ralph Waldo Emerson (1803–82) spent his early adulthood as a schoolteacher and then as a Unitarian minister. But as he grew away from religious orthodoxy and began to promulgate his Transcendental philosophy, Emerson withdrew from the ministry and moved to Concord, living first in The Old Manse where he wrote his manifesto *Nature*. On marrying Lydia Jackson in 1835, he settled into Emerson house, writing essays, organizing lecture tours, and entertaining friends and admirers as the honored "Sage of Concord". Emerson lived in this house until his death in 1882. Much of his furniture, writings, books, and family memorabilia are on display here.

Along the Battle Road, by John Rush, is located in the Minute Man Visitor Center

Concord's Old Manse: home to 19th-century literary giants

⚱ The Old Manse

269 Monument St.
Tel (978) 369-3909.
◷ mid-Apr–Oct: 10am–5pm
Mon–Sat, noon–5pm Sun.

The parsonage by the North Bridge was built in 1770 by the grandfather of writer Ralph Waldo Emerson. Author Nathaniel Hawthorne (1804–64) lived here as a newlywed in 1842–45 and wrote *Mosses from an Old Manse* (1846), giving the house its name. On view are Emerson family possessions and period furniture. The garden was planted by essayist Henry David Thoreau (1817–62) as a wedding gift to Hawthorne.

⚏ Concord Museum

Jct of Lexington Rd and Cambridge Tpk. **Tel** (978) 369-9609. ◷ Jan–Mar: 11am–4pm Mon–Sat, 1–4pm Sun; Apr–Dec: 9am–5pm Mon–Sat, noon–5pm Sun (Jun–Aug: 9am–5pm Sun). 🅿 ♿ **www**.concordmuseum.org

Begun in 1850, the Concord museum contains one of the oldest and best-documented collections of Americana. Holdings include decorative arts from the 17th, 18th, and 19th centuries that can be traced to original Concord owners; the lantern that Paul Revere ordered hung to warn of the British advance; and American Revolution artifacts that include powder horns, muskets, cannonballs, and fifes. The museum is also the repository of the contents of Emerson's study, and the largest collection of personal items that belonged to essayist Henry David Thoreau. The "Why Concord?" exhibit traces the community from initial settlement some 10,000 years ago through the 20th century.

VISITORS' CHECKLIST

🏠 17,750. ✈ Boston.
ℹ 58 Main St. (978) 369-3120.
🎪 Patriots Day (Apr).
www.concordchamberof
commerce.org

A View of the Town of Concord April 19, 1775, Concord Museum

CONCORD TOWN CENTER

Concord Museum ⑦
Emerson House ⑧
Minute Man National
   Historical Park ②
Minute Man Statue ⑤
Monument Square ①

North Bridge ④
North Bridge
   Visitor Center ③
The Old Manse ⑥
Sleepy Hollow
   Cemetery ⑨

0 meters 300
0 yards 1000

Key to Symbols see back flap

Author's Ridge, Sleepy Hollow Cemetery

🏛 Sleepy Hollow Cemetery

Bedford St, east of Monument Sq.
◯ *dawn–dusk daily.*

This rolling green cemetery is the final resting place of many Concord literary giants. Pilgrims seek the graves of Henry David Thoreau (1817–62), Nathaniel Hawthorne (1804–64), Louisa May Alcott (1832–88), and Ralph Waldo Emerson (1803–82), among other notables, on "Author's Ridge." They often leave pebbles on Emerson's head-stone, acorns on Thoreau's, and pennies on the grave of sculptor Daniel Chester French. Although his most famous work is the Lincoln Memorial in Washington, DC, French also sculpted the Civil War Memorial in Sleepy Hollow.

🏛 Orchard House

399 Lexington Rd.
***Tel** (978) 369-4118.* ◯ *Apr–Oct: 10am–4:30pm Mon–Sat, 1–4:30pm Sun; Nov–Mar: 11am–3pm Mon–Fri, 10am–4:30pm Sat, 1–4:30pm Sun.*
📷 🚻 ● *Jan 1–15, Easter, Thanksgiving, Dec 25.*
www.louisamayalcott.org

Louisa May Alcott was the most successful member of the Alcott family, but in his day, her father Bronson was well-regarded as a Transcendental philosopher and founder of the now-defunct Concord School of Philosophy. Orchard House was the Alcott family home from 1858–77, and Louisa May set *Little Women* (1868) here. Since the house has been little altered since the Alcotts lived

in it, visitors often comment that a tour is like walking through the book.

Room at Orchard House, the Alcott family residence from 1858–77

🏛 The Wayside

455 Lexington Rd. ***Tel** (978) 369-6993.* ◯ *Jun–Oct, call for hours.*

This National Historic Site has a long literary history. It was home to the Alcott family while Louisa May was growing up, and became the only home ever owned by author Nathaniel Hawthorne. Children's author Margaret Sidney (1844–1924) of *Five Little Peppers* fame bought it from Hawthorne's daughter. Guided tours are offered at limited hours by Minute Man National Park rangers.

🏛 Walden Pond State Reservation

915 Walden St. ***Tel** (978) 369-3254.*
◯ *call for hours.* 📷 🚻 ♿
www.mass.gov/dcr

Essayist Henry David Thoreau (1817–62) lived at Walden Pond from 1845 to 1847. It was here that he compiled the material for his seminal work *Walden; or, Life in the Woods* (1854), which called for a return to simplicity and a respect for nature, which he cast as the source of all morality. Although he depicted himself living in isolation, Thoreau would visit the Concord Center to have Sunday dinners with the Emerson family, and the pond and its woodlands are no more wilderness than they were in Thoreau's day. His significance in American thought and letters, however, led to the designation of the pond as a National Historic Landmark. The area is popular for walking, fishing, and swimming, though the reservation limits visitors to 1,000 people at any one time. A bronze statue of Thoreau stands outside a re-creation of his cabin.

Directly across busy Route 2 from Walden Pond is the Walden Woods Project which demonstrates the enduring appeal of Thoreau's ideas. A one-mile (1.6-km) walking trail is punctuated by aphoristic inscriptions in granite from Thoreau's writings, and bronze-tipped columns devoted to such issues as pacifism and environmentalism. Within Walden Woods is a "reflection circle." The granite columns surrounding it bear yet more quotations from thinkers who were influenced by Thoreau, including civil rights leader Martin Luther King, Jr. (1929–68) and Sioux chief Luther Standing Bear (1868–1939).

Fisherman on the tranquil waters of Walden Pond

Lexington ⑩

The peaceful prosperity of the modern-day suburb of Lexington belies its role in the birth of American independence. On the village common at dawn on April 19, 1775, British regulars and Colonial militia exchanged shots. The skirmish proved to be the opening salvo of the American Revolution, and Lexington Battle Green has been hallowed ground for Americans ever since. Many visitors like to bicycle the 5.5 miles (9 km) from Alewife "T" station in Cambridge along the Minuteman Bikeway, which roughly parallels the British route on their march to Lexington.

Minute Man Bikeway, part of the Minute Man National Historical Park

🎖 Minute Man National Historical Park – Minute Man Visitor Center

Rte 2A. **Tel** (781) 674-1920. ◻ late Mar–Oct: 9am–5pm daily, Nov: 9am–4pm daily. **www**.nps.gov/mima
This 990-acre (400-ha) park, with access from both Concord (see pp116–18) and Lexington, preserves the site and interprets the story of the first battles of the American Revolution. It explains that British forces were seeking to uncover colonial munitions hidden in the countryside, and how both Massachusetts militia and citizen-soldiers, known as Minute Men, managed to rout the British regulars. The Visitor Center features a massive battle mural and a 22-minute multimedia show, *Road to Revolution*. A significant portion of the national park runs along the five-mile (8-km) Battle Road Trail. This is the path that was followed by British forces as they advanced from Lexington and marched on to Concord – the same route the forces took in retreat.

🏛 Lexington Battle Green

Tranquil churches surround the leafy green where, each year in April, historic re-enactors re-create the Battle of Lexington. The rest of the year, a statue of a Massachusetts militia man erected in 1900 recalls the event, as do the graves of seven of the eight colonial casualties.

Historic re-enactor

🏛 Historical Society Houses

Hancock-Clarke House 36 Hancock St; **Buckman Tavern** 1 Bedford St; **Munroe Tavern** 1332 Massachusetts Ave; **Tel** (781) 862-1703. ◻ call for seasonal opening hours. 🖼 📷 **www**.lexingtonhistory.org
These three structures all played a role in the events of April 19, 1775 (now known as Patriots Day). **Buckman Tavern** served as the meeting place for the Massachusetts militia before the confrontation

VISITORS' CHECKLIST

🏙 31,550. 🚇 Boston. ℹ 1875 Massachusetts Ave. (781) 862-1450. 🎌 Patriots Day (Apr). **www**.lexingtonchamber.org

and as a makeshift hospital for their wounded. Bostonian Paul Revere undertook his "midnight ride" to **Hancock-Clarke House** to warn patriots Samuel Adams and John Hancock, two of the signatories to the Declaration of Independence, of the approaching British (see p21). **Munroe Tavern** was a headquarters for British forces. All display artifacts from the Revolutionary era.

🏛 National Heritage Museum

33 Marrett Rd. (at intersection of Rte 2A and Massachusetts Ave.) **Tel** (781) 861-6559. ◻ 10am–4:30pm daily (from noon Sun). ● Jan 1, Thanksgiving, Dec 24–25. **www**.monh.org
This museum, opened on the bicentennial of the Battle of Lexington, is devoted both to patriotic subjects and a celebration of American popular culture. Among its prized artifacts is a copy of the Lexington Alarm, a broadside detailing the events at Lexington and calling on American colonists to revolt against the British Crown.

Buckman Tavern, where militia met to plan their revolt against British forces

THREE GUIDED WALKS

Given the difficulties of driving in Boston, it is fortunate that its compact layout and ubiquitous sidewalks make it an ideal walking city. These three walks show the city's extremes – the dense riches of a university campus, the unexpected pleasures of an intensely residential neighborhood, and Boston's most famous walking tour along the historic Freedom Trail. While Harvard *(see pp112–7)* gets the lion's share of attention among the Boston-area universities, its younger neighbor in Cambridge, the Massachusetts Institute of Technology (MIT), is known for its modern art. South Boston is a secret often jealously guarded by its inhabitants. Although Dorchester Heights was a critical site in the American Revolution, few Freedom Trail walkers ever make the detour to appreciate the high vantage on Boston's outer harbor. In addition to these three walks, each of the five areas of Boston described in the *Area by Area* section of this book has a walk on its *Street-by-Street* map.

David Faragut statue

CHOOSING A WALK

The Three Walks
This map shows the location of the three guided walks in relation to the main sightseeing areas of Boston.

MIT Campus (p121)

The Freedom Trail continued (pp126–7)

The Freedom Trail (pp124–5)

South Boston (pp122–3)

Grand architecture and extensive parkland at the MIT campus (p121)

0 kilometers 1

0 miles 1

KEY

••• Walk route

A 45-Minute Walk on the MIT Campus

Perhaps best known for its advances in science and engineering, the Massachusetts Institute of Technology has embraced cutting-edge art and architecture as surely as it has pioneered artificial intelligence and robotics. This walking tour samples some of the best of modern and post-modern sculpture and buildings located around the campus. These highlights represent the institute's innovative use of unconventional materials and techniques.

The Stata Center designed by Frank Gehry ⑨

From the Kendall/MIT "T" station, walk to Main Street and turn right. Take the second right down Wadsworth Street to the corner of Amherst Street where Pablo Picasso's *Figure Découpée* ① from 1963 stands in a small garden. Cross the intersection to the Tang Building, where Frank Stella's 1988 abstract wall relief of acrylic and enamel on aluminum, *Heads or Tails* ②, fills the wall at the base of the staircase atrium. Continue down Amherst Street and turn right onto Ames Street at the Media Lab Extension building. Next door, the sleekly banded white box with dark windows is the List Visual Arts Center ③, where galleries display changing exhibitions of innovative, contemporary art. Note Alexander Calder's intermediate model for his

sculpture, *The Big Sail*, in the lobby ④. In the central atrium, Kenneth Noland's 1985 *Here-There* ⑤ carries the minimalist abstraction of the List building to its logical artistic extreme in a four-story interior wall mural.

Join the students rushing to classes as you cross Ames Street to the walkway that leads into the heart of the campus. Set at the edge of the sidewalk on the left is a complex sculpture of curves, angles, and twisted planes commissioned in 1975 from sculptor Louise Nevelson. Although painted, *Transparent Horizon* ⑥ was constructed

of non-rusting corten steel. Continue past the Nevelson and look to the left for a view of Alexander Calder's fully realized, 40-ft- (12-m) high sculpture, *The Big Sail* ⑦.

Here-There mural (1985) by minimalist artist Kenneth Noland ⑤

0 meters | 200
0 yards | 200

KEY

• • • Walk route

Ⓣ "T" station

Turn right to enter the Whitaker Building, where a projection screen in the ground-level corridor shows experimental film and video. The Media Test Wall ⑧, as the installation is called, is emblematic of the school's commitment to technology in the arts. Cross through the Whitaker building for a view of the south side of the Stata Center ⑨. Frank Gehry's metal-sheathed complex constitutes a research and teaching village devoted to computer, information, and intelligence sciences. Walk around the center to return to Main Street and the "T" station.

TIPS FOR WALKERS

Starting point: Kendall/MIT "T"
Length: 0.8 miles (1.3 km).
Stopping-off points: Amelia's Trattoria (111 Harvard St.) serves gourmet pizzas and pasta dishes.
Visitor information: See page 109 for museum opening hours.

A Two-Hour Walk in South Boston

The harbor is the main attraction in quickly gentrifying South Boston. Initially populated by refugees from the mid-19th century Irish famine, the area evolved into the third-largest Irish-American community in the U.S. Recent gentrification has diversified the population and turned Victorian tenements into trendy condominiums. But the defining characteristic of South Boston has always been its relation to the harbor – a bevy of soft sand beaches and headlands that guard the entry to the Port of Boston. The steep hill to Dorchester Heights can be skipped in favor of a continued seaside promenade.

toddler-friendly L Street Beach ⑦, and M Street Beach ⑧. The bath house, which actually stretches between K and M streets, was a municipal gift from notoriously corrupt mayor James Curley (last elected to office from jail) to his friends and cronies of South Boston. The bath house now serves a broad public. Walk east along William J. Day Boulevard as it winds past the yacht club and private moorings and concludes at Pleasure Bay. Standing sentinel over the

Stone column at the entrance to Joe Moakley Park ①

Park, where the Dorchester Heights Monument ③ stands like a lighthouse to mark the spot where George Washington erected cannons in 1776 to force the British withdrawal from Boston. The massive

The last stop of the No. 5 bus is at the playing fields and green walkways of Joe Moakley Park ①, named after the late South Boston-born Congressman. Some of Moakley's sayings celebrate the neighborhood's identity and are etched on granite columns that can be found around the park. One such saying reads "Everyone I knew growing up in South Boston was baptized, issued a union card, and enrolled in the Democratic Party." Cross the park to the broad swath of fine brown sand known as Carson Beach ②, a public swimming beach with a bathhouse and bocce courts.

The steep walk up Old Harbor Street leads to the grand hilltop oval of Thomas

building at one end of the park is South Boston High School ④. Walk along East 7th Avenue past renovated homes to L Street and turn right toward the harbor. Woody's L Street Tavern ⑤, Southie's most old-fashioned pub and the set for scenes in the film *Good Will Hunting*, is at the corner of East 8th Street.

At the foot of the street is the L Street Bath House ⑥, the

harbor on the traffic circle connecting the boulevard to Farragut Road is a bronze of Admiral David Farragut ⑨, commander in chief of the U.S. Navy during the Civil War.

Across the street is the section of South Boston beach known as the "Sugar Bowl" ⑩. This beach lines

TIPS FOR WALKERS

Starting point: *Joe Moakley Park*
Getting there: *No. 5 bus from Andrew Sq. to Moakley Park (McCormack Housing).*
Length: *3 miles (5km).*
Stops: *Sullivan's (next to Fort Independence) and Nicole's Seaside Cafe (at Carson Beach) serve fried clams. Supreme House of Pizza, across from Moakley Park, offers an Italian alternative.*

Time out on Carson Beach ②

Cannons at Fort Independence, Castle Island ⑭

walkway brings you to a pointed obelisk monument ⑬. This granite-block shaft is a memorial to Donald McKay whose shipyard, directly across the channel, launched some of the fastest clipper ships of the mid-19th century and helped cement Boston as an international trading port. Bas-reliefs of some of McKay's most famous vessels are mounted near the base. The shipyard site is now Logan International Airport. Most planes coming to Boston make their final approach and touchdown on the runway directly opposite Castle Island.

Because Castle Island controls the throat of Boston harbor, it has been fortified since 1634. The current structure, Fort Independence ⑭, was erected in 1779 under George Washington's orders so that no enemy could ever again occupy Boston as the British had done. It never saw action, though it did serve as a prisoner of war camp during the Civil War. Author Edgar Allen Poe served here briefly in the 1820s and is said to have based one of his macabre tales, *A Cask of Amontillado*, on a fort legend of a man deliberately confined in a dungeon. (Just such a skeleton was uncovered during a renovation in 1905.) The No. 11 bus, which runs along Day Boulevard, will take you back to downtown Boston.

KEY

••• Walk route

Ⓣ "T" station

Pleasure Bay, a circular body of water protected from the harbor by an extensive breakwater, the Pleasure Bay Causeway ⑪. The causeway walk of nearly 1 mile (1.5 km) is a favorite spot for local mothers to show off their infants, as well as a good exercise route for joggers and speed walkers. Halfway along the causeway is the Head Island light pavilion ⑫, with picnic tables, benches, and sweeping views of the harbor, looking all the way down to the landmark gas storage tank in Dorchester. The tank was

first painted in rainbow colors by abstract artist Corita Kent in 1971.

The causeway concludes at Castle Island, which has not been a real island since the channel to the mainland was filled in 1891. Follow the seaside walkway which passes by a number of memorials to fallen South Boston firefighters, police officers, and soldiers. The

USS *Constitution* gliding past Fort Independence ⑭

A 90-Minute Walk along the Freedom Trail

Boston has more sites directly related to the American Revolution than any other city. The most important of these sites, as well as some relating to other freedoms gained by Bostonians, have been linked together as "The Freedom Trail." This 2.5-mile (4-km) walking route, marked in red on the sidewalks, goes from Boston Common to Bunker Hill in Charlestown *(see pp126–7)*. This first section weaves through the central city and Old Boston. See www.thefreedomtrail.org for more information.

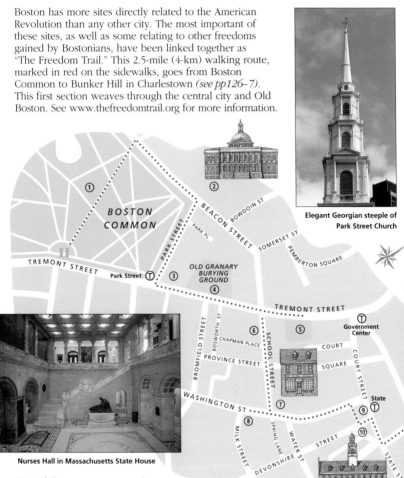

Elegant Georgian steeple of Park Street Church

Nurses Hall in Massachusetts State House

Central City

The Freedom Trail starts at the Visitor Information Center on Boston Common ① *(see pp46–7)*. This is where angry colonials rallied against their British masters and where the British forces were encamped during the 1775–76 military occupation. Political speakers still expound from their soapboxes here, and Boston Common remains a center of much activity.

Walking toward the northwest corner of the Common gives a great view of the Massachusetts State House ② *(see p50)* on Beacon Street, designed by Charles Bulfinch as the new center of state

governance shortly after the Revolution. Along Park Street, at the end of the Common, you will come to Park Street Church ③ *(see p48)*, built in 1810 and a bulwark of the antislavery movement. The church took the place of an old grain storage facility, which in turn gave its name to the adjacent Granary Burying Ground ④, one of Boston's earliest cemeteries and the final resting place of patriots John Hancock and Paul Revere *(see p21)*. Continuing along Tremont Street you will come to King's Chapel and Burying Ground ⑤ *(see p58)*.

The atmospheric cemetery is Boston's oldest, containing, among others, the grave of colonial city founder John Winthrop. As the name suggests, King's Chapel was the principal Anglican church in Puritan Boston, and more than half of its congregation fled to Nova Scotia at the outbreak of the Revolution. The box pew on the right just inside the front entrance was reserved for condemned prisoners to hear their last sermons before going to the gallows on Boston Common.

Heart of Old Boston

Head back along Tremont Street and turn down School Street, where a hopscotch-like mosaic embedded in the sidewalk commemorates the site of the First Public School ⑥, established in 1635. At the end of the street is the Old Corner Bookstore ⑦ (see p59), a landmark more associated with Boston's literary emergence of 1845–65 than with the Revolution.

The Old South Meeting House ⑧, a short way to the south on Washington Street, is a graceful, white-spired brick church, modeled on Sir Christopher Wren's English country churches. As one of the largest meeting halls in Revolutionary Boston, "Old South's" rafters rang with many a fiery speech urging revolt against the British. It was a crucible for free-speech debates and taxation protests. A few blocks along, the Old State House ⑨ presides over the head of State Street. The colonial government building, it also served as the first state legislature, and the merchants' exchange in the basement was where Boston's colonial shipping fortunes were made. The square in front of the Old State House is the Boston Massacre Site ⑩, where British soldiers opened fire on a taunting mob in 1770, killing five and providing propaganda for revolutionary agitators.

Follow State Street down to Congress Street and turn left to reach Faneuil Hall ⑪, known as the "Cradle of Liberty" for the history of patriotic speeches made in its public meeting hall. Donated to the city by Huguenot merchant Peter Faneuil, the building was built primarily as Boston's first central marketplace. Use the red stripe to negotiate your way down to North End and

TIPS FOR WALKERS

Starting point: Boston Common. Maps available at Boston Common Visitors' Center.
Length: 2.5 miles (4 km).
Getting there: Exit at Park Street "T" station to start. Other "T" stations also located on route: State, Haymarket, and Government Center. Follow red stripe on sidewalk for the full route.

Faneuil Hall, popularly known as "the Cradle of Liberty"

Old State House, once the seat of colonial government

the Paul Revere House ⑫ on North Square. Boston's oldest private residence, it was home to the man famously known for his "midnight ride" (see p21). From here, walk to Hanover Street and turn right, following the red stripe towards the next point on the Freedom Trail, Old North Church (see p126).

0 meters   200
0 yards   200

KEY

•••   Walk route

Ⓣ   "T" Station

ℹ   Tourist information

The Freedom Trail continued

Distances begin to stretch out on the second half of the Freedom Trail as it meanders through the narrow streets of the North End, then continues over the Charles River to Charlestown, where Boston's settlers first landed. The key Revolutionary and colonial-era sites here embrace two wars – the War of Independence and the War of 1812.

View from Copp's Hill terrace, Copp's Hill Burying Ground ⑭

The North End

Following the Freedom Trail through the North End from Paul Revere House *(see p125)*, allow time to try some of the Italian cafés and bakeries along the neighborhood's main thoroughfare, Hanover Street. Cross through the Paul Revere Mall to reach Old North Church ⑬ *(see p71)*, whose spire is instantly visible over the shoulder of the statue of Paul Revere on horseback. Sexton Robert Newman famously hung two lanterns in the belfry here, signaling the advance of British troops on Lexington and Concord in 1775. The church retains its 18th-century interior, including the unusual box pews.

Gravestone at Copp's Hill Burying Ground

The crest of Copp's Hill lies close by on Hull Street. Some of Boston's earliest gallows stood here, and Bostonians would gather in boats below to watch the hangings of heretics and pirates. Much of the hilltop is covered by Copp's Hill Burying Ground ⑭. This was established in 1660, and the cemetery holds the remains of several generations of the Mather family – Boston's influential 17th- and 18th-century theocrats – as well as the tombstones of many soldiers of the Revolution slain in the fight for freedom.

Boston's first free African American community, "New Guinea," covered the west side of Copp's Hill. A broken column marks the grave of Prince Hall, head of the Black Masons, distinguished veteran of the Revolution, and prominent political leader in the early years of the Republic. The musketball-chipped tombstone of patriot Daniel Malcolm records that he asked to be buried "in a stone grave 10 feet deep" to rest beyond the reach of British gunfire.

Unusual box pews inside Old North Church ⑬

KEY

 Walk route

Ⓣ "T" station

View of Bunker Hill Monument ⑯
from Charlestown harborfront

| 0 meters | | 200 |
| 0 yards | | 200 |

Charlestown

The iron bridge over the Charles River that links the North End in Boston with City Square in Charlestown dates from 1899. Across the bridge, turn right along Constitution Road, following the signs to Charlestown Navy Yard ⑮. The National Park Service operates the Visitor Center at Building 5, which has exhibits explaining the historic role of the Navy Yard and the history of the warships – one from the late 18th century, another from the mid-20th century – that are berthed at its piers. The colonial navy had been no match for the might of Britain's naval forces during the Revolution, and building a more formidable naval force became a priority. This was one of several shipyards that were set up around 1800. Lying at her berth alongside Pier 1, the 200-year-old wooden-hulled

**Lion carving, U.S.S.
Constitution ⑮**

U.S.S. *Constitution* is probably the most famous ship in U.S. history and still remains the flagship of the U.S. Navy. Built at Hartt's shipyard in the North End, she was completed in 1797. In the War of 1812, she earned the nickname "Old Ironsides" for the resilience of her live oak hull against cannon fire. Fully restored for her bicentennial, the *Constitution* occasionally sails under her own power. The granite obelisk that

towers above the Charlestown waterfront is Bunker Hill Monument ⑯, commemorating the battle of June 17, 1775 that ended with a costly victory for British forces against an irregular colonial army that finally ran out of ammunition. British losses were so heavy, however, that the battle would presage future success for the colonial forces. As a monument to the first large-scale battle of the Revolution, the obelisk, based on those of ancient Egypt, was a prototype for others across the U.S. Catch a bus from Chelsea Street back to the North End and city center.

Defensive guns at Charlestown Navy Yard ⑮ with view of the North End

TRAVELERS'
NEEDS

WHERE TO STAY 130–137

RESTAURANTS, CAFES, AND BARS 138–151

SHOPPING IN BOSTON 152–157

ENTERTAINMENT IN BOSTON 158–163

SPORTS AND OUTDOOR ACTIVITIES 164–167

CHILDREN'S BOSTON 168–171

WHERE TO STAY

Boston offers the visitor almost every type of accommodation: modest guesthouses, luxury hotels, chain motels, Victorian brownstone bed and breakfasts, and elegant, designer "boutique" hotels. Many older hotels have been renovated to provide traditional charm with modern conveniences, while new hotels and B&Bs open in the

Ritz-Carlton door-man *(see p134)*

city every year. Nevertheless, the city has a perennial hotel shortage, which keeps prices high and makes it difficult to book rooms during peak seasons. Even in winter, it's rare to find rooms under $100 per night; in summer "budget" rates can approach $150 or more. Information is available from Boston's tourist information offices *(see p175)*.

The elegant Omni Parker House *(see p133)*

WHERE TO STAY

The centrally located Back Bay has the greatest concentration of hotels and is convenient for tourists as well as business travelers. In the gentrified South End, nearby, an increasing number of restored Victorian brownstones have been converted to B&Bs. Accommodation in the Financial District, close to the waterfront, caters to business people during the week, but often offers good value to vacationers on the weekends. Across the Charles River, Cambridge has a large number of hotels, particularly around Harvard Square and Kendall Square. In more suburban Brookline, situated a little way west of Back Bay, there are several guesthouses, as well as a selection of more upscale B&Bs.

HOTEL GRADING AND FACILITIES

Boston does not have an official hotel grading system. While higher prices generally indicate more amenities, some lodgings in prime locations, or with unique historic features, may

command prices that exceed what the facilities might otherwise warrant. B&Bs generally do not offer fitness facilities, business services, or restaurants, and may be somewhat less expensive, although some at the high end of the price scale now have amenities – and prices – that rival the best hotels. Most large hotels have at least a basic fitness room, while some have arrangements with nearby clubs for guest use. Swimming pools are less common, except at the big hotels, and outdoor pools generally open only between June and early September. One recent development that travelers may find beneficial is that Boston's hotels now house many of the city's top restaurants. High-speed internet access (wired and wireless) has also become increasingly common in hotels.

HOW TO BOOK

Most hotels have toll-free reservation numbers, and some offer discounts for internet booking. Room rates are often quoted for two people sharing a room, not including tax or breakfast, although some B&Bs provide a morning meal. Prepay only the first night in case the accommodation does not meet expectations. There are last-minute rooms during the winter months, but Boston hotels are busy in May and June for college graduations, July and August for summer vacations, and September and October for the fall season.

HIDDEN EXTRAS

If you have a car in Boston, you'll pay dearly for parking. Ask your hotel if parking is included; if not, budget at least $20-25 extra per day. Taxes in Boston will also add 12.45 percent to the hotel bill. If breakfast is not included, expect to spend at least $3 for coffee and a pastry in a nearby café or $15 and up for a full hotel breakfast.

Lobby of the Hyatt Regency Boston *(see p134)*

◁ City Palace Atrium in the Massachusetts State Transport Building

Glass Atrium of the Inn at Harvard *(see p137),* **Cambridge**

DISCOUNTS

Hotel prices vary significantly with the seasons, with the lowest rates found in January and February. Through the year, many hotels catering to business travelers, such as in the Financial District, around Hynes Convention Center, and in Cambridge's Kendall Square, offer discount weekend rates. B&Bs may offer better prices mid-week.

BED AND BREAKFAST

Boston has a good selection of small hotels and B&Bs, offering personal service and charm. If you are looking for a classic B&B – a room or two in the owner's home – contact one of Boston's B&B booking agencies. A recent trend is the "boutique" hotel, a small, elegantly appointed hotel, though prices at these reflect the level of service and luxury.

BUSINESS TRAVELERS

Business travelers will find that all major hotels provide fax and wireless internet access. Some new or newly refurbished hotels offer in-room fax machines, multiline phones, and private voice mail. It is wise to check that older hotels have the facilities you require.

DISABLED TRAVELERS

Disabled travelers may be most comfortable in the city's newer hotels that have been built to conform to access requirements. Some of the large older hotels have been refitted, but many small B&Bs have steps, narrow hallways, or other architectural features that may make access difficult. For information about hotels, transportation, tour services, and other resources, contact the **Massachusetts Network of Information Providers for People with Disabilities**.

CHILDREN

Children are welcome in most of the larger hotels and often stay free in their parents' rooms. Some deluxe hotels provide child-friendly amenities, ranging from bedtime milk and cookies to the telephone "bedtime story line" at the Charles Hotel *(see p137)*. Suites are available in many big hotels, giving families space to spread out. For families on more moderate budgets, some guesthouses, such as the Commonwealth Court Guest House *(see p134)*, offer apartment-style accommodations. Be aware that many B&Bs cannot accommodate young children.

Exterior of Irving House *(see p137),* **Cambridge**

BUDGET OPTIONS

It can be hard finding budget accommodation in Boston. The **Boston International Youth Hostel** has mostly six-bed dormitories, and there are some inexpensive chain hotels, such as **Days Inn**, in the suburbs, which offer functional lodging. The North Shore towns of Salem and Rockport, just north of Boston, have good selections of mid-priced B&Bs and are accessible from the city by M.B.T.A. commuter rail – contact the **North of Boston Convention and Visitors' Bureau** for more details.

DIRECTORY

BED AND BREAKFAST AGENCIES

Bed and Breakfast Agency of Boston
Tel *(617) 720-3540.*
Tel *(800) 248-9262.*
www.boston-bnbagency.com

Bed and Breakfast Associates Bay Colony, Ltd.
P.O. Box 57166, Babson Park Branch, Boston, MA 02457.
Tel *(781) 449-5302.*
Tel *(888) 486-6018.*
Tel 08-234-7113 (toll-free from UK).
www.bnbboston.com

Host Homes of Boston
Box 117, Waban Branch, Boston, MA 02468.
Tel *(617) 244-1308.*
Tel *(800) 600-1308.*
www.hosthomesofboston.com

DISABLED TRAVELERS

Massachusetts Network of Information Providers for People with Disabilities
200 Trapelo Rd, Waltham, MA 02452. *Tel* *(781) 642-0248.*
Tel *(800) 642-0249.*
TTY (for people who cannot hear). *Tel* *(800) 764-0200.*
www.disabilityinfo.org

HOSTELS

Boston International Youth Hostel
12 Hemenway St. **Map** 3 A3.
Tel *(617) 536-9455.*
www.bostonhostel.org

BUDGET AND CHAIN HOTELS

Days Inn
Several locations.
Tel *(800) 329-7466.*
www.daysinn.com

Best Western
Several locations.
Tel *(800) 780-7234.*
www.bestwestern.com

North of Boston Convention and Visitors' Bureau
17 Peabody Sq., Peabody, MA 01960.
Tel *(978) 977-7760.*
www.northofboston.org

Choosing a Hotel

The hotels in this guide have been selected across a
wide range for their good value, facilities, and location.
These listings highlight some of the factors that may
influence your choice. Hotels are listed by area,
beginning with Beacon Hill and West End. All the
entries are alphabetical within each price category.

PRICE CATEGORIES
For a standard double room per night,
inclusive of breakfast, service charges,
and any additional taxes.
$ Under $150
$$ $150–$200
$$$ $200–$250
$$$$ $250–$300
$$$$$ Over $300

BEACON HILL AND WEST END

John Jeffries House $$
14 David G Mugar Way, 02114 **Tel** *(617) 367-1866* **Fax** *(617) 742-0313* **Rooms** *46*   **Map** *1 B3*

This red brick building was opened in 1909 as housing for nurses at the Massachusetts Eye and Ear Infirmary.
Hardwood floors, original moldings, and comfortable traditional furnishings give the feel of a well-lived-in
townhouse. It is conveniently located at the foot of Beacon Hill. **www.johnjeffrieshouse.com**

Beacon Hill Hotel & Bistro $$$$
25 Charles St., 02114 **Tel** *(617) 723-7575* **Fax** *(617) 723-7525* **Rooms** *13*   **Map** *1 B4*

Paris meets Beacon Hill in this smart townhouse renovation, steps from Boston Common and Public Garden. Rooms
are fairly small but chic with soothing colors, plantation shutters, and flat panel televisions. There is a sitting room
and a private roof deck. Rates include breakfast in the ground floor bistro. **www.beaconhillhotel.com**

Holiday Inn Select Government Center $$$$
5 Blossom St., 02114 **Tel** *(617) 742-7630; (800) 972-3381* **Fax** *(617) 742-4192* **Rooms** *303*   **Map** *1 B3*

The location is neither Beacon Hill nor Quincy Market, but a kind of no-man's land of government buildings.
However, walking a few extra steps can yield significant savings. After a major renovation, this hotel now functions
largely as a tour group and conference facility. **www.ichotelsgroup.com**

Onyx Hotel $$$$
155 Portland St., 02114 **Tel** *(617) 557-9955; (866) 660-6699* **Fax** *(617) 557-0005* **Rooms** *112*   **Map** *1 C2*

This sleekly contemporary boutique hotel features modest-sized rooms decorated in a warm palette of black,
taupe, and Chinese-lacquer red. It has comfortable beds with feather and down pillows. There is a car service
to the Financial District each morning. The hotel is pet-friendly. **www.onyxhotel.com**

Bulfinch Hotel $$$$$
107 Merrimac St., 02109 **Tel** *(617) 624-0202; (877) 267-1776* **Fax** *(617) 624-0211* **Rooms** *80*   **Map** *1 C2*

This building near TD Garden boasts big Beaux-Arts windows that flood the sleek, contemporary rooms with
light. The lobby is minimal, but the rooms and mini-suites have large beds and all the modern technology,
including flat-screen televisions. **www.bulfinchhotel.com**

Charles Street Inn $$$$$
94 Charles St., 02114 **Tel** *(617) 314-8900; (877) 772-8900* **Fax** *(617) 371-0009* **Rooms** *9*   **Map** *1 B4*

This Charles Street time capsule was built in 1860 as a demonstration showpiece for new homes under construction
in the Back Bay. Victorian features such as carved marble fireplaces harmonize with European furnishings and
modern whirlpool tubs. This is a good base for exploring the street's antiques shops. **www.charlesstreetinn.com**

Liberty Hotel $$$$$
215 Charles St., 02114 **Tel** *(617) 224-4000; (866) 507-5245* **Fax** *(617) 224-4001* **Rooms** *298*   **Map** *1 B3*

Housed in an imposing granite building that dates back to 1851 (which at one point served as a prison), this
atmospheric hotel sports a stunning central atrium and several trendy bars and restaurants. Guests enjoy stylishly
modern rooms at a convenient location just steps from the Charles River and Beacon Hill. **www.libertyhotel.com**

OLD BOSTON AND THE FINANCIAL DISTRICT

Harborside Inn $$$
185 State St., 02109 **Tel** *(617) 723-7500; (888) 723-7565* **Fax** *(617) 670-6015* **Rooms** *98*   **Map** *2 E3*

This modest boutique hotel is housed in an 1858 granite spice warehouse building near Faneuil Hall Marketplace
and the New England Aquarium. Rooms are small but stylish, with exposed brick walls, wooden floors, sleigh beds,
and Oriental carpets. **www.harborsideinnboston.com**

Key to Symbols *see back cover flap*

Omni Parker House $$$$

60 School St., 02108 **Tel** *(617) 227-8600; (888) 444-6664* **Fax** *(617) 742-5729* **Rooms** *551* **Map** *2 D4*

Memorabilia on display in the ornate lobby emphasizes Parker House's status as the oldest hotel in continuous operation in the US. Rooms have been refurbished, though some remain compact. Boston cream pie was first served here, and Parker's Restaurant and Parker's Bar are favorites with local politicians. **www.omniparkerhouse.com**

Ames Hotel $$$$$

1 Court St., 02108 **Tel** *(617) 979-8100* **Fax** *(617) 979-8101* **Rooms** *114* **Map** *2 D3*

Located just steps from Government Center and Faneuil Hall, in the historic Ames Building, this boutique hotel thrills with its innovative design touches and hip street-level restaurant *(see p143)*. The chic, monochromatic rooms feature state-of-the-art amenities, while the suites have arched windows and original fireplaces. **www.ameshotel.com**

Hilton Boston Financial District $$$$$

89 Broad St., 02110 **Tel** *(617) 556-0006; (800) 996-3426* **Fax** *(617) 556-0053* **Rooms** *362* **Map** *2 E4*

This 1928 Art Deco building was Boston's first skyscraper. A careful conversion in 1999 preserved such Art Deco features as marble floors in the lobby and bathrooms, and polished wood and brass details in the public areas. Rooms are traditionally furnished. It is situated on the edge of the Financial District. **www.hilton.com**

Langham Boston Hotel $$$$$

250 Franklin St., 02110 **Tel** *(617) 451-1900* **Fax** *(617) 423-2844* **Rooms** *318* **Map** *2 D4*

The Langham occupies a Renaissance Revival palace which was constructed to house the Federal Reserve Bank. The painted dome and gilded vaults of the foyer hint at the 19th-century French decor in the rooms. The hotel's Bond Restaurant *(see p143)* and Bar is housed in the former bank vault. **www.langhamboston.com**

Millennium Bostonian $$$$$

26 North St., 02109 **Tel** *(617) 523-3600; (800) 343-0922* **Fax** *(617) 523-2454* **Rooms** *201* **Map** *2 D3*

This upscale hotel is housed in three former warehouse buildings. Rooms vary greatly in size, but all were updated in 2008 and now feature luxury linens and 42" LCD televisions. Some have balconies overlooking Faneuil Hall Marketplace. The lobby boasts a gas-burning fireplace for cool evenings. **www.millenniumhotels.com**

Nine Zero $$$$$

90 Tremont St., 02108 **Tel** *(617) 772-5800; (866) 906-9090* **Fax** *(617) 772-5810* **Rooms** *190* **Map** *4 F1*

Poised between Beacon Hill and Downtown Crossing, the elegant Nine Zero prides itself on winning numerous design awards from the hotel and travel industries. Frette linens, Italian marble, and plenty of stainless steel and glass combine to create a comfortable atmosphere. **www.ninezero.com**

XV Beacon $$$$$

15 Beacon St., 02108 **Tel** *(617) 670-1500; (877) 982-3226* **Fax** *(617) 670-2525* **Rooms** *60* **Map** *1 C4*

This chic hotel occupies a 1903 Beaux Arts office building. Furnishings mix traditional and contemporary styles. All rooms feature gas fireplaces, CD players, and television sets, along with other luxury amenities. A complimentary chauffeured car service is available for trips within the city. **www.xvbeacon.com**

NORTH END AND THE WATERFRONT

Westin Boston Waterfront $$$

425 Summer St., 02210 **Tel** *(617) 532-4600* **Fax** *(617) 532-4630* **Rooms** *793* **Map** *2 D5*

Connected to the Boston Convention & Exhibition Center, this property contains vast amounts of meeting space. Business travelers are well served, but the hotel makes it easy for tourists too, with a complimentary shuttle service for the surrounding area. There are several restaurant and bar options on site. **www.starwoodhotels.com**

Seaport Hotel $$$$

1 Seaport Lane, 02210 **Tel** *(617) 385-4000; (877) 732-7678* **Fax** *(617) 385-4001* **Rooms** *426* **Map** *2 F5*

This modern business hotel, connected by walkway to the World Trade Center, helped revitalize the waterfront district. Regular shuttles run to North Station and the Financial District. A water taxi to Long Wharf, the North End, and Charlestown is a fun way to tour the Freedom Trail *(see pp124–7)*. **www.seaportboston.com**

Boston Harbor Hotel $$$$$

70 Rowes Wharf, 02110 **Tel** *(617) 439-7000; (800) 752-7077* **Fax** *(617) 330-9450* **Rooms** *230* **Map** *2 E4*

Dramatic public spaces and large rooms are trademarks of this classically elegant hotel. Specify harbor or city view when booking. Located in the heart of the waterfront activity, this hotel is known for fine dining, a winter wine festival, and open air films and concerts on its outdoor decks in the summer. **www.bhh.com**

Fairmont Battery Wharf $$$$$

3 Battery Wharf, 02109 **Tel** *(617) 994-9000; (800) 257-7544* **Fax** *(617) 994-9092* **Rooms** *150* **Map** *2 E2*

This swanky hotel enjoys a cozy perch along a quiet stretch of the historic waterfront, with the North End and Quincy Market only a short stroll away. Guests enjoy expert service, sophisticated environs, and a gourmet French restaurant. Many of the elegant guest rooms enjoy stunning harbor views. **www.fairmont.com/batterywharf**

InterContinental Hotel   🖥 $$$$$

510 Atlantic Ave., 02210 **Tel** *(866) 493-6495; (617) 747-1000* **Fax** *(617) 217-5190* **Rooms** *424*   **Map** *2 D5*

A bold hotel clad in reflective blue glass and polished granite, the InterContinental is located on the still-developing South Boston waterfront. Great harbor views and posh rooms are aimed squarely at executive travelers on expense accounts. High rack rates, however, are sometimes offset by excellent specials. **www.intercontinentalboston.com**

Marriott Long Wharf   🖥 P 👔 🎿 🍽 $$$$$

296 State St., 02109 **Tel** *(617) 227-0800; (800) 228-9290* **Fax** *(617) 227-2867* **Rooms** *412*   **Map** *2 E3*

This red-brick hotel stretches along Boston's original China Trade Wharf. Most rooms feature harbor or city skyline views. The seasonal outdoor terrace is a favorite with locals on weekend afternoons. This is a good base for exploring the waterfront or taking a ferry to the Harbor Islands. **www.marriottlongwharf.com**

CHINATOWN AND THE THEATER DISTRICT

Boston Park Plaza   🖥 P 👔 🍽 $$$$

64 Arlington St., 02116 **Tel** *(617) 426-2000; (800) 225-2008* **Fax** *(617) 426-5545* **Rooms** *941*   **Map** *4 D2*

Opened in 1927, this 15-floor hotel is the city's largest historic lodging. Two ballrooms and an elegant lobby make the Park Plaza the scene of many local celebrations, as well as business meetings and small conventions. Afternoon tea is served in Swan's Cafe. **www.bostonparkplaza.com**

Hyatt Regency Boston Financial District   🖥 P 👔 🎿 🍽 $$$$

1 Avenue de Lafayette, 02116 **Tel** *(617) 912-1234* **Fax** *(617) 451-2198* **Rooms** *498*   **Map** *4 D2*

The Hyatt offers spacious rooms with modern decor and is located close to the up-and-coming Ladder District, with several fine restaurants and night-time entertainment venues nearby. It is also one block from the Downtown Crossing shops. It caters to business travelers but also has good-value weekend specials. **regencyboston.hyatt.com**

Four Seasons   🖥 P 👔 🎿 🍽 $$$$$

200 Boylston St., 02116 **Tel** *(617) 338-4400; (800) 819-5053* **Fax** *(617) 423-0154* **Rooms** *274*   **Map** *4 D2*

Low-key contemporary luxury draws rock stars, authors, corporate businesspeople, and visiting dignitaries. The lobby-level Bristol Lounge offers afternoon tea and a full dining menu for children. The Four Seasons is conveniently situated on a corner of the Public Garden at the edge of the Theater District. **www.fourseasons.com**

Ritz-Carlton Boston Common   🖥 P 👔 🎿 🍽 $$$$$

10 Avery St., 02111 **Tel** *(617) 574-7100; (800) 241-3333* **Fax** *(617) 574-7200* **Rooms** *193*   **Map** *4 E2*

Boston's Ritz-Carlton occupies a prime spot across from Boston Common. This is a good alternative for those seeking the trademark pampering of Ritz hotels, but who prefer a more modern decor and sensibility. There is a multi-screen cinema and fine dining on offer. **www.ritzcarlton.com**

W Boston   🖥 👔 🍽 P $$$$$

100 Stuart St., 02116 **Tel** *(617) 261-8700* **Fax** *(617) 261-8725* **Rooms** *235*   **Map** *4 E2*

Located in the center of the Theater District, the high-rise W offers hip rooms and luxurious condos. While there are numerous tourist attractions within walking distance, many guests view the property as an urban oasis and enjoy its stylish amenities, relaxing spa, and trendy restaurant *(see p145)* and bar. **www.starwoodhotels.com**

BACK BAY AND SOUTH END

463 Beacon Street Guest House   P $$

463 Beacon St., 02116 **Tel** *(617) 536-1302* **Fax** *(617) 247-8876* **Rooms** *20*   **Map** *3 A2*

This Back Bay brownstone is a handsome building closer to the Charles River Esplanade than Back Bay attractions. It offers budget lodging in the form of studio rooms and small furnished apartments by day, week, or month. All rooms have at least limited cooking facilities. It is popular with young European travelers. **www.463beacon.com**

Chandler Inn Hotel   🖥 $$

26 Chandler St., 02116 **Tel** *(617) 482-3450; (800) 842-3450* **Fax** *(617) 542-3428* **Rooms** *55*   **Map** *4 D3*

Located in the South End just two blocks from Tremont Street's restaurant row, this tastefully decorated budget inn is well-situated for walking around Back Bay. The immediate neighborhood is primarily a low-rise residential area, giving the Chandler a homely feel in the heart of the city. **www.chandlerinn.com**

Commonwealth Court Guest House $$

284 Commonwealth Ave., 02116 **Tel** *(617) 424-1230; (888) 424-1230* **Fax** *(617) 424-1510* **Rooms** *17* **Map** *3 A2*

On the corner of Gloucester Street, the Commonwealth is convenient to upper Back Bay, especially the Hynes Convention Center and Berklee College of Music. The former private brownstone residence oozes historic architectural detail. Rooms are often rented by the week or month and include kitchenettes. **www.commonwealthcourt.com**

Key to Price Guide *see p132* **Key to Symbols** *see back cover flap*

Hotel 140

⬛🅿️🍴📺 $$

140 Clarendon St., 02116 **Tel** *(617) 585-5600; (800) 714-0140* **Fax** *(617) 585-5699* **Rooms** *54*   **Map** *3 C3*

Literally around the corner from the Back Bay Amtrak rail station, Hotel 140 is a stylish budget-priced renovation of America's first YWCA building. Rooms are small but the trendy minimalist design makes efficient use of space. There is a secure key card access system for both rooms and elevator. **www.hotel140.com**

Midtown Hotel

⬛🅿️🍴♒ $$

220 Huntington Ave., 02115 **Tel** *(617) 262-1000; (800) 343-1177* **Fax** *(617) 262-8739* **Rooms** *159*   **Map** *3 B4*

A rarity in Back Bay, this is a classic 1960s-era motor inn. Renovated rooms offer simple style and good value in an otherwise expensive area. The outdoor swimming pool and low-cost parking are significant bonuses. The on-site Italian café has a child-friendly menu. **www.midtownhotel.com**

The Back Bay Hotel

⬛🅿️🍴📺 $$$

350 Stuart St., 02116 **Tel** *(617) 266-7200; (877) 587-9774* **Fax** *(617) 266-7203* **Rooms** *225*   **Map** *4 D2*

Located in an attractive stone building that once housed the headquarters of the Boston Police Department, this hotel is ideal for tourists and shoppers. The well-appointed rooms and chic environs, complete with a two-story glass waterfall and an illuminated glass staircase, create a contemporary atmosphere. **www.doylecollection.com**

Charlesmark Hotel

⬛📺🅿️ $$$

655 Boylston St., 02116 **Tel** *(617) 247-1212* **Fax** *(617) 247-1224* **Rooms** *40*   **Map** *3 C2*

Very much in the mode of a contemporary European boutique hotel, the Charlesmark occupies an 1892 Back Bay townhouse on Copley Square. Custom-made designer furniture, light-toned woodwork, imported Italian tile, and European lighting fixtures decorate the 40 rooms. The Charlesmark offers good value. **www.charlesmarkhotel.com**

Newbury Guest-House

⬛🅿️ $$$

261 Newbury St., 02116 **Tel** *(617) 670-6000; (800) 437-7668* **Fax** *(617) 670-6100* **Rooms** *32*   **Map** *3 B2*

When three Victorian homes were linked to form this cozy inn, owners were careful to preserve such period details as ceiling medallions, parquet floors, and decorative fireplaces. The rooms feature a comfortable mix of older furniture. Newbury Street can be noisy so ask for a room at the back. **www.newburyguesthouse.com**

Lenox Hotel

⬛🅿️🍴📺 $$$$

61 Exeter St., 02116 **Tel** *(617) 536-5300; (800) 225-7676* **Fax** *(617) 267-1237* **Rooms** *214*   **Map** *3 B2*

This landmark hotel, just off Copley Square behind the Boston Public Library, features sumptuous Edwardian detail in its public areas. Several deluxe corner suites with wood-burning fireplaces rival any upscale room in town. Mahogany furniture, marble baths, and muted tones create a soothing, elegant atmosphere. **www.lenoxhotel.com**

The Colonnade Hotel

⬛🅿️🍴♒🏊🏋️📺 $$$$$

120 Huntington Ave., 02116 **Tel** *(617) 424-7000; (800) 962-3030* **Fax** *(617) 425-3222* **Rooms** *285*   **Map** *3 B3*

The spacious and comfortable rooms at the Colonnade have been updated in modern style with rich, soothing colors. This family-friendly hotel is also favored by upscale bus groups. Amenities include a rooftop pool and a ground-level bistro. **www.colonnadehotel.com**

Copley Square Hotel

⬛🅿️🍴 $$$$$

47 Huntington Ave., 02116 **Tel** *(617) 536-9000; (800) 225-7062* **Fax** *(617) 421-1402* **Rooms** *143*   **Map** *3 C3*

Opened in 1891 as the first hotel in Back Bay, this establishment is now an ultra-modern hotel with free Wi-Fi throughout. All rooms feature efficient workspaces as well as fine linens and big TVs. Ask for an interior room for the utmost tranquility. Basement-level Saint is one of the city's trendiest nightspots. **www.copleysquarehotel.com**

Eliot Suites Hotel

⬛🅿️🍴📺 $$$$$

370 Commonwealth Ave., 02215 **Tel** *(617) 267-1607; (800) 443-5468* **Fax** *(617) 536-9114* **Rooms** *95* **Map** *3 A2*

The suites with separate sleeping and sitting rooms here are equally convenient for guest musicians playing at nearby Symphony Hall, business people, and families (children under 18 stay free). Guests enjoy complimentary access to Boston Sports Club. Restaurant Clio *(see p147)* is one of the city's best. **www.eliothotel.com**

Fairmont Copley Plaza Hotel

⬛🅿️🍴 $$$$$

138 St. James Ave., 02116 **Tel** *(617) 267-5300; (866) 540-4417* **Fax** *(617) 267-7668* **Rooms** *383*   **Map** *3 C2*

A red carpet leads guests into the opulent lobby of this 1912 Boston landmark, the sister hotel to New York's Plaza. Interior rooms can be small, but a $34-million restoration updated the traditional style of dark woods and rich fabrics. Extravagant furnishings help make the Oak Room the city's favorite steak house. **www.fairmont.com/copleyplaza**

Mandarin Oriental

⬛🍴🏋️📺🅿️ $$$$$

776 Boylston St., 02199 **Tel** *(617) 535-8888; (866) 526-6567* **Fax** *(617) 535-8893* **Rooms** *148*   **Map** *3 B3*

Connected to the Prudential Center, in the heart of Back Bay, the Mandarin Oriental offers some of the city's largest rooms, all of which feature luxurious amenities like designer linens, large bathtubs, and state-of-the-art electronics. Guests also enjoy the full-service spa and numerous dining options. **www.mandarinoriental.com/boston**

Taj Boston Hotel

⬛🅿️🍴🏋️📺 $$$$$

15 Arlington St., 02116 **Tel** *(617) 536-5700; (877) 482-5267* **Fax** *(617) 536-1335* **Rooms** *273*   **Map** *4 D2*

Opened in 1927, this was the first hotel of the Ritz-Carlton chain, and the progenitor of Ritz style. The property became part of the Taj Hotel Group in 2007, but continues to emphasize elegance and excellent service. **www.tajhotels.com**

FARTHER AFIELD

A Friendly Inn   P $$

1673 Cambridge St., Cambridge, 02138 **Tel** *(617) 547-7851* **Fax** *(617) 547-0202* **Rooms** *17*

Visiting scholars, prospective students, and parents visiting their Ivy League offspring tend to frequent this aptly named bed and breakfast. It is located in a quiet residential neighborhood just north of Harvard Yard and east of Harvard Divinity School. **www.afinow.com**

Beech Tree Inn $$

83 Longwood Ave., Brookline, 02446 **Tel** *(617) 277-1620; (800) 544-9660* **Rooms** *9*

This rambling Victorian home is located in a leafy neighborhood near Longwood Medical Center and the Green Line's "E" branch. The rooms have an old-fashioned decor with solid furnishings and a television set, but some rooms share bathrooms. Read a book and sip tea under the backyard apple tree. **www.thebeechtreeinn.com**

Constitution Inn   P $$

150 Third Ave., Charlestown, 02129 **Tel** *(617) 241-8400; (800) 495-9622* **Fax** *(617) 241-2856* **Rooms** *147* **Map** *2 D1*

Convenient to the Freedom Trail *(see pp124–7)*, this unique property offers the lowest rates to Armed Services personnel. However, it also welcomes casual visitors and its well-maintained rooms, fitness center, pool, and sauna are a good deal for all. Kitchenette rooms available. **www.constitutioninn.org**

Days Hotel Boston   P $$

1234 Soldiers Field Rd., 02135 **Tel** *(617) 254-1234; (800) 329-7466* **Fax** *(617) 254-4300* **Rooms** *117*

This hotel along the Charles River provides easy access to the popular river banks and their jogging paths. The slightly dated rooms are cheerful and spacious. Fitness buffs may want to undertake the one-mile walk to Harvard Square. **www.dayshotelboston.com**

Holiday Inn Express   P $$

250 Monsignor O'Brien Hwy., Cambridge, 02141 **Tel** *(617) 577-7600; (800) 972-3381* **Fax** *(617) 354-1313* **Rooms** *112*

Close to the Lechmere "T" stop, this hotel is also designed for business travelers who arrive by car. It is one of the rare newer hotels to offer rooms for smokers and a choice of room sizes. On-site parking is limited, however free parking is offered across the street. **www.hiecambridge.com**

Hotel Indigo $$

339 Grove St., Newton, 02462 **Tel** *(617) 454-3399* **Rooms** *191*

Located near several highways and bus/rail lines, this boutique hotel provides modern, eco-friendly accommodations. Guests enjoy state-of-the-art rooms and the interiors of the common areas are regularly changed to reflect the season. The outdoor pool has private cabanas, and there's a classy restaurant. **www.newtonboutiquehotel.com**

Kendall Hotel $$

350 Main St., Cambridge, 02142 **Tel** *(617) 577-1300; (866) 566-1300* **Fax** *(617) 577-1377* **Rooms** *77*

The memorabilia here celebrates this boutique hotel's former life as a century-old Queen Anne-style firehouse. Eleven of the guest rooms were once the firemen's dormitory. The rest of the spacious rooms occupy newer extensions. It is convenient to Massachusetts Institute of Technology and the "T"'s Red Line. **www.kendallhotel.com**

Mary Prentiss Inn   P $$

6 Prentiss St., Cambridge, 02140 **Tel** *(617) 661-2929* **Fax** *(617) 661-5989* **Rooms** *20*

The strong architectural features of this 1843 Greek Revival mansion are accentuated by the bold wallpapers, period furniture, antiques, and rich fabrics. Some rooms have wood-burning fireplaces and whirlpool tubs. Breakfast is served in the parlor or on the outdoor terrace in summer. **www.maryprentissinn.com**

Ramada Inn Boston $$

800 Morrissey Blvd., Dorchester, 02122 **Tel** *(617) 287-9100* **Fax** *(617) 265-9287* **Rooms** *177*

The Ramada Inn is well located for making daytrips into the city. The hotel offers a free shuttle to Logan Airport, JFK/UMass stop on the "T"'s Red Line, and to the World Trade Center. It is a convenient spot for travelers also planning to go to Cape Cod. **www.bostonhotel.com**

Best Western Roundhouse Suites $$$

891 Massachusetts Ave., 02118 **Tel** *(617) 989-1000; (888) 468-3562* **Fax** *(617) 541-9588* **Rooms** *92*

This unique 1900s round building was transformed into an all-suites hotel in 2001. Sofa beds, microwaves, and refrigerators make Roundhouse Suites an appealing option for families. A shuttle service is available and parking is free for those who arrive by car. **www.bestwesternboston.com**

Harvard Square Hotel $$$

110 Mt. Auburn St., Cambridge, 02138 **Tel** *(617) 864-5200; (800) 458-5886* **Fax** *(617) 864-2409* **Rooms** *73*

This four-story motor-inn boasts an excellent location in the midst of Harvard Square. There is a small lobby and basic but comfortable guest rooms featuring light wood furnishings and warm colors. Register for special deals offered only by email. **www.harvardsquarehotel.com**

Key to Price Guide *see p132* **Key to Symbols** *see back cover flap*

Hotel Tria 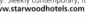 $$$

220 Alewife Brook Pkwy., Cambridge, 02138 **Tel** *(617) 491-8000; (866) 333-8742* **Fax** *(617) 491-4932* **Rooms** *121*

Though outside the usual tourist districts, this hotel is big on contemporary style and comfort. Guest-pleasing perks include fresh cookies in the afternoon and hand-cut scented soaps. Children under 18 stay free. There is a complimentary shuttle service to Alewife on the T's Red Line and to Harvard Square. **www.hoteltria.com**

Irving House ▣ $$$

24 Irving St., Cambridge, 02138 **Tel** *(617) 547-4600; (877) 547-4600* **Fax** *(617) 576-2814* **Rooms** *44*

This bed and breakfast is housed in a large, wood-framed Victorian building with a welcoming front porch. Rooms vary greatly in size and some share baths. Its friendly service, quiet location, and proximity to Harvard Yard and Harvard Square make it a favorite with visiting scholars on a budget. **www.irvinghouse.com**

Isaac Harding House ▣ $$$

288 Harvard St., Cambridge, 02138 **Tel** *(617) 876-2888; (877) 489-2888* **Fax** *(617) 497-0953* **Rooms** *14*

This bed and breakfast occupies an 1860s Victorian house in a quiet Cambridge residential neighborhood halfway between Central and Harvard squares. Public areas combine comfort with elegance. Guest rooms are spacious and bright, and some share baths. Free parking is available. **www.harding-house.com**

Le Méridien Cambridge $$$

20 Sidney St., Cambridge, 02139 **Tel** *(617) 577-0200; (800) 543-4300* **Fax** *(617) 494-8366* **Rooms** *210*

Built as the Hotel @ MIT, the high-tech Méridien is an interface between investors and the professors, biotech engineers, and electronics visionaries at the adjacent Massachusetts Institute of Technology. Sleekly contemporary, it is also handy to the music bars and ethnic restaurants of Cambridge's Central Square. **www.starwoodhotels.com**

Hotel Commonwealth 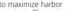 $$$

500 Commonwealth Ave., 02215 **Tel** *(617) 933-5000; (866) 784-4000* **Fax** *(617) 266-6888* **Rooms** *150*

The opening of this ultra-modern hotel in 2002 signaled the gentrification of student-oriented Kenmore Square. French Second Empire decor is combined with hi-tech amenities. The Foundation Lounge is a popular drinking spot. Lunch and dinner are served outdoors in good weather. **www.hotelcommonwealth.com**

Hotel Marlowe 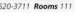 $$$$

25 Edwin H. Land Blvd., Cambridge, 02141 **Tel** *(617) 868-8000; (800) 825-7140* **Fax** *(617) 868-8001* **Rooms** *236*

Next to the Cambridgeside Galleria, this sleek hotel has something for everyone: fitness center, a complimentary wine reception each evening by the fireplace in the lobby, and special packages for pets. A short walk to the Charles River, Museum of Science, and the "T"'s Green Line. **www.hotelmarlowe.com**

Hyatt Harborside $$$$

101 Harborside Dr., East Boston, 02128 **Tel** *(617) 568-1234* **Fax** *(617) 567-8856* **Rooms** *270*

Located on the East Boston waterfront near Logan Airport, this modern hotel was designed to maximize harbor views from the lobby, restaurant, and indoor pool. Half of the spacious rooms also have harbor views. The water taxi to downtown docks nearby. **www.harborside.hyatt.com**

Inn at Harvard $$$$

1201 Massachusetts Ave., Cambridge, 02138 **Tel** *(617) 491-2222; (800) 458-5886* **Fax** *(617) 520-3711* **Rooms** *111*

The four-story atrium of this modern hotel was modeled on Isabella Stewart Gardner's Italian-style palazzo turned museum. Rooms are comfortably appointed and filled with period furniture. Access to the nearby Harvard Faculty Club and its dining room is extended to all guests. **www.theinnatharvard.com**

Sheraton Commander $$$$

16 Garden St., Cambridge, 02138 **Tel** *(617) 547-4800; (800) 325-3535* **Fax** *(617) 234-1396* **Rooms** *175*

Harvard Square's original hotel, built in 1927, sits across from Cambridge Common and a short walk from Harvard Yard. Though the hallways are narrow and some rooms are small, consistent refurbishment maintains the hotel's comfortable style. The restaurant specializes in traditional New England fare. **www.sheraton.com/commander**

Charles Hotel $$$$

1 Bennett St., 02138 **Tel** *(617) 864-1200; (800) 882-1818* **Fax** *(617) 864-5715* **Rooms** *294*

Handmade quilts on the beds add a cozy touch to the restrained modern decor. The hotel's location on the edge of Harvard Square is a plus. A top-notch jazz club, restaurant, and hip bar serve visitors and locals alike. The weekly farmers market and outdoor dining enliven the hotel's plaza in warm weather. **www.charleshotel.com**

Hotel Veritas $$$$$

1 Remington St., Cambridge, 02138 **Tel** *(617) 520-5000; (888) 520-1050* **Fax** *(617) 520-5004* **Rooms** *30*

This luxury four-story boutique hotel near Harvard University features mostly queen-bedded, intimate rooms with rich linens, and relaxed contemporary styling. Breakfast and bar service are offered in the entry lobby. Limited underground parking is available. Nine rooms have private balconies. **www.thehotelveritas.com**

Royal Sonesta Hotel $$$$$

5 Cambridge Hwy., Cambridge, 02142 **Tel** *(617) 806-4200; (800) 766-3782* **Fax** *(617) 806-4232* **Rooms** *400*

The Royal Sonesta boasts a prime location on the pathway along the Charles River. Many of the comfortable rooms have river views and public areas are noted for outstanding art works. It is within easy walking distance to the "T"'s Green Line. Family packages often include bicycles. **www.sonesta.com/boston**

RESTAURANTS, CAFÉS, AND BARS

For a number of years Boston had a reputation of serving stodgy, old New England fare. Today, however, this is no longer the case, as the city now has a wide variety of exciting places to eat. Along with more traditional cuisine, Boston restaurants show many diverse influences, with immigrant restaurateurs and innovative chefs transforming local restaurant culture. Celebrated chefs also bring traditional Boston cuisine to life for modern palates, and restaurants all delight in fresh New England produce. The top restaurants serve a medley of styles, such as French and Italian, often using other Mediterranean and Asian accents. For other flavors of the world, Boston has many Indian, Southeast Asian, Latin American, Caribbean, and Japanese restaurants, which are located in small neighborhoods and fashionable streets alike.

Murals at the Casablanca restaurant, a Cambridge institution (see p149)

EATING THE BOSTONIAN WAY

If your lodgings don't include breakfast, join locals on their way to work and have a bagel and a cup of steaming coffee in one of the city's many delis and coffee bars. Most places also offer pastries, muffins, coffee cake, tea, and fruit juices. Diners offer richer, more substantial breakfasts of bacon, eggs, potatoes, and toast, with a "bottomless" cup of coffee – one with free refills.

Lunches in Boston may also be a simple sandwich or a larger meal in a restaurant, depending on how much time you have, and how hungry you are. Business districts abound with lunch options – join office workers Downtown at a lunch counter for a grinder (long filled roll).

Dinner is the biggest meal of the day for Bostonians. The most exclusive and elegant restaurants are in the Financial District and Downtown. Those in the Back Bay, North End and South End tend to be trendy and youthful, while in Cambridge they are more relaxed. The websites www.bostonchefs.com and www.boston.menupages.com are useful for menus and prices.

OPENING HOURS

The types of meals served at many restaurants vary according to the type of establishment and its location. Many downtown lunch counters are open only for breakfast and lunch, while some finer restaurants are open only for dinner. Some restaurants close for a few hours between lunch and dinner, while smaller family-run places may stay open throughout the afternoon, making them a good bet for eating at more unusual times. Generally, lunch is served from 11:30am to 2:30pm, and dinner from 5:30 to 10:30pm. Massachusetts state law prohibits the sale of alcohol, including beer and wine, after 2am, so bars and most restaurants will close by then. There are some very late night restaurants in Chinatown and Kenmore Square, supported mostly by the ravenous crowds leaving dance clubs and bars. On Sundays, restaurants begin serving alcohol at noon. Cocktails at brunch are very popular, especially in the South End.

Attractive exterior of the Terramia restaurant (see p144)

PAYING AND TIPPING

Most restaurants with table service will bring you your bill at the end of the meal. The bill will have a 7 percent state and local meals tax added to the total. All restaurants with table service expect you to tip your waiter, who is paid a very low rate

The fashionable Sonsie restaurant in Boston's Back Bay (see p147)

A typically Italian atmosphere is created at Caffé Vittoria *(see p150)*

with the expectation that tips will fill out their salary. The standard tip is 20 percent of the pre-tax bill. If service is especially good or bad, adjust the tip accordingly. If paying by credit card, you may include the tip in the charged amount. Fast food restaurants may have optional tip jars next to the cashier.

BOOKING

Finer restaurants often require a reservation, though in most cases (especially on weeknights) reservations can be made at short notice. There are a few very popular places that do not accept reservations, and customers must put their names on the waiting list. The host will tell you how long you can expect to wait.

ALCOHOL AND SMOKING

The tide has turned in favor of non-smokers throughout Greater Boston, with complete bans on indoor smoking in public places including restaurants and bars. Outdoor smoking is also prohibited at playgrounds and other posted areas.

Twenty-one is the legal drinking age, so under-age travelers should be aware that they will be denied access to most bars. They will not be able to order wine with dinner in restaurants, either. If there is any doubt that a person is old enough, proof will be required, so use your I.D. or passport if asked.

ETIQUETTE

Bostonians tend to dress casually when dining out. Restaurants that enforce dress codes usually require a reservation, so ask when booking. For the top dining rooms, a jacket and tie for men is expected. Ladies may wear slacks, though skirts or dresses are more traditional. Formal evening wear is uncommon but not out of place in the finer restaurants. Cell phone use is strongly discouraged.

CHILDREN

Children are welcome in most mid-range restaurants, although in the business areas restaurants are often less accustomed to them. Avoid restaurants that feature a large bar and young crowds, as they are less likely to permit under-21s on the premises.

DISABILITIES

A number of restaurants in Boston and Cambridge are accessible by wheelchair *(see pp142–9)*, and many more are accessible to people with other disabilities. Doors may be fitted with an automatic opener, and rest rooms usually include the appropriate stalls and sinks.

FAST FOOD

Being a college city, Boston is teeming with fast food options. Sandwiches come in infinite varieties, the classic sandwich being found along with "wraps" (fillings wrapped up in a flatbread), "grinders" (long rolls stuffed with meats), and gourmet sandwiches on baguette or *focaccia*. Pizza is another ubiquitous meal, and bagels, spread with cream cheese, are a popular snack eaten on the go. Burritos are hearty portable meals of meat, beans, and cheese rolled into a flour tortilla. Downtown and Harvard Square are good places for fast food, with their many lunch counters catering to business people. These are reliable and easy on the wallet.

Enjoying a beer outside at one of Quincy Market's bars *(see p64)*

The Flavors of Boston

Geography and history have given New England some fine and highly distinctive culinary traditions. Its long coastline accounts for the region's abundance of superb seafood. Early settlers brought dishes from England, such as boiled dinners and puddings, that remain popular to this day, as do a range of staples introduced to them by Native Americans, such as corn, maple syrup, and cranberries. The ethnic make-up of Boston has also led to some surprising culinary highlights. Thanks to a large Italian community, Boston boasts some of the best and most authentic pizza in America, and the large Irish population ensures there are plenty of hearty Irish dishes to enjoy.

New England apples

Lobster meal at one of Boston's seafood restaurants

GIFTS FROM THE SEA

Seafood is king in New England. The cold waters along the coast yield a bounty of delicious fish such as scrod (young cod), haddock, and swordfish. Lobster is a particularly coveted delicacy. Tanks of live lobsters are shipped to restaurants all around America, but nowhere are they as succulent and sweet as they are in their home region. Several of Boston's best restaurants serve mouth-watering lobster dishes, where diners can pick their own freshly-caught lobster from a tank, then sit back and relax while it is steamed or boiled, according to their wishes. Lobster dishes are usually served up with an accompaniment of melted butter for dipping the meat into and cups of clear, steaming seafood broth.

THE MIGHTY CLAM

No food is more ubiquitous in New England than clams. They are served in so many different ways: steamed, stuffed, baked, minced in fish cakes or in the famous New England clam chowder. The large hard-shelled quahog clam – a delicacy from nearby Rhode Island – is used to make stuffed clams known as "stuffies". Many regional states have their own

Corn on the cob   Baked potato   Steamed clams   Melted butter   Boiled lobster

A typical New England clambake dinner

LOCAL DISHES AND SPECIALITIES

Like most Americans, New Englanders tend to have a light lunch and their main meal in the evening. Perhaps because of the cold winters, breakfasts are hearty. Some New England dining experiences are too good to miss. At least one breakfast should include wild blueberry pancakes or muffins, and another an omelette made with tangy Vermont cheddar. Other musts are a lunch of lobster roll (chunks of sweet lobster meat in a mayonnaise-based dressing, stuffed into a toasted bun), New England clam chowder,

Maple Syrup

and one of the region's famous clambake dinners. A visit to Boston is hardly complete without sampling the superb local scrod and its rich, classic Boston cream pie, both found on menus all over the city, along with Vermont's favorite ice cream, Ben and Jerry's.

Blueberry pancakes *Small wild blueberries are stirred into batter to make a stack of these thick pancakes.*

Colorful display of pumpkins at a local farmers' market

version of clam chowder. Boston has a distinctive interpretation of this broth, made with a cream sauce, potatoes, and onions, which makes it much richer than the clear tomato-based version served in Manhattan.

SWEET OFFERINGS

Sugar maples, which bring a dazzling display of color to the hillsides in autumn, yield yet another bonus in late winter. They can then be tapped and their sap boiled down to produce maple syrup. This is served on pancakes and made into candy (sweets) and sauces. New England's vast acres of wild blueberries, along with its many apple orchards and pumpkin fields, also lend themselves to a variety of delectable desserts. In the

19th century, molasses from the Caribbean was used as a sweetener, and it is still added to many traditional sweet treats, such as Indian pudding, a delicious slow-baked confection of spiced cornmeal, molasses, and milk.

Freshly picked wild blueberries, from the bumper summer harvest

NEW AMERICAN CUISINE

Boston's best chefs are masters of "New American" cuisine, emphasizing the use of the freshest ingredients, in-season fruits and vegetables, and light, healthy sauces. Often dishes have touches of Mediterranean and Asian spices. Seasonal menus include game in winter and fall, and fresh seafood year round. In the growing season, many dishes also feature fresh fruit and berries. To ensure freshness, produce comes from nearby growers. Presentation is important, with dishes planned to please the eye as well as the palate.

WHAT TO DRINK

Poland Spring water This bottled water from Maine is popular with Bostonians.

Frappé A New England-style milk shake made with ice cream and chocolate syrup.

Westport Rivers wines These are always a favorite at the annual Boston wine festivals.

Samuel Adams and Harpoon beers New England's best known brands are brewed in Boston.

Micro-brewery beers Sample Boston Beer Works' "Boston Red," named after the city's Red Sox baseball team, or any one of the English-style pale ales made by Tremont Brewery.

Baked scrod *Fillets of young cod (scrod) are rolled in breadcrumbs, baked, and then served with tartare sauce.*

New England clam chowder *Fresh clams, either left whole or chopped, and chunks of potato fill this creamy soup.*

Boston cream pie *Layers of sponge cake, sandwiched with egg custard, are topped with chocolate icing.*

Choosing a Restaurant

The restaurants in this guide have been selected for their good value, exceptional food, or interesting location. These listings highlight some of the factors that may influence your choice, such as whether you can opt to eat outdoors or if the venue offers live music. Entries are alphabetical within each price category.

PRICE CATEGORIES
Include a three-course meal for one, half a bottle of house wine, and all unavoidable extra charges such as sales tax and service.

$ Under $20
$$ $20–$30
$$$ $30–$45
$$$$ $45–$60
$$$$$ Over $60

BEACON HILL AND WEST END

King and I $$
145 Charles St., 02114 **Tel** *(617) 227-3320*   **Map** *1 B3*

Located on scenic Charles Street, King and I is one of Beacon Hill's most affordable options, serving authentic Thai food in a simply appointed dining room. Spice levels run high, but the kitchen can adjust any dish to suit individual tastes. Any item on the menu can be prepared without meat, so vegetarians are well served. Closed Fri lunch; Sun.

Artú $$$
89 Charles St., 02114 **Tel** *(617) 227-9023*   **Map** *1 B3*

The secret weapon of this casual eatery is the ferociously hot oven, which produces sumptuous roast pork and lamb that go perfectly with such grilled Italian vegetables as marinated eggplant. Prepare for a long wait at lunch: savvy office workers come here for sandwiches. Dinner is quieter, and more romantic. Closed lunch Mon, Sun.

Figs $$$
42 Charles St., 02114 **Tel** *(617) 742-3447*   **Map** *1 B4*

This small, casual eatery (a side operation of a local superchef) launched Boston's love for grilled pizzas. The signature pizza is topped with caramelized figs, prosciutto, and gorgonzola cheese, and the rich baked pastas are extremely popular too. The portions are so generous that virtually every entrée provides enough food to feed two people.

Lala Rokh $$$
97 Mt. Vernon St., 02114 **Tel** *(617) 720-5511*   **Map** *1 B4*

North Africa's fine cuisine was born in Persia, and dining at Lala Rokh is like taking a gastronomic tour through the greatest hits of Persian cuisine. Dishes are redolent of herbs, citrus, and exotic spices, often featuring lamb and game birds. Most of the desserts are built around dates and nuts.

Panificio $$$
144 Charles St., 02114 **Tel** *(617) 227-4340*   **Map** *1 B3*

A popular bakery that specializes in rustic Italian breads and also structures light meals, served all day, from their baked goods. Piles of meat and heaps of vegetables fill the sandwiches, but the soups are less hearty. Look out for fancy egg dishes such as frittatas, French toast, and different versions of eggs Benedict at the weekend brunches.

Paramount Deli-Restaurant $$$
44 Charles St., 02114 **Tel** *(617) 720-1152*   **Map** *1 B4*

This hangout has been a comfort-food destination since 1937. The busiest times are at breakfast and during the day when there is a cafeteria-style service. The evening table service emphasizes stir-fries and unfussy American bistro dishes, usually a grilled piece of meat atop a starch and graced with a light sauce. All the meals provide good value.

Beacon Hill Bistro $$$$
25 Charles St., 02114 **Tel** *(617) 723-1133*   **Map** *1 B4*

Located in the Beacon Hill Hotel *(see p132)*, this Irish-run restaurant features American staples for breakfast and lunch but offers an American interpretation of French bistro cuisine at night. Steak-frites, for example, is made with New York strip steak, while local codfish gets a Mediterranean treatment with roasted tomatoes and Greek olives.

Bin 26 Enoteca 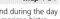 $$$$
26 Charles St., 02114 **Tel** *(617) 723-5939*   **Map** *1 B4*

True to its name, this stylishly contemporary restaurant puts a strong emphasis on its extensive wine list, with delicious *stuzzichini* ("small bites") to munch while enjoying a glass of wine. The cuisine is predominantly Italian and definitely more adventurous than traditional. Try the cocoa pasta with wild mushrooms.

No. 9 Park $$$$$
9 Park St., 02108 **Tel** *(617) 742-9991*   **Map** *1 C4*

Sports stars, state politicians, and hard-charging business people frequent this upscale room near the State House for bold American bistro food accompanied by an imaginative list of unusual wines. The chef-owner has a magical touch with duck, so the duck special of the night is often worth trying.

Key to Symbols *see back cover flap*

Scampo

215 Charles St., 02114 **Tel** (617) 536-2100

Map 1 B3

Located in the stylish Liberty Hotel, this trendy restaurant serves modern Italian fare with flair. Items like suckling pig and baby lamb are given the star treatment, but it's the homemade pastas and fresh mozzarella bar that get the most attention. With lively crowds and high energy levels, this is not a spot for a quiet conversation.

OLD BOSTON AND THE FINANCIAL DISTRICT

Anthem

$$$

101 South Market Building, Faneuil Hall Marketplace, 02115 **Tel** (617) 720-5570

Map 2 D3

A greenhouse-like box on the corner of South Market facing Faneuil Hall, Anthem serves American steakhouse grub in modest portions (along with original-recipe pizzas) in a congenial setting that includes two separate bar areas. Hanger steak or shrimp "corndogs" go well with the beer and cocktails.

Durgin Park

$$$

340 Faneuil Hall Marketplace, 02109 **Tel** (617) 227-2038

Map 2 D3

Legendary for its generous portions, Durgin Park began in 1826 as a lunch hall for produce and meat market workers. Family-style seating at long tables in the dining room makes for lively conversation. Traditional favorites include baked beans, Indian pudding, and grilled prime rib of beef big enough to hang over the edge of the plate.

Union Oyster House

$$$

41 Union St., 02110 **Tel** (617) 227-2750

Map 2 D3

Some dishes have probably not changed much since Daniel Webster was a regular in the 1830s, and people still point to the booth where John F. Kennedy used to have Sunday brunch and read the paper. Apart from Boston scrod, the best bet by far is the raw bar. Savor the differences in oysters from various waters of the world.

Bond

$$$$

250 Franklin St., 02110 **Tel** (617) 451-1900

Map 2 D4

The Langham Hotel's *(see p133)* restaurant attracts the local cool crowd thanks to its cosmopolitan setting and inventive offerings. A globe-spanning menu of small plates and shareable dishes (Colombian empanadas, Korean short ribs) pairs well with the bar's designer cocktails. DJs and stylish servers contribute to the hip atmosphere.

Woodward

$$$$

1 Court St., 02108 **Tel** (617) 979-8200

Map 2 D3

Befitting its home in the quirky Ames Hotel *(see p133)*, this modern tavern is full of offbeat artifacts, though most patrons come for the carefully crafted comfort fare. The restaurant serves luxury cocktails, gourmet burgers, and thin-crust pizzas from early morning until late at night, pleasing Downtown's trendy workers.

Oceanaire

40 Court St., 02108 **Tel** (617) 742-2277

Map 2 D5

Part of a small national chain of upmarket fish restaurants, Oceanaire retains the marble glamor of the bank that once occupied this space, while offering up a constantly changing menu of outstanding seafood. Unlike most Boston seafood restaurants, Oceanaire makes no bones about flying in fish not available from local waters. Closed at lunch.

Radius

8 High St., 02110 **Tel** (617) 426-1234

Map 2 D5

This restaurant is often ranked as one of America's temples of trendy cuisine. The kitchen imbues dishes with explosive sensuality for those who can afford both the prices and the calories. Solo diners can join the convivial crowd at an elevated bar in one corner of the room. Closed lunch Sat; Sun.

NORTH END AND THE WATERFRONT

Ernesto's Pizzeria

$

69 Salem St., 02113 **Tel** (617) 523-1373

Map 2 D4

This simple pizza shop with plastic seating offers 24 different combinations of toppings and delivers to most Boston hotel rooms, beating the pizza chains at their own game. The signature *mala femina* pie is topped with artichoke hearts, fresh tomatoes, and blue cheese.

Antico Forno

93 Salem St., 02108 **Tel** (617) 723-6733

Map 2 D2

This North End eatery stands out from its culinary neighbors thanks to its wood-fired pizzas and affordable prices. The casual twin dining rooms are often packed with a mix of tourists and locals, and while there are colorful murals, it's the brickwork decor that catches the eye. Besides the thin-crusted pies, the menu offers homemade pastas.

Barking Crab

88 Sleeper St., 02110 **Tel** *(617) 426-CRAB* $$$

Map *2 E5*

Although it is open all year, this Fort Point Channel restaurant is best in summer, when diners can sit outdoors at picnic tables and wield heavy stones to crush lobster and crab shells. Local cod, haddock, flounder, tuna, halibut, clams, and crab are available fried, steamed, or broiled. The Boston skyline views are an added bonus.

La Famiglia Giorgio

112 Salem St., 02113 **Tel** *(617) 367-6711* $$$

Map *2 D2*

Upbeat Italian meals with generous portions at a price that will not break the bank. Great for couples and families on a casual night out. The menu is simple: pizzas, pastas with a choice of sauces, and filling chicken or veal dishes. Unlike many North End restaurants, they do serve dessert and coffee.

Maurizio's Ristorante Italiano

364 Hanover St., 02113 **Tel** *(617) 367-1123* $$$

Map *2 E2*

The Sardinian chef-owner has an affinity for fish dishes, and the menu features Sardinian and Ligurian white wines that complement the bold flavors. The handmade filled pastas (like lobster ravioli) are tender and luscious. There is an open kitchen and close quarters on the main floor, as well as a basement room below. Closed lunch Mon–Fri.

Pomodoro

319 Hanover St., 02113 **Tel** *(617) 367-4348* $$$

Map *2 E2*

The tiny Pomodoro often has long lines of diners waiting for tables. The eponymous tomato sauce is one of the North End's best, and the kitchen shines with its vegetable dishes. Even dedicated meat-eaters will find pleasure in a meal of cold grilled vegetable antipasti, great bread, and a warming bowl of soup.

Bricco

241 Hanover St., 02113 **Tel** *(617) 248-6800* $$$$

Map *2 E2*

Bricco's kitchen keeps finding new twists on traditional Italian cooking, like spicing up steamed mussels with smoked red pepper and braised broccoli rabe. The windows swing wide open onto busy Hanover Street to make Bricco a popular spot for socializing over Venetian-style sardines or saddle of rabbit. Closed lunch.

Carmen

33 North Sq., 02113 **Tel** *(617) 742-6421* $$$$

Map *2 E2*

This cozy little trattoria specializes in small dishes for those who just want a bite while sipping wine – maybe a bowl of mussels or some oil-drizzled cheese. Fine pasta dishes with classic sauces are also available. Close quarters and below-street seating combine to give Carmen a romantic atmosphere. Closed lunch (except Fri and Sat).

Sel de la Terre

255 State St., 02109 **Tel** *(617) 720-1300* $$$$

Map *2 E3*

A study in contrasts, this casually elegant dining room near the Aquarium specializes in the rustic dishes of Provence. The fish dishes make good use of produce sold at the morning fish auction a few piers down the harbor. There are also great breads and charcuterie, and the boulangerie by the door sells breakfast breads and lunchtime sandwiches.

Terramia

98 Salem St., 02113 **Tel** *(617) 523-3112* $$$$

Map *2 D2*

This snug trattoria (the sister restaurant to Antico across the street) eschews the red-sauce neighborhood heritage in favor of Piemontese roasted meats, deeply savory dishes with dark mushrooms and caramelized onions, and bright Ligurian-style seafood lightly dressed with capers and lemon. There is sadly no coffee or dessert.

Meritage

70 Rowes Wharf, 02110 **Tel** *(617) 439-3995* $$$$$

Map *2 E4*

Exquisite regional and seasonal contemporary American dishes are laid out on the menu to match choices from the extensive wine list. Thus, the list leads with dishes for sparkling wines and light whites, proceeds through robust reds and ends with rich desserts or a platter of fine cheeses matched to ports and Sauternes.

Prezza

24 Fleet St., 02113 **Tel** *(617) 227-1577* $$$$$

Map *2 E1*

Prezza bases its menus on the mountain and shore cuisine of Abruzzi, with delicate handmade pastas and chunky meat and fish dishes cooked on a wood-burning grill. Roughly four dozen Italian and New World wines by the glass complement the food. Unlike many neighboring restaurants, Prezza makes its own desserts. Closed lunch.

Sensing

3 Battery Wharf, 02118 **Tel** *(617) 994-9001* $$$$$

Map *2 E2*

The Michelin-starred Parisian chef Guy Martin chose the Fairmont Battery Wharf as the site of his first U.S.-based restaurant. Knowledgeable servers patrol the minimalist dining room while explaining the menu's intricacies. The kitchen applies a modern French spin on local, seasonal ingredients such as Maine lobster and Rhode Island scallops.

Sportello

348 Congress St., 02116 **Tel** *(617) 737-1234* $$$$$

Map *2 E5*

This sleek, welcoming eatery whips up trattoria-inspired treats such as homemade pastas, gourmet soups, and grilled panini sandwiches. Heartier fare, like veal sweetbreads and day boat scallops, rounds out the menu. A counter provides a gourmet takeout spot for freshly baked breads and imported Italian treats.

Key to Price Guide *see p142* **Key to Symbols** *see back cover flap*

CHINATOWN AND THE THEATER DISTRICT

Xinh Xinh $

7 Beach St., 02111 **Tel** *(617) 422-0501*   **Map** 1 C5

Popular with many of Boston's Vietnamese residents, Xinh Xinh (pronounced "sin-sin") is a Saigon-style bistro offering the soothing noodle soups that many Western diners associate with Vietnamese cuisine and also classic dishes such as lemongrass chicken with rice-paper wrappers and smoky, tangy roasted whole quail.

Chau Chow City $$$

83 Essex St., 02111 **Tel** *(617) 338-8158*   **Map** 1 C5

Modern Hong Kong seafood dishes, such as scallops with green beans and macadamia nuts, top the menu on the lower two floors, while the third level is the reigning king of Boston's dim sum palaces. Shrimp dumpling is the benchmark of good dim sum, and this one is a perfect tender wrapper around sweet and crunchy shrimp.

Jacob Wirth Company Restaurant $$$

31 Stuart St., 02116 **Tel** *(617) 338-8586*   **Map** 1 B5

This Boston landmark *(see p85)* has been around since 1868, and is an old-fashioned restaurant best known for its bratwurst with sauerkraut and homemade potato salad. The sauerbraten may not be up to Munich standards, but the price is right and the evening piano bar can be a lot of fun.

Legal Sea Foods $$$

26 Park Plaza, 02116 **Tel** *(617) 426-4444*   **Map** 4 E2

Now that Legal has gone national with airport restaurants, this flagship of the local chain is less of a novelty, but it is still a national leader in setting quality standards for fresh fish. This location features an extensive wine cellar and a lounge popular for Back Bay business lunches and after-dinner drinks. It also offers a gluten-free menu for celiacs.

Peach Farm $$$

4 Tyler St., 02111 **Tel** *(617) 482-1116*   **Map** 4 F2

In the heart of Chinatown and popular with the locals. The sound of Hong Kong pop music fills the series of interconnected rooms and you should step inside the door to peruse the live tanks. Chinese seafood is its specialty, such as sesame jellyfish and salt and pepper eel, or just ask for what is fresh. Open late.

Shabu-Zen $$$

16 Tyler St., 02111 **Tel** *(617) 292-8828*   **Map** 2 D5

"Shabu-shabu" means "swish-swish" – the sound chopsticks make as they swirl raw vegetables and slivers of meat and fish in hot broth. Season your chicken broth with scallions, soy sauce, and hot pepper, settle on a meat or fish and a type of noodles, and assemble your own dinner. Perfect for diners who always wanted their sushi cooked.

Taiwan Cafe $$$

34 Oxford St., 02111 **Tel** *(617) 426-8181*   **Map** 4 F2

Locals flock here for Taiwanese comfort food that makes few concessions to western tastes. If you are hunting for homestyle delicacies such as duck tongue, steamed taro, or meatballs in clay hot pots, this small second-story restaurant is the place. Luncheon specials (fish ball soup, for example) are a rare steal. Cash only.

Teatro $$$$

177 Tremont St., 02111 **Tel** *(617) 778-6841*   **Map** 4 E2

The high arched mosaic ceiling and open kitchen of this erstwhile synagogue-turned-restaurant creates a theatrical atmosphere worthy of the name. Reservations aren't required, but make one if you need to eat in time for a curtain opening. Teatro offers a light grill menu and broad selection of northern Italian seafood and veal dishes.

Bina Osteria $$$$$

581 Washington St., 02116 **Tel** *(617) 956-0888*   **Map** 1 C5

This hotspot provides lovers of modern Italian cuisine with an inviting dining room in which to enjoy homemade pastas, thin-crust pizzas, and intricate salads. Those looking for heartier fare gravitate toward braised wild boar or Florentine-style porterhouse steaks. There's also a store selling fresh breads, gelati, pastas, and prepared meals.

Locke-Ober $$$$$

3 Winter Place, 02139 **Tel** *(617) 542-1340*   **Map** 1 C4

One of Boston's historic gems, this storied restaurant dates back to the 1870s and has hosted many dignitaries. The lavish environs and extensive menu remain popular with the city's elite, with upscale European classics like Dover sole and duck à l'orange sharing table space with more exotic fare like Singapore lobster curry. Closed Sun.

Market $$$$$

100 Stuart St., 02111 **Tel** *(617) 310-6790*   **Map** 4 E2

Jean-Georges Vongerichten's first New England restaurant sits on the ground floor of the W Hotel *(see p134)*, enabling guests and local foodies to sample his multicultural cuisine. Eclectic drinks complement the range of small plates. Local, seasonal ingredients are used in items such as rice cracker-crusted tuna and sweet-and-sour striped bass.

BACK BAY AND SOUTH END

Mike's City Diner   ⬛🚶   ⑤
1714 Washington St., 02118 **Tel** *(617) 267-9393*   **Map** *3 C5*

Show up early – very early. Mike's is open 6am–3pm every day, and there is usually a line of customers outside the door waiting for the breakfast specials, rendered with a little more care and finesse than you would normally expect. Political candidates always come by for a photo op during the quadrennial presidential nominating race.

Parish Cafe   🚶♿🔳   ⑤⑤
361 Boylston St., 02116 **Tel** *(617) 247-4777*   **Map** *3 B2*

Think of this casual bar-restaurant as a sampler of Boston's most famous chefs. The owners convinced each to dream up a signature sandwich, and the results are unusual, lobster salad on pepper brioche, for one. Landing one of the few outdoor tables can be hard so come early or sit at the bar inside.

Steve's Greek Restaurant   🚶   ⑤⑤
316 Newbury St., 02116 **Tel** *(617) 267-1817*   **Map** *3 A3*

Maybe the cheapest place to eat well in Back Bay, Steve's is an old-fashioned Greek restaurant where spinach-feta pastries, eggplant dishes, and salads studded with dark olives are the standard fare. Steve's gets a deal on locally-caught octopus, since few other restaurants serve it, but aficionados rave loudest about the lamb dishes.

Orinoco   ⑤⑤⑤
477 Shawmut Avenue, 02118 **Tel** *(617) 369-7075*   **Map** *3 C5*

This dining room with a tin ceiling in an 1890s building is the hot spot for listening to the new wave in Latin music while enjoying *arepas* (meat-filled grilled corn muffins) and plantain-stuffed *empanadas*. There is limited seating and no reservations.

B&G Oysters   ⑤⑤⑤⑤
550 Tremont St., 02116 **Tel** *(617) 423-0550*   **Map** *4 D4*

A side venture of the famed chef of No. 9 Park, this subterranean spot for mollusk lovers consists of a marble bar surrounded by stools and an open stainless steel kitchen that preps the raw bar offerings. At least a dozen varieties of oysters are available at any given time. There is also a broad selection of sparkling and mineral-rich white wines.

Bouchée   ⑤⑤⑤⑤
159 Newbury St., 02116 **Tel** *(617) 450-4343*   **Map** *3 B2*

Boston's love affair with French food goes back at least to the American Revolution, and Bouchée delivers all the classics you'd look for in a Parisian brasserie, from steak *frites* and *coq au vin* to *bouillabaisse* and *cassoulet*. The excellent French wine list gets past the obvious names to include many lesser-known appellations. Open daily.

Brasserie Jo   🅿🚶♿🔳   ⑤⑤⑤⑤
120 Huntington Ave., 02116 **Tel** *(617) 425-3240*   **Map** *3 B3*

One advantage of this Alsatian restaurant in the Colonnade Hotel *(see ρ135)* is that you can get a meal from dawn until after midnight. French beers are on tap, and the menu is replete with all the brasserie classics from steak-frites to *tarte tatin* (form of apple pie). This place is popular after-work for sharing glasses of kir and a plate of pâté.

Ciao Bella   🚶♿🔳   ⑤⑤⑤⑤
240 Newbury St. #A, 02116 **Tel** *(617) 536-2626*   **Map** *3 A3*

The outdoor tables on Newbury Street at Fairfield are as big a draw as the reasonably priced retro Italian-American menu that runs from minestrone to chicken parmesan. Local sports figures and visiting minor celebrities often seem to end up eating here, so the paparazzi provide some good additional street entertainment.

Jasper White's Summer Shack   🚶♿   ⑤⑤⑤⑤
50 Dalton St., 02116 **Tel** *(617) 867-9955*   **Map** *3 A3*

The Back Bay venue of this chain of casual seafood restaurants, started by one of New England's best chefs, sits right above a bowling alley and within easy walking distance of Symphony Hall and Fenway Park. Look out for the daily fish specials and weekend brunches featuring White's signature lobster hash.

Masa   🅿🚶♿   ⑤⑤⑤⑤
439 Tremont St., 02116 **Tel** *(617) 338-8884*   **Map** *4 D3*

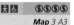

A rarity in Boston, Masa draws inspiration from the gourmet cuisine pioneered in the American Southwest. The chef is apt to serve mushrooms in a pumpkin seed mole sauce or grilled trout with a chile-pepper rub. This is not a salsa-and-chips tequila bar, but Masa does pour tasting flights of different styles of tequila. Closed lunch Mon–Fri.

Post 390   ♿🚶🅿   ⑤⑤⑤⑤
406 Stuart St., 02118 **Tel** *(617) 399-0015*   **Map** *3 C3*

Located near the Back Bay–South End border, this handsome urban tavern serves as a meeting spot for business types and neighborhood foodies. Two bars and an open kitchen are spread over two floors, giving diners plenty to ponder when not perusing the lengthy menu of upscale comfort fare, like turkey pot pie and house-smoked BBQ ribs.

Key to Price Guide *see p142* **Key to Symbols** *see back cover flap*

Rocca
 ⑤⑤⑤⑤

500 Harrison Ave., 02118 **Tel** *(617) 451-5151*

Map *1 C5*

Boston's only restaurant focusing on Ligurian cuisine (the herb-infused dishes and ocean-oriented food of Genoa and the Italian Riviera), Rocca stands out by serving intensely flavored but light Italian food. The lively scene is fueled in part by an excellent cocktail bar and on-site parking, which is almost unheard of in the South End. Closed lunch.

Sibling Rivalry
 ⑤⑤⑤⑤

525 Tremont St., 02116 **Tel** *(617) 338-5338*

Map *4 D4*

The name refers to the two vastly different menus by brothers who have achieved chef stardom elsewhere in the country. Located on the ground level of a fashionably designed luxury condo complex, Sibling Rivalry offers a choice of French food as favored by one brother, and American cuisine as favored by the other.

Sonsie
⑤⑤⑤⑤

327 Newbury St., 02116 **Tel** *(617) 351-2500*

Map *3 A3*

Everybody loves the look of this upper-Newbury Street stalwart, especially when they swing open the glass doors in the summer and the outdoor tables fill up with patrons more interested in being seen than in eating the truly delicious food. Most dishes hail from the French and Italian rivieras, with the occasional Indochinese delight.

Stephanie's on Newbury
⑤⑤⑤⑤

190 Newbury St., 02116 **Tel** *(617) 236-0990*

Map *3 B2*

Stephanie's has become an institution with its dinner salads and pasta dishes that are so big that diners routinely leave with "doggie bags" for the next meal. Signature plates include smoked salmon potato pancakes and meatloaf layered with cheese and caramelized onions. The restaurant offers some of Back Bay's best outdoor tables.

Tapeo
 ⑤⑤⑤⑤

266 Newbury St., 02116 **Tel** *(617) 267-4799*

Map *3 B2*

Authentically Spanish, this restaurant and tapas bar specializes in small plates that would be served with a glass of sherry in Spain. One of the few restaurants in Boston to serve true *jamón serrano* (the Spanish answer to Italian prosciutto), Tapeo also prepares exquisite bites like boneless pheasant breast and garlicky squid. Closed lunch Mon–Fri.

Toro
 ⑤⑤⑤⑤

1704 Washington St., 02118 **Tel** *(617) 536-4300*

Map *3 C5*

The name is a bilingual pun of the Spanish for "bull" and the Japanese for bluefin tuna belly sashimi – no surprise, given the chef-owner's love of Spanish tapas and Japanese sushi and sashimi bars. The food is a hybrid of the two. Sushi is much less expensive here than at the chef's upscale restaurant Clio. Closed lunch.

Tremont 647
 ⑤⑤⑤⑤

647 Tremont St., 02118 **Tel** *(617) 266-4600*

Map *3 C4*

The extensively tattooed chef-owner is no shrinking violet, and his style of cooking favors big portions, bold flavors, and lots of smoke with the meat. South End trend-followers are always stopping in to determine what's *au courant*, whether it is high-alcohol caipirinhas or the weekend pajama brunches when diners show up in sleepware.

Union Bar & Grille
⑤⑤⑤⑤

1357 Washington St., 02118 **Tel** *(617) 423-0555*

Map *4 D4*

An anchor for the rapidly gentrifying SoWa (south of Washington) neighborhood, this restaurant is popular with owners of the stylish new loft conversions. A sleek restaurant serving unpretentious American food, its attentive service, sharp design, and deft bar make it a hit with those who love to dine out. Closed lunch.

Via Matta Plaza
 ⑤⑤⑤⑤

79 Park Place, 02116 **Tel** *(617) 422-0008*

Map *4 D2*

"Crazy Street" is as good a name as any for this hip bar-restaurant scene on the back side of Park Square. The food is solidly northern Italian – risottos and game from the Piedmont, tender veggie plates from Liguria, roasted meats of Tuscany, and heavenly sauces and cheeses from Emilia Romagna. The menu changes daily.

Clio
⑤⑤⑤⑤⑤

370-A Commonwealth Ave., 02215 **Tel** *(617) 536-7200*

Map *3 A2*

Clio's chef-owner is widely celebrated as one of country's most inventive chefs. Small plates and appetizers often feature arcane Asian spices, dabs of various caviars, and decorative techniques worthy of an origami master. Entrées are simpler, with the emphasis on exquisite cuts of meat and fish. Closed lunch; Mon.

Grill 23
 ⑤⑤⑤⑤⑤

161 Berkeley St., 02116 **Tel** *(617) 542-2255*

Map *4 D2*

Although a horde of chain steakhouses has descended on Boston in recent years, Grill 23 has been the genuine article since 1983. Beef is certified hormone- and antibiotic-free, and the bar serves exquisite martinis. The constantly evolving menu is based on seasonal availability. The 900-plus label wine list is among the city's best. Closed lunch.

Hamersley's Bistro
⑤⑤⑤⑤

553 Tremont St., 02116 **Tel** *(617) 423-2700*

Map *4 D4*

A French country restaurant translated into an urban setting adjacent to the Boston Center for the Arts. Chicken roasted with garlic, lemon, and parsley under the skin has been a signature dish for decades. The summertime tables on the plaza are some of the most sought-after in the city.

L'Espalier $⑤⑤⑤⑤⑤

774 Boylston St., 2138 **Tel** *(617) 262-3023*   **Map** *3 B3*

One of Boston's premier restaurants enjoys a stylish perch next to the luxe Mandarin Oriental Hotel *(see p135)*. The award-winning, modern French cuisine emphasizes local, artisanal ingredients, yielding items like butter-poached Maine lobster and cocoa-rubbed venison. Note that only the pricy prix fixe and tasting menus are offered at dinner.

Oak Room $⑤⑤⑤⑤

138 St. James Avenue, 02116 **Tel** *(617) 267-5300*   **Map** *1 A5*

The aromas that strike you as you enter are seared beef and old money. The oak paneling helps preserve the Edwardian men's club atmosphere in this venerable steak house where even the small portions could feed two. The anteroom bar is one of the most elegant in the city.

Oishii 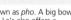 $⑤⑤⑤⑤⑤

1166 Washington St., 2116 **Tel** *(617) 482-8868*   **Map** *4 E4*

This South End eatery is widely regarded as one of the city's top-rated, and priciest, places for gourmet Japanese fare. Exceptionally fresh ingredients are diced, rolled, and torched into artfully presented platters of heavenly sushi and sashimi. The minimalist interior and respectful servers ensure that the diner's focus falls firmly on the cuisine.

Sorellina $⑤⑤⑤⑤⑤

1 Huntington Avenue, 02116 **Tel** *(617) 412-4600*   **Map** *3 A4*

Contemporary northern Italian cuisine is on offer in this impressive restaurant with its highly designed decor. Dishes range from the traditional, such as herb-roasted chicken and plain, grilled steaks, to the more adventurous, such as venison carpaccio with cherries. Closed lunch.

FARTHER AFIELD

Mr. Bartley's Burger and Salad Cottage $⑤

1246 Massachusetts Ave., Cambridge, 02138 **Tel** *(617) 354-6559*

Harvard Square's quintessential burger shop specializes in whopping pieces of meat. Some sandwiches have humorous names linked to a celebrity or politician, but most importantly, the prices are right, the food is fresh, and it fills you up. On weekends, it can take up to an hour to get in the door to order.

Le's 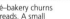 $⑤⑤

36 Dunster St., Cambridge, 02138 **Tel** *(617) 864-4100*

Asian students at Harvard head to this congenial restaurant for bowls of Vietnamese soup known as *pho*. A big bowl of noodles and broth with beef, chicken, or seafood is perhaps the ultimate comfort food, but Le's also offers a range of other noodle dishes, as well as healthy and inexpensive entrées and rice plates.

Sofra $⑤⑤

1 Belmont St., Cambridge, 02138 **Tel** *(617) 661-3161*

Situated on a busy corner where Cambridge meets Watertown, this inviting Middle Eastern café–bakery churns out modern interpretations of Old World treats like hummus, tzatziki, kibbeh, and stuffed flatbreads. A small seating area enables patrons to enjoy them on the spot, but many customers opt to take their treats to go.

Tanjore $⑤⑤

18 Eliot St., Cambridge, 02138 **Tel** *(617) 868-1900*

Located on the river side of Harvard Square, Tanjore, owned by a local family, is the most eclectic of Indian restaurants. The menu carefully identifies the regions from which all the dishes come, from the mild dosas of the south to the coastal vindaloos to the tandoori dry roasts of the north. Authentic Indian desserts are available.

Betty's Wok & Noodle $⑤⑤⑤

250 Huntington Ave., 02116 **Tel** *(617) 424-1950*   **Map** *3 A4*

Offering tongue-in-cheek dining close to the Huntington Theatre and Symphony Hall, Betty's is decorated in 1950s retro chic. The menu, though, is all about modern choice. Pick a rice or noodle base, then a protein (fish, chicken, tofu), then a sauce to create your own combo dish. Traditional American desserts include chocolate layer cake.

Hungry Mother $⑤⑤⑤

233 Cardinal Medeiros Ave., Cambridge, 02478 **Tel** *(617) 499-0090*

Tucked away in a corner of Kendall Square, this restaurant thrills with Southern fare made with local ingredients. The kitchen's specialties are its house-cured meats, smoked fish, and house-made preservatives. Drink-lovers enjoy artfully made cocktails, some of which feature garnishes like bacon or boiled peanut. Closed Mon.

Petit Robert Bistro $⑤⑤⑤

468 Commonwealth Ave., 02215 **Tel** *(617) 375-0699*

Once you have eaten here, you will wonder how any other restaurant in the neighborhood can stay in business. French bistro fare in French bistro portions (smaller than American) by a French Master Chef at these prices is a steal. Simple, clean executions of the classics from *coquilles St-Jacques*, to steak-frites, to profiteroles.

Key to Price Guide *see p142* **Key to Symbols** *see back cover flap*

Tory Row

                                 $$$

3 Brattle St., Cambridge, 02142 **Tel** *(617) 876-8769*

This sophisticated, minimally decorated hangout gets all the atmosphere it needs from its location in the heart of Harvard Square. Students, tourists, and locals navigate an eclectic menu of multicultural comfort food, alternating between bites of croque monsieur, baked raclette, and homemade roasted red pepper hummus.

Casablanca

                               $$$$

40 Brattle St., Cambridge, 02138 **Tel** *(617) 876-0999*

Few Harvard alumni can return without a nostalgic meal at this Bogart-themed boite. Casablanca approaches Mediterranean cuisine from North Africa, so cumin and coriander figure prominently in the lamb and bulgar meatballs, and spicy hummus is often a side dish. The bar in the rear is a watering hole for local literati.

Craigie on Main

                               $$$$

853 Main St., Cambridge, 02138 **Tel** *(617) 497-5511*

With its relentless focus on the best local, seasonal, and organic ingredients available, this handsome Central Square restaurant remains a favorite with the city's gourmands. The à la carte, tasting, and bar menus change daily, and patrons can expect intricate preparations of rustic ingredients like cockscombs, pork belly, and monkfish cheeks.

East Coast Grill

                               $$$$

1271 Cambridge St., Cambridge, 02139 **Tel** *(617) 491-6568*

The chef that runs this colorful, casual restaurant is an acknowledged master of open-fire grilling, having written seven books and counting. Grilled fish with tropical salsas, pulled barbecued pork, and icy oysters are among the greatest hits. The Bloody Mary bar inevitably draws an overflow crowd during Sunday brunch. Closed Mon–Sat lunch.

Il Casale

                               $$$$

50 Leonard St., Belmont, 02462 **Tel** *(617) 209-4942*

Lovers of Italian fare flock to this old fire station in Belmont to gorge on homemade pasta dishes – some of which come from the chef's family recipes – and wood-grilled meats and fish. The atmospheric interior can get noisy when packed, but most patrons are too focused on their lamb stew, or gnocchi with boar ragout to notice. Closed Mon.

Les Zygomates

                               $$$$

129 South St., 02111 **Tel** *(617) 542-5108*
                                 ***Map** 4 F2*

The name refers to the facial muscles involved in smiling, which is what most diners will be doing when they discover the relaxed French bistro fare, the live jazz, and the extensive selection of wines by the glass. The wine bar is located in the old Leather District close to South Station. The menu always includes a few vegetarian entrées.

Sandrine's Bistro

                               $$$$

8 Holyoke St., Cambridge, 02138 **Tel** *(617) 497-5300*

It is hard to resist the Alsatian flatbread topped with farmer's cheese blended with spices, and bacon, mushrooms, or asparagus – and those are just starters on this classical Alsatian menu. Here charcuterie is king and cabbage isn't eaten until it is sauerkraut. Modestly priced daily menu, as well as pull-out-the-stops tasting menu. Closed Sun lunch.

Temple Bar

                               $$$$

1688 Massachusetts Ave., Cambridge, 02138 **Tel** *(617) 547-5055*

This local hangout between Harvard and Porter Squares takes the kitchen as seriously as it does the busy bar. Burgers, sandwiches, and gourmet pizzas (lamb and roasted tomatoes, for example) are always available, but evening entrées are more ambitious New American bistro fare presented with considerable panache. Closed lunch.

Blue Ginger

          $$$$$

583 Washington St., Wellesley, 02113 **Tel** *(781) 283-5790*

Blue Ginger lures adventurous gourmands to quiet Wellesley. Signature items like sake-miso marinated Alaskan butterfish, and foie gras-shiitake shumai demonstrate the kitchen's blending of ingredients and techniques from Asia and Europe. The welcoming interior sports bamboo accents and a lively open kitchen. Closed Sat lunch, Sun.

Oleana

                               $$$$$

134 Hampshire St., Cambridge, 02139 **Tel** *(617) 661-0506*

Oleana's chef-owner is the winner of many culinary accolades. Her dishes are inspired by the cuisines of all sides of the Mediterranean Sea, so she is likely to wax Lebanese in one dish, Moroccan in the next, and Catalan in another. Aromatic spices and intense sauces characterize most dishes. There is a nightly vegetarian tasting menu. Closed lunch.

Olives

                               $$$$$

10 City Square, Charlestown, 02129 **Tel** *(617) 242-1999*
                                 ***Map** 1 C1*

Home base for superchef Todd English, Olives pioneered a style of rustic Italian/Mediterranean cooking in Boston. Bold baked pastas and giant roasts of meat and fish pour out of the kitchen with admirable consistency. Its Charlestown location is near USS *Constitution* at the end of the Freedom Trail and there is a vigorous bar scene. Closed lunch.

Rialto

                               $$$$$

1 Bennett St., Cambridge, 02138 **Tel** *(617) 661-5050*

High-end, sophisticated decor makes this the special event restaurant of choice around Harvard Square. But Rialto is friendly and more relaxed than most *haute cuisine* temples. The chef takes a luscious approach to the classic Mediterranean cuisines, where rosemary is magic and basil an herb to conjure with. Closed lunch.

Cafés and Bars

The social fabric of Boston is held together through its abundance of places to meet with friends and while away the hours. A city with a rich mix of students, working folk, and executives provides a selection of cafés and bars that cater to all tastes, and to people who keep all hours. There are places where you can find a pick-me-up, rest your feet, and meet local people. A further selection of bars is listed on pp162–3.

CAFÉS

Cafés tend to cluster in a few areas of the city, most notably Harvard Square and its environs, the South End, the North End, and Beacon Hill. **Crema Café**, one of Harvard Square's long line of cafés, serves both hot and iced tea, along with delicious pastries and sandwiches. The oldest of the square's coffee culture joints, the hip **Café Pamplona**, dates back to the Beatnik days. For an especially genteel treat, make your way to **L.A. Burdick's Handmade Chocolates** and order a sampler plate of their innovative chocolates or one of their superb buttery fruit tarts. They also have some fine teas, including herbals. There are two branches of the **1369 Coffeehouse**, which are spacious, upbeat and frequented by a clientele of all ages, who come mainly for the excellent cookie bars.

The South End's secluded cafés are home to a thriving café society. Many are popular with the vibrant gay community *(see p163)* that has made its home in this neighborhood, but also happily welcome all visitors, regardless of sexual preference. **Berkeley Perk** is colorful and spacious, with a wide selection of juices, quality sodas, and sweet treats. Pastry chef Joanne Chang's first **Flour Bakery & Café**, in the South End, met with such overwhelming neighborhood support that she opened a second one on Fort Point Channel, near the Children's Museum. Either location is a surefire venue for artisanal breads, generous sandwiches, and warming soups, as well as fine tarts, cakes, cookies, and breakfast breads.

Cafés cluster around the main thoroughfares of the North End, where many local restaurants do not even bother to serve coffee or dessert because the cafés in this lively Italian neighborhood do it so much better – espresso or cappuccino with *tiramisu* or *cannoli* are a must. **Caffè Vittoria**, decorated in marble and chrome, has a wide array of pastries and liqueurs, and its own cigar parlor. **Caffè Pompei** is a more chaotic place, which features murals of its doomed namesake crowding the walls. While many like **Mike's Pastry** for their *cannoli*, it is said that the best are found alongside the nougat at **Maria's Pastry Shop**, which sadly does not have seating. **Lulu's Bake Shop** is known for its tempting variety of cupcakes. On Beacon Hill, **Café Vanille** has a range of exquisite Parisian pastries.

TEA ROOMS

A couple of grand hotels have preserved a genteel tradition of offering afternoon tea: **The Bristol Lounge** at the Four Seasons Hotel serves a lovely tea (especially enjoyable if you are seated by the fireplace), while on weekends the **Taj Boston** continues the formal afternoon tea tradition established by its predecessor the Ritz-Carlton, complete with a full Old World service. More recently, tea has found aficionados among the college-aged crowd, and a number of tea houses designed for the younger and more budget-conscious flourish in Harvard Square and on Newbury Street. **Tealuxe**, which has a branch on Newbury Street and in Harvard Square, lets customers peruse an impressive catalog of hundreds of teas from around the world. Fine Asian teas, with a touch of tranquillity and a hint of enlightenment, are the specialty at **Dado Tea**, which is situated both in and east of Harvard Square in Cambridge. Near the theater district and in Harvard Square is **Finale**, famous for specializing in producing the most delicious desserts.

ICE CREAM PARLORS

Bostonians eat more ice cream, per person, year round, than anyone else in America. They are highly discerning customers, and fiercely loyal to their favorite parlor. Many restaurants make a point of serving one of the locally made ice creams with their dessert menus. When ordering ice cream, you can get it served in a dish with a spoon, or in a cone to lick. You get a choice of wafer cone (light, crispy, slightly bland) or a sugar cone (thin, crisp, sweet cookie wafer). Some may decide to order one of the enormous waffle cones, which is really just an overgrown sugar cone custom-made for the truly indulgent. Parlors are open most of the day and late into the evening. In central Boston the best ice creams are hard to find, but Newbury Street *(see p93)* has some of the best options. **J.P. Licks** is an old favorite, its bizarre tiled decor a landmark. The New England ice cream giant **Ben and Jerry's** has several parlors featuring all their flavors.

If possible, the ice-cream talent in Cambridge is even greater than in Boston. Adult lovers of gourmet ice cream swear by the Burnt Caramel and Earl Grey flavors at **Toscanini's**, in Central Square With the demise of Herrell's, **Lizzy's Ice Cream** has emerged as the new standard bearer of Harvard Square. Try the Charles River Crunch (dark chocolate ice cream with almond toffee nuggets).

Competition for most inventive flavors is stiff. For example, **Christina's** in Inman Square makes the best green tea ice cream in the city, as well as a wide range of other flavors, ranging from the sublime to the simply gooey.

A little farther afield, **Ron's Gourmet Homemade Ice Cream & Bowling** features specialty flavors such as peanut sunrise, as well as a chance to work off some calories on their candlepin bowling lanes.

BARS

The legal drinking age in Boston is 21, and you may be asked to show proof of identification (see p174).

Boston has scores of bars which offer live music and other types of entertainment (see also pp162–3). Those listed here are a good place to relax and simply have a drink, though some of them can still be quite lively.

For good, down-to-earth bars, you cannot go wrong with the youthful **Shay's Pub**

and Wine Bar, The Sevens, the slightly tacky **Purple Shamrock,** the well-heeled **21st Amendment,** or the kitschy lounge paradise of **The Good Life. Parker's Bar** at the Omni Parker House Hotel has the atmosphere of a gentleman's club, while around the city are dotted a number of good wine bars, notably **Les Zygomates** and **Troquet. Jacob Wirth** (see p85), which is also a restaurant, is situated in the Theater District and has good beer and a lively ambience.

DIRECTORY

CAFÉS

Berkeley Perk
69 Berkeley St. **Map** 4 D3.
Tel (617) 426-7375.

Café Pamplona
12 Bow St., Cambridge.
Tel (617) 492-0352.

Café Vanille
70 Charles St. **Map** 1 B2.
Tel (617) 523-9200.

Caffè Pompei
278 Hanover St. **Map**
2 E2. *Tel (617) 227-1562.*

Caffè Vittoria
290–296 Hanover St.
Map 2 E2.
Tel (617) 227-7606.

Crema Café
27 Brattle St., Cambridge.
Tel (617) 876-2700.

**Flour Bakery
& Café**
1595 Washington St. **Map**
3 C5. *Tel (617) 267-4300.*
12 Farnsworth St. **Map** 2
E5. *Tel (617) 338-4333.*

**L.A. Burdick's
Handmade
Chocolates**
52 Brattle St.,Cambridge.
Tel (617) 491-4340.

Lulu's Bake Shop
227 Hanover St. **Map** 2
E2. *Tel (617) 720-2200.*

**Maria's
Pastry Shop**
46 Cross St. **Map** 2 D3.
Tel (617) 523-1196.

Mike's Pastry
300 Hanover St. **Map** 2
E2. *Tel (617) 742-3050.*

1369 Coffeehouse
1369 Cambridge St.,
Cambridge.
Tel (617) 576-1369.
757 Massachusetts Ave.
Tel (617) 576-4600.

TEA ROOMS

The Bristol Lounge
200 Boylston St.
Map 4 D2.
Tel (617) 338-4400.

Dado Tea
955 Massachusetts Ave.,
Cambridge.
Tel (617) 497-9061.
50 Church St., Cambridge.
Tel (617) 547-0950.

Finale
1 Columbus Ave.
Map1 B5.
Tel (617) 423-3184.
30 Dunster St.,
Cambridge.
Tel (617) 441-9797.

Taj Boston
15 Arlington St.
Map 4 D2.
Tel (617) 536-5700.

Tealuxe
Brattle St., Cambridge.
Tel (617) 441-0077.
108 Newbury St.
Map 3 C2.
Tel (617) 927-0400.

ICE CREAM
PARLORS

Ben and Jerry's
174 Newbury St.
Map 3 B2.
Tel (617) 536-5456.
20 Park Plaza.
Map 4 D2.
Tel (617) 426-0890.
36 John F. Kennedy St.,
Cambridge.
Tel (617) 864-2828.

Christina's
1255 Cambridge St.
Tel (617) 492-7021.

J.P. Licks
352 Newbury St.
Map 3 A3.
Tel (617) 236-1666.

Lizzy's Ice Cream
29 Church St.,
Cambridge.
Tel (617) 354-2911.

**Ron's Gourmet
Homemade
Ice Cream &
Bowling**
1231 Hyde Park Ave.,
Hyde Park, MA 02136.
Tel (617) 364-5274.

Toscanini's
899 Main St., Cambridge.
Tel (617) 491-5877.

BARS

The Good Life
28 Kingston St.
Map 2 D5.
Tel (617) 451-2622.

Jacob Wirth
31–37 Stuart St.

Map 4 E2.
Tel (617) 338-8586.

Les Zygomates
129 South St.
Map 4 F2.
Tel (617) 542-5108.

Parker's Bar
60 School St.
Map 2 D4.
Tel (617) 227-8600.

**Purple
Shamrock**
1 Union St.
Map 2 D3.
Tel (617) 227-2060.

The Sevens
77 Charles St.
Map 1 B3.
Tel (617) 523-9074.

**Shay's Pub
and Wine Bar**
58 John F. Kennedy St.,
Cambridge.
Tel (617) 864-9161.

Troquet
140 Boylston St.
Map 4 E2.
Tel (617) 695-9463.

21st Amendment
150 Bowdoin St.
Map 1 C3.
Tel (617) 227-7100.

SHOPPING IN BOSTON

Shopping in Boston has evolved dramatically in recent years. Long known as an excellent center for antiques, books, and quality clothing, the city's shopping options now cover a much broader spectrum, influenced both by its booming economy and its large, international student population. From the fashionable boutiques of Newbury Street, to the many stores selling cosmopolitan home furnishings or ethnic treasures, to the varied art and crafts galleries, Boston caters to every shopping need. Whether you are looking for the latest fashion accessory, an unusual antique, or a special souvenir, choices abound to accommodate every sense of style and budget. Boston is no longer simply traditional, and now holds its own in providing a vibrant, eclectic and world-class shopping experience.

Red Sox baseball cap

Large glass atrium of the busy Prudential shopping mall

SALES

There are two major sale seasons in Boston: July, when summer clothes go on sale to make room for fall fashions, and January, when any winter clothing and merchandise is cleared after the holidays. Most stores also have a sale section or clearance rack throughout the year.

PAYMENT AND TAXES

Major credit cards and traveler's checks with identification are accepted at most stores. There is a tax of 6.25 percent on all purchases except groceries and clothing, although any item of clothing over $175 will be taxed.

OPENING HOURS

Most stores open at 10am and close at 6pm from Monday to Saturday, and from noon to 5 or 6pm on Sunday. Many stores stay open later on Thursday nights, and most department stores stay open until 7:30 or 8pm throughout the week. Weekday mornings are the best times to shop. Saturdays, lunch hours, and evenings can be very busy.

SHOPPING MALLS

Shopping malls – clusters of shops, restaurants, and food courts all within one large and open complex – have become top destinations for shopping, offering variety, dining, and entertainment. With long winters and a fair share of bad weather, New Englanders flock to malls to shop, eat, and, in the case of teenagers, simply hang out.

Copley Place, with its elegant restaurants, and more than 75 shops over two levels, is based around a dazzling 60-ft (18-m) atrium and waterfall. Across a pedestrian overpass, **Shops at Prudential Center** encompasses **Saks Fifth Avenue** department store, a food court, and many smaller specialty shops. The most upscale mall in town, **Heritage on the Garden** looks out over Boston's Public Garden, and features the boutiques of top European designers, fine jewelers, and stores selling other luxury goods. Outside the center of town, across the Charles River, **Cambridgeside Galleria** has over 100 shops and a pond-side food court. For last-minute purchases, **Boston Landing**, at Logan Airport (Terminal C), has shops, restaurants, banking, and internet access.

DEPARTMENT STORES

There are four major department stores in Boston offering a large and varied selection of clothing, accessories, cosmetics, housewares, and gifts. Some also have restaurants and beauty salons, and provide a variety of personal shopping services. For those wanting to shop at several stores, **Concierge of Boston** provides a shopping service in metropolitan Boston. At

Farm produce on display on Charles Street

Downtown Crossing *(see p82)*, a bustling shopping district between Boston Common and the Financial District, generations of Bostonians once shopped at Filene's, now closed. The department store's underground cut-price offspring, **Filene's Basement**, pioneered the "automatic markdown," in which goods are discounted more heavily the longer they remain unsold. This branch of Filene's Basement is closed through 2012 for renovations.

Directly across the street, **Macy's**, the legendary New York emporium, offers an equally impressive array of fashions, cosmetics, housewares, and furnishings.

Heading uptown, through Boston Common and Public Garden to Boylston Street, you can spot the Prudential Tower, centerpiece of a once nondescript but now revitalized complex of shops, offices, and restaurants. This includes the venerable and elegant **Saks Fifth Avenue**, which caters to its upscale clientele with renowned service, a luxurious ambiance, and strikingly stylish displays. For the ultimate high fashion, high profile shopping experience, stop by **Neiman Marcus**,

which specializes in haute couture, precious jewelry, furs, and gifts. The store is well known for its Christmas catalog, with presents that have included authentic Egyptian mummies, vintage airplanes, a pair of two-million-dollar diamonds, and robots to help out around the house – or mansion. Other Copley Place merchants include Ralph Lauren, Christian Dior, Louis Vuitton, Gucci, and Emporio Armani, as well as Boston's first outlet of popular Manhattan trendsetter, Barney's.

Boutiques of genteel Newbury Street

DISCOUNT AND OUTLET STORES

Dedicated bargain hunters may want to consider making a day trip to one of New England's famed outlet centers, where many top designers and major brand manufacturers offer last-season and overstocked clothing and goods at big discounts. Generally sold at 20 to 30 percent less than their regular retail prices, some items can be found reduced by as much as 75 percent.

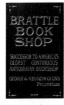
Brattle Bookshop's sign

Wrentham Village

Premium Outlets are about 40 miles (65 km) south of Boston. The stores here sell designer clothing, housewares, and accessories from many of the leading manufacturers.

Kittery, 50 miles (80 km) north of Boston, is an even larger outlet destination, with more than 125 shops selling everything from footwear and designer clothes, to sports equipment, perfume, books, china, glass, and gifts. There are also numerous restaurants.

Freeport, Maine, is one of the largest and most famous outlet centers, being home to the renowned outdoor equipment specialist **L.L. Bean**. Over two hours' drive from Boston, it is only worth the journey for the dedicated shopper, or for those already visiting Maine.

DIRECTORY

SHOPPING MALLS

Boston Landing
Terminal C,
Logan International
Airport, East Boston.
www.massport.com

Cambridgeside Galleria
100 Cambridgeside Pl.,
Cambridge.
Tel (617) 621-8666.

Copley Place
100 Huntington Ave.
Map 3 C3.
Tel (617) 369-5000.
www.simon.com

Heritage on the Garden
300 Boylston St. **Map** 4 D2.
Tel (617) 426-9500.

Shops at Prudential Center
800 Boylston St. **Map** 3 B3.
Tel (800) 746-7778.
www.prudential
center.com

DEPARTMENT STORES

Concierge of Boston
165 Newbury Street.
Map 3 C2.
Tel (617) 266-6611.
www.concierge.org

Filene's Basement
426 Washington St. **Map** 4 F1. *Tel (617) 542-2011.*

Macy's
450 Washington St. **Map** 4 F1. *Tel (617) 357-3000.*

Neiman Marcus
5 Copley Place, 100 Huntington Ave. **Map** 3 C3. *Tel (617) 536-3660.*

Saks Fifth Avenue
Prudential Center. **Map** 3 B3. *Tel (617) 262-8500.*

DISCOUNT AND OUTLET STORES

Freeport Merchants Association
Freeport, Maine.

Tel (207) 865-1212.
Tel (800) 865-1994.
www.freeportusa.com

Kittery Outlets
Route 1, Kittery, Maine.
Tel (888) 548-8379.
www.thekitteryoutlets.com

L.L. Bean
Route 1, Freeport, Maine.
Tel (877) 552-3268.

Wrentham Village Premium Outlets
1 Premium Outlets Blvd,
Wrentham.
Tel (508) 384-0600.

Fashion

From chain stores stocked with popular brand labels to specialists selling vintage clothing, Boston offers choices in every area of fashion. Well-heeled shoppers frequent high-fashion boutiques, students flock to vintage emporiums, bargain hunters converge at Filene's Basement, and businessmen visit both traditional outlets and the many fashionable men's outfitters. In this stylish, international city, many stores feature fine clothes from Italy, France, England, and Japan, along with the more prevalent fashions from top American designers.

MIXED FASHION

Many stores in Boston offer quality clothing for both men and women. **Louis Boston**, which has abandoned its historic Back Bay home for a store in the up-and-coming Seaport waterfront, has long been known as the city's most exclusive men's outfitters. It also features similarly beautiful clothing for women. **Barney's New York**, a branch of the world-famous Manhattan fashion icon, offers an extensive range of cutting-edge designer labels.

Nearby on Newbury Street, **Giorgio Armani**, **Riccardi**, and **Burberry** all cater to the well-heeled, who love to browse through their extravagantly stylish and outrageously expensive clothing and accessories. **Alan Bilzerian** attracts celebrities in search of both his own label and the latest avant-garde looks from Europe and Japan. Donna Karan's **DKNY** features a wider range of fashion, from casual sportswear to glamorous evening attire, as well as housewares and baby clothes. In Cambridge, **American Apparel** features casual sportswear for men and women. **Urban Outfitters** offers an eclectic collection of clothing and accoutrements for the young and trendy, and stocks Kikit, Girbaud, and Esprit. America's favorite chain, **Gap**, has simple styles which remain stylish enough for movie stars, yet affordable for the masses. **Banana Republic** is ideal for those after a sleeker more modern look.

The Swedish retailer **H&M**, which stocks trend-setting fashion for adults and children at affordable prices, has shops both downtown and in Back Bay. The Back Bay store is particularly known for its large selection of accessories. For clothing more suited to the great outdoors, visit **Eddie Bauer**, which sells a range of no-nonsense sporting gear, or **Patagonia**, a mecca for serious climbers, skiers, and sailors, which also carries sophisticated, high-tech sporting equipment.

Visitors don't mind going a little out of the way for huge discounts (up to 70 percent) on athletic and street shoes and apparel at the **New Balance Factory Outlet** store. The locally based athletic-shoe company stocks virtually every size – short and narrow to long and wide.

WOMEN'S FASHION

No woman need leave Boston empty-handed, whether her taste is for the *haute couture* of **Chanel** in Boston's Taj Hotel or the earthy ethnic clothing at **Nomad**. Newbury Street is filled with sumptuous, high-fashion boutiques, including **Kate Spade**, **Betsy Jenney**, and **Max Mara**, Italy's largest and most luxurious ready-to-wear manufacturer for women. Casual clothes with optimistic mottoes are the specialty of **Life is Good**, while **Oilily**, the Dutch boutique, blazes with colorful prints and youthful designs. On Boylston Street, **Ann Taylor** is undoubtedly the first choice for refined, modern career clothes, while **Talbots**, a Boston institution, features enduring classics. **Anthropologie** stocks an eclectic mix of exotic and whimsical clothing and accessories from around the world.

In Harvard Square, **Oona's** has been selling vintage clothing for 35 years, while **A Taste of Culture** offers beautiful knit and woollen garments from Peru. **Clothware** features natural-fiber clothes from local designers, and **Settebello** carries elegant European apparel and accessories.

MEN'S FASHION

Gentlemen seeking a quintessential New England look need go no farther than **Brooks Brothers** on Newbury Street, longtime purveyors of traditional, high-quality men's and boys' wear.

America's foremost fashion house, **Polo/Ralph Lauren** offers top-quality and highly priced sporting and formal attire, while **Jos. A. Bank Clothiers** sells private label merchandise as well as most major brands at discounted prices.

Academics and college students alike head to Cambridge, where the venerable **Andover Shop** and **J. Press** provide a selection of Ivy-League essentials of impeccable quality.

DISCOUNT AND VINTAGE CLOTHES

The legendary Boston bargain emporium **Filene's Basement** began by selling discounted clothing nearly a century ago and soon became known for the frenzied atmosphere of its counters and its complex automatic markdown scheme. Bargain hunters eagerly await the store's return (scheduled for 2012) once the 1912 Downtown Crossing building is restored. Meantime, the twice-annual "Running of the Brides" for deeply discounted wedding gowns continues at other locations. First among the other discount chains is **Marshall's**, promising "brand names for less" and offering bargains on clothing, shoes, housewares, and accessories.

Vintage aficionados will love the vast collections at **Bobby from Boston**, a longtime costume source for Hollywood and top fashion designers. In Cambridge, **Keezer's** has provided generations of Harvard students with everything from used tuxedos to sports jackets and loafers. **Second Time Around**, with consignment shops in both Cambridge and Boston, offers a select array of top-quality, gently worn contemporary clothing for women.

SHOES AND ACCESSORIES

Many stores in Boston specialize in accessories and footware. **Helen's Leather** on Charles Street is well known for leather jackets, briefcases, purses, shoes, and Birkenstock sandals, as well as its huge selection of Western boots. At Downtown Crossing, **Foot Paths** carries a range of shoes from Timberland, Kenneth Cole, Rockport, and others.

Stylish Spanish shoes and bags are the specialty at **Stuart Weitzman** at Copley Place, while the adventurous will find more fashionable and unusual shoes at **Berk's** and **The Tannery** in Cambridge. For sports gear, the large and opulent **Niketown** on Newbury Street shows video re-runs of sports events while shoppers peruse the latest designs in athletic clothing and footwear.

DIRECTORY

MIXED FASHION

Alan Bilzerian
34 Newbury St.
Map 4 D2.
Tel (617) 536-1001.

American Apparel
47 Brattle St., Cambridge.
Tel (617) 661-2770.

Banana Republic
28 Newbury St. **Map** 4 D2.
Tel (617) 267-3933.

Barney's New York
Copley Place. **Map** 3 C3.
Tel (617) 385-3300.

Burberry
2 Newbury St. **Map** 3 C2.
Tel (617) 236-1000.

DKNY
37 Newbury St. **Map** 3 C2.
Tel (617) 236-0476.

Eddie Bauer
500 Washington St. **Map**
2 D4. **Tel** (617) 423-4722.

Gap
201 Newbury St. **Map** 3
C2. **Tel** (617) 247-1754.

Giorgio Armani
22 Newbury St. **Map** 3 C2.
Tel (617) 267-3200.

H&M
350 Washington St.
Map 4 F1.
Tel (617) 482-7081.
100 Newbury St. **Map** 3
C2. **Tel** (617) 859-3192.

Louis Boston
60 Northern Ave.
Map 2 F5.
Tel (617) 262-6100.

**New Balance
Factory Outlet**
40 Life St., Brighton.
Tel (877) 623-7867.

Patagonia
346 Newbury St. **Map**
3 A3. **Tel** (617) 424-1776.

Riccardi
116 Newbury St. **Map** 3
C2. **Tel** (617) 266-3158.

Urban Outfitters
361 Newbury St. **Map** 3
A3. **Tel** (617) 236-0088.

WOMEN'S FASHION

Ann Taylor
800 Boylston St. **Map** 3 B3.
Tel (617) 421-9097.

Anthropologie
799 Boylston St. **Map** 3 B3.
Tel (617) 262-0545.

A Taste of Culture
1160 Massachusetts Ave.,
Cambridge.
Tel (617) 868-0389.

Betsy Jenney
114 Newbury St. **Map** 3
C2. **Tel** (617) 536-2610.

Chanel
5 Newbury St. **Map** 4 D2.
Tel (617) 859-0055.

Clothware
52 Brattle St., Cambridge
Tel (617) 661-6441.

Kate Spade
117 Newbury St. **Map**
3 C2. **Tel** (617) 262-2632.

Life is Good
285 Newbury St. **Map** 3
B2. **Tel** (617) 262-5068.

Max Mara
69 Newbury St. **Map** 3 C2.
Tel (617) 267-9775.

Nomad
1741 Massachusetts Ave.,
Cambridge.
Tel (617) 497-6677.

Oilily
32 Newbury St.
Map 4 D2.
Tel (617) 247-9299.

Oona's
1210 Massachusetts Ave.,
Cambridge.
Tel (617) 491-2654.

Settebello
52 Brattle St., Cambridge.
Tel (617) 864-2440.

Talbots
500 Boylston St.
Map 3 C2.
Tel (617) 262-2981.

MEN'S FASHION

Andover Shop
22 Holyoke St.,
Cambridge.
Tel (617) 876-4900.

Brooks Brothers
46 Newbury St.
Map 4 D2.
Tel (617) 267-2600.

**Jos. A. Bank
Clothiers**
399 Boylston St.
Map 4 D2.
Tel (617) 536-5050.

J. Press
82 Mount Auburn St.,
Cambridge.
Tel (617) 547-9886.

Polo/Ralph Lauren
93/95 Newbury St.
Map 3 C2.
Tel (617) 424-1124.

DISCOUNT AND VINTAGE CLOTHES

Bobby from Boston
19 Thayer St. **Map** 4 E4.
Tel (617) 423-9299.

Filene's Basement
426 Washington St.
Map 4 F1.
www.filenesbasement.
com/bridal.php

Keezer's
140 River St., Cambridge.
Tel (617) 547-2455.

Marshall's
500 Boylston St. **Map** 3 C2.
Tel (617) 262-6066.

**Second Time
Around**
176 Newbury St. **Map**
3 B2. **Tel** (617) 247-3504.

SHOES AND ACCESSORIES

Berk's
50 John F. Kennedy St.,
Cambridge.
Tel (617) 492-9511.

Foot Paths
489 Washington St.
Map 4 F1.
Tel (617) 338-6008.

Helen's Leather
110 Charles St. **Map** 1 B3.
Tel (617) 742-2077.

Niketown
200 Newbury St. **Map** 3
B2. **Tel** (617) 267-3400.

Stuart Weitzman
Copley Place. **Map** 3 C3.
Tel (617) 266-8699.

The Tannery
39 Brattle St., Cambridge.
Tel (617) 491-1811.

Antiques, Fine Crafts, and Gifts

Visitors hoping to take home a special memento will find an enormous number of antique, craft, and gift stores in Boston. From the huge antique markets and cooperatives, to specialty shops selling everything from rugs to rare books, there are abundant opportunities to indulge a passion for the past. Those favoring more contemporary *objets d'art* will find crafts guilds, galleries, and gift shops selling unique glassware, ceramics, textiles, jewelry, and much more produced by New England artisans, as well as items from every corner of the world.

ANTIQUES

Charles Street is Boston's antiques Mecca, with more antique stores than any other part of town. The neighborhood is extremely affluent with many exclusive and expensive stores, though the occasional bargain may be found in some of the larger stores. One of the larger places is **Antiques at 80 Charles**, which has three floors of merchandise ranging from silver tea sets to jewelry, paintings, clocks, and collectables. **Upstairs Downstairs** also sells "affordable antiques," and has four rooms full of furniture, lamps, prints, and a large selection of smaller items.

Collectors of fine Asian antiques should not miss **Alberts-Langdon, Inc.** and **Judith Dowling Asian Art**, for everything from screens and scrolls to lacquer-ware, ceramics, paintings, and furniture from all over Japan. A prime source for antique pine and painted furniture, **Danish Country** carries antique *armoires* and other furniture from Scandinavia, as well as Royal Copenhagen china and tall case clocks. The shop also carries Chinese lacquered antique furniture that blends well with the Scandinavian pieces.

Antique jewelry from around the world is a specialty at **Marika's Antiques Shop**, along with paintings, glass, porcelain, and silver. Collectors of Art Deco furniture and decorative pieces inevitably gravitate to **A Room with a Vieux Antiques**, where the owners do most of their buying in France. **Twentieth Century Ltd.** excels particularly in glittery costume jewelry from top designers. They also offer pieces in sterling silver.

In Cambridge, **Reside** specializes in mid-20th century modern furniture and accessories, with ethnic pillows and weavings. For an eclectic mix of antiques both fine and funky from the 19th century to the 1950s, head to **Easy Chairs**.

ANTIQUE MARKETS AND COOPERATIVES

If browsing through mountainous inventories with the broadest range of quality, price, and stock is your idea of heaven, then there are several multi-dealer antiques emporiums worth exploring. On Charles Street, **Boston Antiques Cooperative I and II** has everything from quilts, candlesticks, and wicker furniture to chandeliers and furniture. In the Leather District, situated near South Station, is **JMW Gallery**, which specializes in fine 19th- and early 20th-century American furniture, ceramics, and printed materials associated with the Arts and Crafts Movement. In Cambridge, **Cambridge Antique Market** encompasses more than 100 dealers, offering estate antiques, collectibles, furniture, jewelry, and a vast selection of many other items.

If you have scoured Charles Street, scrutinized the cooperatives and still not found what you are looking for, try **Skinner Inc.** in Boston, which holds auctions throughout the year featuring furniture and fine arts, as well as ethnic art and books.

SPECIALTY DEALERS

Collectors in pursuit of more specific pieces will find shops in Boston that specialize in everything from nautical antiques to rare books, maps, jewelry, and rugs. Fine antiques and jewelry featuring Victorian and Art Nouveau designs are beautifully displayed and described by the knowledgeable staff at **Small Pleasures**. Vintage watches from Rolex, Cartier, Vacheron, Constantia, and others are a specialty at **Paul A. Duggan Co.**; while **The Bromfield Pen Shop** has been purveyor of thousands of new, antique, and limited edition pens for over 50 years. For nautical antiques, including model ships and marine paintings, **Lannan Ship Model Gallery** boasts an extensive and high quality inventory. Antique rugs, carpets, and tapestries from around the world are the mainstay at **Decor International**, and at **Mario Ratzki Oriental Rugs**, which has a discriminating selection of antique Persian carpets and tribal rugs from the 1860s to the 1930s. Bibliophiles will also find an extraordinary range of stores in Boston. In business since 1825, **Brattle Book Shop** (*see p83*) is the oldest and best known, with a huge selection of used, out-of-print and rare books, magazines, and vintage photographs. Rare books in the fine arts are the focus of **Ars Libri Ltd.**, while **Eugene Galleries** features antiquarian maps, prints, and etchings, in addition to its comprehensive selection of books. Fans of graphic novels, comic books, Japanese and Korean manga, and all sorts of visual storytelling flock to **Million Year Picnic** to get their fix of current titles. A few toys and T-shirts round out the collection, but comics are the main draw. Also in Cambridge, **Schoenhof's Foreign Books** and **Grolier Poetry Book Shop** cater to those seeking specialty volumes. The **Bryn Mawr Bookstore** stocks used books and some rare volumes covering every conceivable subject.

FINE CRAFTS

Collectors with a more contemporary bent will find several distinguished galleries and shops featuring a wide variety of American crafts by both local and nationally recognized artists. **Mobilia** in Cambridge has a national reputation for its jewelry, ceramics, and other objects. The **Society of Arts and Crafts**, established in 1897, has a shop and gallery, with exhibits from the 350 artists it represents. Works are largely in wood, fiber, metal, glass, and mixed media. The **Cambridge Artists' Co-operative**, owned and run by over 250 artists, offers an eclectic collection of items, ranging from hand-painted silk jackets to ornaments and other larger items. **The Artful Hand Gallery** also has a range of fine items, again crafted primarily by American artists.

GIFTS

In addition to the plethora of souvenir shops that threaten to drown tourists in tasteless, predictable merchandise, Boston has numerous shops specializing in original and distinctive gifts that you will not find anywhere else. On Newbury Street browse the **International Poster Gallery**, for original, vintage posters from the 19th and 20th centuries. In Cambridge, **Joie de Vivre** has a fantastic collection of toys, clocks, jewelry, jack-in-the-boxes, and much more beside. Next door, **Paper Source** carries a selection of fine handmade papers, gift wrap, rubber stamps, and other materials for creative indulgence.

DIRECTORY

ANTIQUES

Alberts-Langdon, Inc.
135 Charles St. **Map** 1 B3.
Tel (617) 523-5954.

Antiques at 80 Charles
80 Charles St. **Map** 1 B4.
Tel (617) 742-8006.

Danish Country
138 Charles St. **Map** 1 B3.
Tel (617) 227-1804.

Easy Chairs
375 Huron Ave.,
Cambridge.
Tel (617) 491-2131.

Judith Dowling Asian Art
133 Charles St. **Map** 1 B3.
Tel (617) 523-5211.

Marika's Antiques Shop
130 Charles St. **Map** 1 B3.
Tel (617) 523-4520.

Reside
266 Concord Ave.,
Cambridge.
Tel (617) 547-2929.

A Room with a Vieux Antiques
20 Charles St. **Map** 1 B4.
Tel (617) 973-6600.

Twentieth Century Ltd.
73 Charles St. **Map** 1 B4.
Tel (617) 742-1031.

Upstairs Downstairs
93 Charles St. **Map** 1 B4.
Tel (617) 367-1950.

ANTIQUES MARKETS AND COOPERATIVES

Boston Antiques Cooperative I and II
119 Charles St. **Map** 1 B3.
Tel (617) 227-9810.

Cambridge Antique Market
201 Msgr. O'Brien Hwy,
Cambridge.
Tel (617) 868-9655.

JMW Gallery
144 Lincoln St.
Map 4 F2.
Tel (617) 338-9097.

Skinner Inc.
63 Park Plaza. **Map** 1 C4.
Tel (617) 350-5400.

SPECIALTY DEALERS

Ars Libri Ltd.
500 Harrison Ave.
Map 4 E4.
Tel (617) 357-5212.

Brattle Book Shop
9 West St. **Map** 1 C4.
Tel (617) 542-0210.

The Bromfield Pen Shop
5 Bromfield St. **Map** 1 C4.
Tel (617) 482-9053.

Bryn Mawr Bookstore
373 Huron Ave.,
Cambridge.
Tel (617) 661-1770.

Decor International
61 North Beacon St.,
Allston.
Tel (617) 262-1529.

Eugene Galleries
76 Charles St. **Map** 1 B4.
Tel (617) 227-3062.

Grolier Poetry Book Shop
6 Plympton St.,
Cambridge.
Tel (617) 547-4648.

Lannan Ship Model Gallery
99 High St. **Map** 2 E5.
Tel (617) 451-2650.

Mario Ratzki Oriental Rugs
139 Charles St. **Map** 1
B4. **Tel** (617) 227-3592.

Million Year Picnic
99 Mt. Auburn St.,
Cambridge.
Tel (617) 492-6763.

Paul A. Duggan Co.
333 Washington St.,
Suite 435. **Map** 1 C4.
Tel (617) 742-0221.

Schoenhof's Foreign Books
76A Mt. Auburn St.,
Cambridge.
Tel (617) 547-8855.

Small Pleasures
142 Newbury St.
Map 3 C2.
Tel (617) 267-7371.

FINE CRAFTS

The Artful Hand Gallery
Copley Place. **Map** 3 C3.
Tel (617) 262-9601.

Cambridge Artists' Cooperative
59a Church St.,
Cambridge.
Tel (617) 868-4434.

Mobilia
358 Huron Ave.,
Cambridge
Tel (617) 876-2109.

Society of Arts and Crafts
175 Newbury St. **Map**
3 B2. **Tel** (617) 266-1810.

GIFTS

International Poster Gallery
205 Newbury St. **Map**
3 B2. **Tel** (617) 375-0076.

Joie de Vivre
1792 Massachusetts Ave.,
Cambridge.
Tel (617) 864-8188.

Paper Source
1810 Massachusetts Ave.,
Cambridge.
Tel (617) 497-1077.

ENTERTAINMENT IN BOSTON

From avant-garde performance art to serious drama, and from popular dance music to live classical performances, Boston offers an outstanding array of entertainment options, with something to appeal to every taste: the Theater District offers many excellent plays and musicals, the Wang Theater hosts many touring productions, and Symphony

Quincy Market entertainer

Hall is home of the renowned Boston Symphony Orchestra. Boston is also well acquainted with jazz, folk music, and blues as well as being a center for more contemporary music, played in big city nightclubs. In summer, entertainment often heads outdoors, with many open-air plays and concerts, such as the famous Boston Pops at the Hatch Shell.

PRACTICAL INFORMATION

The best sources for information on current films, concerts, theater, dance, and exhibitions include the Thursday and Friday *G* section of *The Boston Globe* and the Friday entertainment weekly *The Boston Phoenix*. Even more up-to-date listings can be found online at the following sites: www.boston.city search.com; *The Boston Globe* (www.boston.com); *The Boston Phoenix* (www.thephoenix.com).

Boston entertainment listings magazines

BOOKING TICKETS

Tickets to popular musicals, theatrical productions, and touring shows often sell out far in advance, although theaters sometimes have a few returns

or restricted-view tickets available. You can either get tickets in person at theater box offices, or use one of the ticket agencies in Boston. For advance tickets these are **Ticketmaster** and **Live Nation Tickets**. Tickets can be purchased from both of these agencies over the telephone, in person, or online. Half-price tickets to most noncommercial arts events as well as to some commercial productions are available from 11am on the day of the performance at **BosTix** booths. Purchases must be made in person and only cash is accepted. BosTix also sells advance full-price tickets. Special Boston entertainment discount vouchers, available from hotel lobbies and tourist offices, may also give a saving on some shows.

Tchaikovsky's *Nutcracker*, danced by the Boston Ballet *(see p160)*

DISTRICTS AND VENUES

Musicals, plays, comedies, and dance are generally performed at venues in the Theater District, although larger noncommercial theater companies are distributed throughout the region, many being associated with colleges and universities.

The area around the intersection of Massachusetts and Huntington Avenues hosts a concentration of outstanding concert venues, including Symphony Hall, Berklee Performance Center at Berklee College of Music, and Jordan Hall at the New England Conservatory of Music.

Many nightclub and dance venues are on Lansdowne and other streets by Fenway Park and around Boylston Place in the Theater District. The busiest areas for bars and small clubs offering live jazz and rock music are Central and Harvard Squares in Cambridge, Davis Square in Somerville, and Allston. The principal gay scene in Boston is found in the South End, with many of the older bars and clubs in neighboring Bay Village.

Boston's Symphony Orchestra performing at Symphony Hall *(see p160)*

OPEN-AIR AND FREE ENTERTAINMENT

Boston's best free outdoor summer entertainment is found at the Hatch Shell *(see p92)* on the Charles River Esplanade. The Boston Pops *(see p160)* performs here frequently during the week around July 4, and all through July and August jazz, pop, rock, and classical music is played. On Friday evenings from late June to the week before Labor Day, the Hatch Shell also shows free big-screen family films.

Music is also performed in the summer months at the **Bank of America Pavilion** on the waterfront, which holds live jazz, pop, and country music concerts. City Hall Plaza and Copley Plaza have free concerts at lunchtimes and in the evenings, and the **Museum of Fine Arts, Boston** *(see pp104–7)* operates a summer

Free open-air music concert outside New City Hall

musical concert series in its courtyard. Most of the annual concerts and recitals of the **New England Conservatory of Music** are free, although some require advance reservations.

Other open-air entertainment includes a series of free plays staged on Boston Common by the **Commonwealth Shakespeare Company** in July and August, and ticketed performances of various plays by the **Publick Theater** at Christian Herter Park on the Charles River.

An area that has more unusual open-air entertainment is Harvard Square, famous for its nightly and weekend scene of street performers. Many recording

Entrance to the Shubert Theatre *(see p160)*

artists paid their dues here, and other hopefuls still flock to the square in the hope of being discovered – or at least of earning the cost of dinner.

Details of all free entertainment happening in the city are listed in the Thursday and Friday *G* section of *The Boston Globe*.

DISABLED ACCESS

Many entertainment venues in Boston are wheelchair accessible. **Very Special Arts Massachusetts** offers a full Boston arts access guide. Some places, such as **Jordan Hall**, the **Cutler Majestic Theater**, and the **Wheelock Family Theater**, have listening aids for the hearing impaired, while the latter also has signed and described performances.

DIRECTORY

BOOKING TICKETS

BosTix
Faneuil Hall Marketplace.
Map 2 D3.
Copley Square.
Map 3 C2.
Tel (617) 482-2849.
www.bostix.com

Live Nation Tickets
Downtown Crossing.
Map 1 C4.
Various outlets.
Tel (800) 431-3462.
www.livenation.com

Ticketmaster
Various outlets.
Tel (800) 745-3000.
www.ticketmaster.com

OPEN-AIR/FREE ENTERTAINMENT

Bank of America Pavilion
290 Northern Ave.,
South Boston. **Map** 2 F5.
Tel (617) 728-1600.
www.bankofamerica
pavilion.com

Commonwealth Shakespeare Company
Parkman Bandstand,
Boston Common. **Map** 1
C4. **Tel** (617) 426-0863.
http://commshakes.org

Museum of Fine Arts, Boston
465 Huntington Ave.
Tel (617) 369-3306.
www.mfa.org

New England Conservatory of Music

290 Huntington Ave.
Tel (617) 585-1260.
www.newengland
conservatory.edu

Publick Theater
Christian A. Herter Park,
1175 Soldiers Field Rd.,
Brighton. **Tel** (617)
933-8600. www.publick
theater.com

DISABLED ACCESS

Cutler Majestic Theater
219 Tremont St.
Map 4 E2.
Tel (617) 824-8000.
www.maj.org

Jordan Hall

30 Gainsborough St.
Tel (617) 585-1260.

Very Special Arts Massachusetts
89 South St.
Map 4 F2.
Tel (617) 350-7713.
TTY (617) 350-6385.
www.vsamass.org

Wheelock Family Theater
200 Riverway,
Brookline.
Tel (617) 879-2300.
TTY (617) 879-2150.
www.wheelock.edu/wft

The Arts in Boston

Performing arts are vital to Boston's cultural life. Since the 1880s, the social season has revolved around openings of the Boston Symphony Orchestra and many Brahmins *(see p45)* occupy their grandparents' seats at performances. In the past, theaters in Boston were heavily censored *(see p87)*, but today's Bostonians are avid theatergoers, patronizing commercial venues for plays bound to, or coming from, Broadway and attending ambitious contemporary drama at repertory theaters. Many noncommercial theater and dance companies perform in smaller venues in local neighborhoods and at the colleges. Although some theaters are closed on Mondays, there is rarely a night in Boston without performing arts.

CLASSICAL MUSIC AND OPERA

Two cherished Boston institutions, the **Boston Symphony Orchestra** and its popular-music equivalent, the Boston Pops, have a long history of being led by some of America's finest conductors. The BSO performs a full schedule of concerts at Symphony Hall from October through April. The Boston Pops takes over for May and June, performing at the Charles River Esplanade *(see p92)* for Fourth of July festivities that are the highlight of the summer season.

The students and faculty of the **New England Conservatory of Music** present more than 450 free classical and jazz performances each year, many in Jordan Hall *(see p159)*. **Boston Lyric Opera** has assumed the task of reestablishing opera in Boston, through small-cast and light opera at venues around the city.

Boston's oldest musical organization is the **Handel & Haydn Society**, founded in 1815. As the first American producer of such landmark works as Handel's *Messiah* (performed annually since 1818), Bach's *B-Minor Mass* and *St. Matthew Passion*, and Verdi's *Requiem*, H & H is one of the country's musical treasures. Since 1986, the society has focused on performing and recording Baroque and Classical works using the period instruments for which the composers

wrote. H & H gives regular performances in Boston at Symphony Hall, Jordan Hall, and other venues.

Classical music is ubiquitous in Boston. **Emmanuel Music**, for example, performs the entire Bach cantata cycle at regular services at Emmanuel Church on Newbury Street. The Isabella Stewart Gardner Museum *(see p103)* hosts a series of chamber music concerts, continuing a 19th-century tradition of professional "music room" chamber concerts in the homes of the social elite.

The **Celebrity Series** brings world-famous orchestras, soloists, and dance companies to Boston, often to perform at Jordan Hall, as well as several other venues. Some 40 to 50 events are organized.

THEATER

Though much diminished from its heyday in the 1920s, when more than 40 theaters were in operation throughout Boston, the city's Theater District *(see pp80–89)* today still contains a collection of some of the most architecturally eminent, and still commercially productive, early theaters in the United States. Furthermore, during the 1990s, many of the theaters that are currently in use underwent programs of restoration to their original grandeur, and visitors today are bound to be impressed as they catch a glimpse of these theaters' past glory.

The main commercially run theaters of Boston – the **Colonial**, **Wilbur**, and **Shubert** theaters, the **Opera House** and the **Wang Theatre** *(see pp84–7)* – often program Broadway productions that have aleady premiered in New York and are touring the United States. They also present Broadway "try outs" and local productions.

In stark contrast to some of the mainstream shows on offer in Boston, the most avant-garde contemporary theater in the city is performed at the **American Repertory Theater (ART)**, an independent, non-commercial company associated with Harvard University *(see pp112–13)*. ART often premieres new plays, particularly on its second stage, but is best known for its often radical interpretations of traditional and modern classics. By further contrast, the **Huntington Theatre**, allied with Boston University, is widely praised for its traditional direction and interpretation. For example, the Huntington was the co-developer of Pulitzer-Prize winning plays detailing 20th-century African American life, by the late August Wilson, an important chronicler of American race relations.

Several of the smaller companies, including **Lyric Stage**, devote their energies to showcasing local actors and directors and often premiere the work of Boston-area playwrights. Many of the most adventurous companies perform on one of the four stages at the **Boston Center for the Arts**.

DANCE

The city's largest and most popular resident dance company, the **Boston Ballet** performs an ambitious season of classics and new choreography between October and May at the restored Opera House *(see p83)*. The annual performances of the *Nutcracker* during the Christmas season are a Boston tradition. The somewhat more modest

José Mateo's Ballet Theater has earned a reputation for developing a strong and impressive program of repertory choreography. The company performs in the attractive neo-Gothic Old Cambridge Baptist Church, which is situated near Harvard Square. Modern dance in Boston is represented by many small companies, collectives, and independent choreographers, who often perform in the **Dance Complex** and **Green Street Studios** in Cambridge. Boston also hosts many other visiting dance companies, who often put on performances at the **Cutler Majestic Theater**.

CINEMA

Situated in Harvard Square, close to Harvard Yard (see pp110–11), the **Brattle Theater**, one of the very last repertory movie houses in the Greater Boston area, primarily shows classic films on a big screen. For example, the Brattle was instrumental in reviving moviegoers' interest in the Humphrey Bogart, black-and-white classic *Casablanca*. Something of a Harvard institution, the Brattle has long served as a popular "first date" destination for couples with a shared passion for the movies.

Serious students of classic and international cinema patronize the screening programs of the **Harvard Film Archive**. The **Kendall Square Cinema** multiplex is the city's chief venue for non-English language films, art films and documentaries. Multiplex theaters showing mainstream, first-run Hollywood movies are found throughout the Boston area. Some of the most popular are **Loews Theaters**, located at Boston Common, and the **Regal Fenway 13** in the suburb of Brookline. Tickets for every kind of movie in Boston are often discounted for first shows of the day on weekends and all weekday shows before 5pm.

DIRECTORY

CLASSICAL MUSIC AND OPERA

Boston Lyric Opera
Various venues.
Tel (617) 542-6772.
www.blo.org

Boston Symphony Orchestra
Symphony Hall,
301 Massachusetts Ave.
Map 3 A4.
Tel (617) 266-1200, (617) 266-1492. www.bso.org

Celebrity Series
Various venues.
Tel (617) 482-6661.
www.celebrityseries.org

Emmanuel Music
Emmanuel Church, 15 Newbury St. **Map** 4 D2.
Tel (617) 536-3356.
www.emmanuelmusic.org

Handel & Haydn Society
Various venues. *Tel (617) 266-3605.* www.handelandhaydn.org

New England Conservatory of Music
Jordan Hall,
30 Gainsborough St.
Map 3 A4.
Tel (617) 585-1260.
www.newengland conservatory.edu

THEATER

American Repertory Theater
Loeb Drama Center,
64 Brattle St., Cambridge.
Tel (617) 547-8300.
www.amrep.org

Boston Center for the Arts
539 Tremont St.
Map 4 D3.
Tel (617) 933-8600.
www.bostontheater scene.com

Colonial Theatre
106 Boylston St. **Map** 4 E2.
Tel (617) 426-9366.
www.broadway acrossamerica.com

Huntington Theatre
264 Huntington Ave.
Map 3 B4.
Tel (617) 266-0800.
www.huntington theatre.org

Lyric Stage
140 Clarendon St.
Map 3 C3.
Tel (617) 585-5678.
www.lyricstage.com

Opera House
539 Washington St.
Map 4 E1.
Tel (617) 931-2787.
www.broadway acrossamerica.com

Shubert Theatre
265 Tremont St.
Map 4 E2.
Tel (617) 482-9393.
www.citicenter.org

Wang Theatre
270 Tremont St. **Map** 4 E2. *Tel (617) 482-9393.* www.citicenter.org

Wilbur Theatre
246 Tremont St.
Map 4 E2. *Tel (617) 931-2000.* www.thewilbur theatre.com

DANCE

Boston Ballet
Various venues.
Tel (617) 695-6955.
www.bostonballet.org

Cutler Majestic Theater
219 Tremont St.
Map 4 E2. *Tel (617) 824-8000.* www.maj.org

Dance Complex
536 Massachusetts Ave., Cambridge.
Tel (617) 547-9363.
www.dancecomplex.org

Green Street Studios
185 Green St, Cambridge.
Tel (617) 864-3191.
www.greenstreet studios.org

José Mateo's Ballet Theater
400 Harvard St,
Cambridge.
Tel (617) 354-7467.
www.ballettheatre.org

CINEMA

Brattle Theater
40 Brattle St., Cambridge.
Tel (617) 876-6837.

Harvard Film Archive
24 Quincy St.,
Cambridge.
Tel (617) 495-4700.
hcl.harvard.edu/hfa/

Kendall Square Cinema
1 Kendall Square,
Cambridge.
Tel (617) 499-1996.

Loews Theaters
Boston Common.
Map 4 E2.
Tel (617) 423-5801.

Regal Fenway 13
201 Brookline Ave.
Tel (617) 424-6266.

Music and Nightlife

Boston's mix of young professionals and tens of thousands of college students produces a lively nightlife scene, focused on live music, clubs, and bars. Ever since the 1920s, Boston has been especially hospitable to jazz, and it still has an interesting jazz scene, with Berklee College of Music playing an important part. Cambridge is an epicenter of folk and acoustic music revivals and alt-rock, while Lansdowne Street near Fenway Park *(see p166)* is the main district for nightclubs. Virtually every neighborhood has a selection of friendly bars, often with live music.

ROCK MUSIC

The **House of Blues** chain of rock clubs was born in Greater Boston, and its return to the city has spawned its largest and most successful club yet, on Lansdowne Street, near Fenway Park. There are standing-room concerts on most nights. With four performance spaces, the **Middle East** in Cambridge's Central Square leads the alternative rock scene, featuring both local bands and touring newcomers. Larger rock concert venues are the **Orpheum Theater** and the arena seating of **TD Garden**, used at other times for hockey and basketball games.

JAZZ AND BLUES

The city's premier, large concert venue for jazz is **Berklee Performance Center** in Back Bay, which draws on faculty and students from Berklee College of Music as well as touring performers. More intimate settings include **Scullers Jazz Club** overlooking the Charles River in Brighton, the small-hall for aficionados at the **Real Deal Jazz Club** in East Cambridge, and the suave elegance of the **Regatta Bar** just off Harvard Square. No-frills, neighborhood jazz thrives at **Ryles Jazz Club** in Cambridge's Inman Square. The musical parent of jazz, the blues, is also alive and well. **Wally's** in the South End has an ambience that is pure 1940s juke joint, but there's no denying the veracity of the jazz wailing

from its narrow confines. The **Cantab Lounge** in Cambridge's Central Square is a music lover's delight, and features open mic sessions on Mondays and bluegrass on Tuesdays, while the weekends feature live blues, R&B, funk, and soul. The Cantab also runs popular Wednesday night poetry "slams."

FOLK AND WORLD MUSIC

Harvard Square's **Club Passim** is a folk music legend, the hangout in the late 1950s and early 1960s for the likes of Joan Baez and Van Morrison, and still one of the United States' key clubs in the touring life of singer-songwriters. **The Independent** in Somerville's Union Square is a good place to catch unplugged rock, Irish bands, and aspiring troubadours who write their own material Davis Square is a couple of Red Line stops farther out from Harvard station, but well worth the trip for **Johnny D's Uptown Restaurant & Music Club**, where the program offers an eclectic mix ranging from solo singer-songwriters, to zydeco bands, and acoustic and amplified rockabilly. To enjoy some local Caribbean tunes and dancing, one of the the best options is a weekend night at **The Western Front**, which kicks it up near the river in Cambridgeport.

International acts ranging from Afro-pop to ska play at many large venues across Boston in a concert series presented by the music promoters **World Music**.

NIGHTCLUBS AND DISCOS

Boston has a club for just about every type of dance music. Like club scenes everywhere, little happens until late at night; in Boston nothing gets going until at least 11pm. Expect everything from country music and salsa lessons to a weekly Goth night at **An Tua Nua**, near Boston University. **The Grand Canal** near North Station features techno and house music for a youthful clientele. Located in the rear of a stylish restaurant, **The Gypsy Bar** has a Latin night as well as house and techno music. Sleek **Venu** is the top spot where the young and chic go for post-midnight dancing. **Precinct** attracts a gothic crowd for Crypt on Wednesdays, lesbian clubbers for Tuesday's popular Dyke Night, and a multi-gender motley for Heroes on Saturdays. More middle-of-the-road is the **Royale** in the Theater District, with classy touches such as doormen instead of bouncers, marble walls, and a vast dance floor.

BARS

The legal drinking age in Boston is 21, and you may be asked to show proof of identification *(see p174)*.

Boston has many bars *(see also p151)*, but many, such as those listed below, are specifically themed, offer live entertainment, or place a strong emphasis on being "party" venues. The bar at **Mistral** is typical of the increasingly upscale places springing up in Boston, where the young and the beautiful like to meet and play. More down to earth are some of Boston's Irish bars offering live music and the obligatory pints of Guinness. Among these are **The Phoenix Landing Bar and Restaurant**, a mock Irish pub in Central Square lined with mahogany and featuring English football on cable television as well as Celtic and dance rock performances on weekend nights, **The Burren** that features some of the finest musicians in the city, and the smaller **Druid**, where as the evening wears on, crowds of young professionals give way to recent Irish immigrants.

Bostonians love sports, and the city has dozens of sports bars. The **Cask 'N' Flagon** is adjacent to Fenway Park, perfect for celebrating victory or softening the pain of defeat. At **Kings** big-screen sports TVs vie with bowling lanes, while the **Sports Depot** is just mammoth. The area near North Station is filled with bars catering to Boston Celtics and Boston Bruins fans.

GAY CLUBS AND BARS

Boston's gay scene comes into sharpest focus in the South End and Bay Village, but gay and gay-friendly bars and clubs are found throughout the city. The perpetually packed **Fritz Lounge**, which is attached to the Chandler Inn, is a stalwart South End bar. Boston's longest-running gay club, **Jacques**, features rock acts Friday through Monday and female impersonator cabaret during the rest of the week. The weekly *Bay Windows* newspaper provides wider information as do other Boston listings.

COMEDY CLUBS

Many clubs and bars program occasional evenings of standup comedy, and several specialize in this form of entertainment. The **Comedy Connection** at the Wilbur Theatre, brings laughter to the historic hall with an impressive line-up of comedians, who are familiar from their work on national television. **Nick's Comedy Stop** in the Theater District, on the other hand, tends to concentrate more on homegrown talent, grooming performers who often go on to the "big time."

DIRECTORY

ROCK MUSIC

House of Blues
15 Lansdowne St.
Tel (888) 693-2583.

Middle East
472/480 Massachusetts Ave., Cambridge.
Tel (617) 864-3278 ext. 221.
www.mideastclub.com

Orpheum Theater
1 Hamilton Pl. **Map** 1 C4.
Tel (617) 679-0810.

TD Garden
1 Causeway St. **Map** 1 C2.
Tel (617) 624-1000. www.
tdbanknorthgarden.com

JAZZ AND BLUES

Berklee Performance Center
Berklee College of Music, 136 Massachusetts Ave.
Tel (617) 266-7455.
www.berklee.edu

Cantab Lounge
738 Massachusetts Ave., Cambridge.
Tel (617) 354-2685.

Real Deal Jazz Club
41 Second St., Cambridge.
Tel (617) 876-7777.
www.concertix.com

Regatta Bar
Charles Hotel,
1 Bennett St., Cambridge.
Tel (617) 395-7757.
www.regattabarjazz.com

Ryles Jazz Club
212 Hampshire St., Cambridge. *Tel (617) 876-9330.* www.rylesjazz.com

Scullers Jazz Club
Doubletree Guest Suites, 400 Soldiers Field Rd., Brighton.
Tel (617) 562-4111.
www.scullersjazz.com

Wally's Cafe
427 Massachusetts Ave.
Tel (617) 424-1408.

FOLK AND WORLD MUSIC

Club Passim
47 Palmer St., Cambridge.
Tel (617) 492-7679.
www.clubpassim.org

The Independent
75 Union Square, Somerville. *Tel (617) 440-6022.* www.theindo.com

Johnny D's Uptown Restaurant & Music Club
17 Holland St., Somerville.
Tel (617) 776-2004.
www.johnnyds.com

Western Front
343 Western Ave, Cambridge.
Tel (617) 492-7772.

World Music
Box Office:
Tel (617) 876-4275.
www.worldmusic.org

NIGHTCLUBS AND DISCOS

An Tua Nua
835 Beacon St.
Tel (617) 262-2121.

Grand Canal
57 Canal St.
Map 2 D2.
Tel (617) 523-1112.

The Gypsy Bar
116 Boylston St.
Tel (617) 482-7799.

Precinct
70 Union Sq., Somerville.
Tel (617) 623-9211.
www.precinctbar.com

Royale
279 Tremont St.
Map 4 E2.
Tel (617) 338-7699.

Venu
100 Warrenton St.
Map 4 D3.
Tel (617) 338-8061.

BARS

The Burren
247 Elm St., Somerville.
Tel (617) 776-6896.

The Cask 'N' Flagon
62 Brookline Ave.
Tel (617) 536-4840.

Druid
1357 Cambridge St., Cambridge.
Tel (617) 497-0965.

Kings
50 Dalton St. **Map** 3 A3.
Tel (617) 266-2695.

Mistral
223 Columbus Ave.
Map 4 D3.
Tel (617) 867-9300.

The Phoenix Landing Bar and Restaurant
512 Massachusetts Ave., Cambridge.
Tel (617) 576-6260.

Sports Depot
353 Cambridge St., Allston.
Tel (617) 783-2300.

GAY BARS AND CLUBS

Fritz Lounge
26 Chandler St. **Map** 4 D3. *Tel (617) 482-4428.*

Jacques
79 Broadway. **Map** 4 F4.
Tel (617) 426-8902.

COMEDY CLUBS

Comedy Connection
Wilbur Theatre, 246 Tremont St. **Map** 4 E2.
Tel (617) 931-2000.
www.thewilburtheatre. com

Nick's Comedy Stop
100 Warrenton St.
Tel (617) 423-2900.
www.nickscomedy stop.com

SPORTS AND OUTDOOR ACTIVITIES

Bostonians have a wealth of recreational opportunities, thanks largely to the city's many spacious parks, its long, well-maintained riverfront, sizeable harbor, and excellent sports facilities. Visitors can enjoy many outdoor activities, whether it is going for an early morning jog on Boston Common, sailing on the Charles River, taking to one of the extensive cycle paths, or playing a round at a public golf course. In the winter there is also outdoor ice-skating, and farther afield, skiing. For those who watch sports rather than participate, major-league baseball, football, soccer, basketball, and ice-hockey are played at different times through the year.

Rollerblading

WATER SPORTS

During all but the winter months, dozens of small pleasure craft can be seen navigating the Charles River between Cambridge and Boston. At long-established **Community Boating**, only experienced sailors are able to rent sailboats, while farther upriver at the **Charles River Canoe & Kayak Center**, canoes, rowboats, and adult and children's kayaks can be rented.

For those who enjoy swimming or sunbathing, there are several good beaches near Boston, and one supervised beach on the **Boston Harbor Islands**, reached by ferry from Long Wharf. Carson Beach and the beach at Castle Island in South Boston are two of the closest, while Revere Beach to the north is larger and busier and served by the subway. From June to September swimmers can use the **Department of Conservation and Recreation** outdoor swimming pools.

BICYCLING, JOGGING, AND SKATING

The gentle Boston topography makes sightseeing by bicycle ideal. A number of good trails and bicycle paths crisscross the city, the most popular of which is the Dr. Paul Dudley White Bike Path. This links central Boston with outlying Watertown via a circular 17-mile (27-km) trail that runs along both sides of the Charles River. The Southwest Corridor cycle route links the Back Bay with Roxbury along a section of the Emerald Necklace (see p103), and the Boston harborfront pathways also attract many cyclists. Farther afield, an old railroad line has been transformed into the Minuteman Bikeway, which runs between Cambridge and Bedford via historic Lexington. **Urban AdvenTours** offers cycle tours along with rental bikes, while other rental stores include **Back Bay Bicycles** and **Community Bicycle Supply**.

In-line skating and jogging are also popular activities in Boston, with riverside esplanades and Boston Common being the favorite areas. If you are looking to buy some gear, try **City Sports**.

Cyclist on the Dr. Paul Dudley White Bike Path

GOLF AND TENNIS

Along with its many excellent private golf clubs, the Boston area also boasts a number of public golf courses, including some municipal links. The **William J. Devine Golf Course** in Franklin Park is the city's public golf course and there is also the nine-hole **Fresh Pond Golf Course** in Cambridge.

The **Department of Conservation and Recreation** maintains a dozen public tennis courts in Boston. Those in North End Park on Commercial Street and Charlesbank Park on the Charles River Esplanade are the most central. Court time cannot usually be reserved, so availability is on a first-come-first-served basis.

Sailboats on the Charles River with Back Bay in the distance

WINTER SPORTS

Freezing winter weather sees large groups of heavily clothed ice skaters heading for the Frog Pond on Boston Common. A modest fee is charged for skating, and skate rental is available in the pavilion by Frog Pond, or else a few blocks away at the **Beacon Hill Skate Shop**. Each winter, the Department of Conservation and Recreation also opens its many indoor rinks in Boston and Cambridge to the public, including Steriti Rink in the North End, which also has an indoor bocce court.

Most of the best skiing in New England is found a long way from Boston, in Vermont, Maine, and New Hampshire. Closer options include **Blue Hills Ski Area** in Canton for downhill skiing, and **Middlesex Fells Reservation** in Stoneham for cross-country. These areas depend a lot on the weather, however, and have only a few slopes.

Tentative ice-skaters take to the frozen Boston Common pond

FITNESS FACILITIES

Amenities at most of Boston's large hotels include fitness facilities. Those hotels that don't have facilities on-site usually have an arrangement whereby guests can use a private club in the immediate area. Otherwise, choose from the many other public gyms and health clubs found throughout the city. **Fitcorp** has excellent, modern exercise facilities at numerous city locations, while **Boston Athletic Club** in Downtown has both a well-equipped gym, and also a swimming pool, tennis, and squash courts. Across the river, **Cambridge Athletic Club** offers various racquet sports and a good gym.

DIRECTORY

WATER SPORTS

Boston Harbor Islands National Park Area
Tel *(617) 223-8666.*
www.bostonislands.com

Charles River Canoe & Kayak Center
Soldiers Field Rd., Allston.
Tel *(617) 965-5110.*
www.ski-paddle.com

Community Boating
21 David G. Mugar Way.
Map 1 A3. Tel *(617) 523-1038.* www.
community-boating.org

BICYCLING AND SKATING

Back Bay Bicycles
362 Commonwealth Ave.
Map 3 A2.
Tel *(617) 247-2336.*
www.backbay
bicycles.com

City Sports
44 Brattle St., Cambridge.
Tel *(617) 492-6000.*
www.citysports.com

Community Bicycle Supply
496 Tremont St.
Map 4 D3.
Tel *(617) 542-8623.*
www.community
bicycle.com

Urban AdvenTours
Boston Common.
Map 1 C4.
Tel *(617) 670-0637.*
www.urban
adventours.com

GOLF COURSES

Fresh Pond Golf Course
691 Huron Ave.,
Cambridge.
Tel *(617) 349-6282.*

William J. Devine Golf Course at Franklin Park
1 Circuit Drive,
Dorchester.
Tel *(617) 265-4084.*

WINTER SPORTS

Beacon Hill Skate Shop
135 South Charles St.
Map 4 E2.
Tel *(617) 482-7400.*

Blue Hills Ski Area
Canton, MA 02021.
Tel *(781) 828-5070.*
www.ski-bluehills.com

Middlesex Fells Reservation
MDC, 4 Woodland Rd.,
Stoneham, MA 02180.
Tel *(781) 662-2340.*
www.mass.gov/dcr/parks

FITNESS FACILITIES

Boston Athletic Club
653 Summer St.
Tel *(617) 269-4300.*
www.bostonathletic
club.com

Cambridge Athletic Club
215 First St., Cambridge.
Tel *(617) 491-8989.*
www.cambridge
fitness.com

Fitcorp
1 Beacon St.
Map 1 C4.
Tel *(617) 248-9797.*

Prudential Center.
Map 3 B3.
Tel *(617) 262-2050.*

125 Summer St.
Map 2 D4.
Tel *(617) 261-4855.*

197 Clarendon St.
Map 3 C2.
Tel *(617) 933-5090.*
www.fitcorp.com

USEFUL ADDRESSES

Boston Parks and Recreation Department
1010 Massachusetts Ave.
Tel *(617) 635-4505.*
www.cityofboston.gov/
parks

Department of Conservation and Recreation
251 Causeway St.
Tel *(617) 626-1250.*
www.mass.gov/dcr/parks

Spectator Sports

Bostonians watch sporting events with a passion that is unmatched in most other U.S. cities. Boston has had a team in every major professional league for many years, and some of popular sports' greatest athletes have played for home sides. Moreover, such widely known annual competitions as the Boston Marathon and the Head of the Charles Regatta draw amazingly large and enthusiastic crowds, as do the metropolitan area's many college teams, which have long traditions and avid fans.

A Boston Bruin waiting for the pass at TD Garden

BASEBALL

No matter whether they win or lose, the **Boston Red Sox** have an emotional following, especially when the New York Yankees come to town. The Red Sox beloved Fenway Park stadium is the oldest in the country, and is famous for its enormous 37-ft (11-m) left-field wall known as the "Green Monster." The small seating capacity, however, means that tickets can be difficult to obtain for the bigger games. Tickets are sold at the gate on the day of the game and are also available from the Fenway Park hotline. The "Bosox" are in the Eastern Division of the American League, one of the country's two major professional leagues. The baseball season runs from early April to the end of September, with championship games in October. In 2004, Boston ended a long drought to win the World Series in dramatic, come-from-behind fashion, and they won again in 2007.

Red Sox baseball player

BASKETBALL

Despite a fluctuating record, the **Boston Celtics** have been the most successful of all of Boston's major-league sports teams. They were the dominant team during the 1960s and 80s, winning 16 National Basketball Association (NBA) championships. Banners hung above their home court, the modern 19,000-seat TD Garden arena, pay testament to this record. Even when not playing to their full potential, the Celtics normally draw big crowds, hoping to see the team rekindle past glories. Tickets are usually available for most games, although they can be pricey – good seats cost at least $50. The season runs from October to April.

AMERICAN FOOTBALL

The home football team, the **New England Patriots**, once dominated the sport, winning the Superbowl Championships in 2002, 2004, and 2005. They play against their National Football League (NFL) opponents in the Gillette Stadium, about an hour's drive south of downtown Boston. Most NFL games are played during the fall on Sundays, or sometimes on Monday evenings to attract a national television audience. Tickets sell out a long way in advance, so the chances of picking one up are remote.

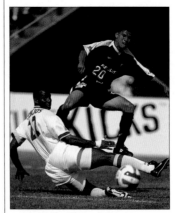

New England Revolution playing soccer against Miami Fusion

ICE HOCKEY

Five Stanley Cup wins make the **Boston Bruins** one of the most successful teams in National Hockey League (NHL) history, although their form has been changeable. The hockey season runs from September to April, with the hard-charging "B's" playing in the NHL's Eastern Conference. End-of-season Stanley Cup Championship games are often sold out well in advance, but for other games, tickets are usually available for between $10 and $175. Games are played at TD Garden.

OTHER SPORTS

Boston's major-league professional soccer team, the **New England Revolution**, plays all of its home games at Gillette Stadium after the New England Patriots have finished their season. The soccer season runs from April through to July, and the game is slowly gaining more widespread support, due partly to its increasing popularity as a college sport.

Suffolk Downs is the Boston area's only thoroughbred racetrack, where bets are taken on both live and simulcast races. The year's biggest attraction is the Massachusetts Handicap, or "Mass 'Cap," race in July.

Greyhound racing is simulcast at **Wonderland Park** in north-suburban Revere. The track can be reached on the subway's Blue Line.

Each August, many of the world's top-seeded players compete in the week-long U.S. Pro Tennis Championships at Brookline's **Longwood Cricket Club**. Despite the suggestive name, no cricket is actually played here.

Boats taking part in the Head of the Charles Regatta in October

Each year on Patriot's Day (a city holiday on the third Monday of April,) the largest event on the sports calendar takes place. The **Boston Marathon** has burgeoned since its inception in 1897, and now approximately 15,000 participants, including many top runners from all over the world, take on the challenge of the 26.2-mile (42.2-km) course. The marathon starts in the town of Hopkinton, west of Boston, and finishes Downtown at the Boston Public Library on Boylston Street. More than half a million people line the entire length of the course to cheer on the runners.

The other major event of the sporting year is the **Head of the Charles Regatta**. The world's largest two-day rowing competition is held annually during the third weekend of October on the Charles River. It involves more than 6,000 crew members, who represent clubs, universities, and colleges from around the world. The 3-mile (5-km) course runs upstream from Boston University boathouse to Eliot Bridge. With up to 80 boats in each race, crews set off at short intervals and are timed along the course.

This is a major social event, as well as a sports one, with as many as 300,000 spectators

Detail from plaque celebrating the Boston Marathon

crowding both banks of the river, spread out on blankets and enjoying picnics and beer as they cheer on the rowers.

COLLEGE SPORTS

Boston's major colleges actively compete in a number of sports, with the major events occurring during the winter and fall. The annual Harvard–Yale football game takes place on the Saturday before Thanksgiving and is usually a fun and spirited event, both on and off the field. The sport that Boston colleges are best at, however, is ice-hockey, and the biggest event on the calendar is the fiercely contested "Beanpot" hockey tournament. This is held at TD Garden over two weekends in early February and involves most of the area's major colleges.

DIRECTORY

BASEBALL

Boston Red Sox
Fenway Park,
4 Yawkey Way.
Tel (617) 267-1700.
www.redsox.com

BASKETBALL

Boston Celtics
TD Garden, 1 Causeway
St. **Map** 1 C2.
Tel (617) 931-2222
(Ticketmaster).
www.celtics.com

AMERICAN FOOTBALL

New England Patriots
Gillette Stadium,
Route 1, Foxboro.
Tel (617) 931-2222
(Ticketmaster).
www.ticketmaster.com
www.patriots.com

ICE HOCKEY

Boston Bruins
TD Garden
(see Boston Celtics).
www.bostonbruins.com

OTHER SPORTS

Boston Marathon
Boston Athletic
Association, 40 Trinity
Place **Map** 3 C3. *Tel*
(617) 236-1652. **www**.
bostonmarathon.org

Head of the Charles Regatta
www.hocr.org

Longwood Cricket Club
564 Hammond St.,
Chestnut Hill. *Tel* (617)
731-2900. **www**.
longwoodcricket.com

New England Revolution
Gillette Stadium (see New
England Patriots). **www**.
revolutionsoccer.net

Suffolk Downs
Route 1a, East Boston.
Tel (617) 567-3900.
www.suffolkdowns.com

Wonderland Park
Route 1a, Revere.
Tel (781) 284-1300.
www.wonderland
greyhound.com

CHILDREN'S BOSTON

First-time visitors to Boston may wonder what this city, famous for its history and learning, has to offer families with children. The answer is more than can possibly be explored in one visit, with an enormous variety of children's attractions and entertainment, as well as many helpful services and facilities. Whether you begin your adventure at Boston's acclaimed Children's Museum, head out to sea on a whale-watching expedition, take a specially designed children's walking

Children's teddy bear

tour of The Freedom Trail, or visit Franklin Park Zoo, families will soon discover that Boston's unique heritage has as much to interest children as it does adults. A good starting point is the Prudential Center Skywalk (see p98), a 360-degree observatory from where children can locate the city's major landmarks, parks, and attractions. For parents hoping to find some time on their own, a few attractions have supervised children's activities and entertainment, and there are also various baby-sitting agencies.

Boston's Duck Tours – from dry land to the Charles River

PRACTICAL ADVICE

A useful monthly publication, found free at many local children's attractions, is *The Boston Parent's Paper*. This has detailed listings of events, attractions, and activities for kids throughout the Boston region. Children's events are also listed in Thursday's edition of *The Boston Globe*. Short-term baby-sitting can be arranged through **Parents-in-a-Pinch**. **CVS Pharmacy** (see p177) is open until late for supplies. Boston is easy to explore on foot, but be cautious before crossing streets with children, as Boston's drivers can be very assertive. Boston's subway system (see pp182–3), is free for children under 12 with an adult.

TOURS AND HISTORICAL SIGHTS

There are many tours and historical sights in Boston which children will find both fun and interesting. They can board an amphibious World

War II vehicle for a land and water tour of historic Boston with **Boston Duck Tours** (see p185). These drive past the city's historic neighborhoods and landmarks and then splash into the Charles River for a spectacular view of the Boston skyline. Boston's inner harbor and islands can be explored with **Boston Harbor Cruises**, whose cruises also stop at the U.S.S. *Constitution*, commonly known as "Old Ironsides" (see p115). Even more breathtaking are the whale-watching trips, run all through the summer by the New England Aquarium (see pp76–7).

Even if tickets to see the Red Sox games are sold out, baseball fans can still take the 40-minute tour of **Fenway Park** for a behind-the-scenes glimpse of the press box, private suites, and dugouts of this historic ballpark.

The experienced guides of **Boston by Foot** conduct special 60-minute family walking tours of the heart of The Freedom Trail (see pp124–7). History comes alive for children as they walk along the old cobblestone streets, and visit many sites of architectural and historical significance. Tours begin and end in front of the statue of Samuel Adams at Faneuil Hall. This is the gateway to **Quincy Market** (see p64), a lively emporium that sees flocks of tourists and locals alike, attracted by the enormous array of restaurants, shops, and entertainment. Children in particular will enjoy the jugglers, mime artists, musicians, and magicians who perform all around the attractive and traffic-free cobblestone marketplace.

Street entertainer, Quincy Market

MUSEUMS

Known as a pioneer of hands-on interactive learning, **Boston Children's Museum** *(see p75)* calls itself "Boston's Best Place for Kids," offering four floors of fun-filled education for toddlers to pre-teens in one building and three stories of exhibits in a new adjoining structure. Children can explore a 170-year-old house transplanted from Tokyo, create giant bubbles or conduct experiments in the Science Playground, and learn about healthy, active lifestyles in the KidPower exhibition. Children aged under three have their own Playspace, a stimulating second-floor area designed especially for them. The **Museum of Science** *(see p53)* could be another full-day stop, housing over 550 permanent exhibits exploring astronomy, energy, industry, anthropology, and nature. Younger children will enjoy the Human Body Connection, while older kids can explore basic scientific principles in Investigate. All will be impressed by the life-sized Tyrannosaurus Rex and The Computing Revolution, which recreates milestones of computing from giants of the 1940s to the PDAs of today. Attached to the museum there is also a Planetarium and an Omni IMAX film theater.

Few art museums have made their collections so accessible to families as the **Museum of Fine Arts, Boston** *(see pp104–7)*. Art classes and workshops are offered for children and adults in several media, including drawing, painting, mixed media, sculpture, and weaving. Family Place is open weekends with art materials, games, and activities for children aged four and up accompanied by an adult. A visitor's guide is available for families. During February and

Playspace activity, Children's Museum

April school vacations, performances and art-making activities are organized throughout the galleries.

The unique history of Boston's African-American community is presented at two sites. The centerpiece of the **Museum of African American History** *(see p49)* is the oldest black church in the U.S., and the **Abiel Smith School** *(see p49)* was the first schoolhouse for black children in America. The schoolhouse has interactive computer stations where children can learn about slavery, the American abolitionist movement, and the Underground Railroad *(see p49)*, as well as more contemporary issues affecting African-Americans in New England. Older children may be interested in the **Black Heritage Trail** *(see p49)*, a 1.5-mile (2.5-km) guided walking tour that visits 14 sites significant to the history of free African-Americans. The **Boston Tea Party Ships & Museum** *(see p74)*, with models of the three brigantine ships involved in the infamous rebellion, may possibly reopen on Congress Street in 2012.

Sports enthusiasts will want to take a trip to the **Sports**

Hands-on exhibit at Boston's Museum of Science

Having fun, Boston Museum of Science

Museum of New England, where interactive exhibits, mini-presentations, and a vast collection of sports memorabilia chronicle the region's sporting history. Children will be fascinated by the life-size wooden statues of Larry Bird, Carl Yastrzemski, and Bobby Orr, and enthusiastically take the chance to try out a variety of sports equipment.

DIRECTORY

PRACTICAL ADVICE

Parents-in-a-Pinch
45 Bartlett Crescent, Brookline.
Tel *(617) 739-5437.*
Tel *(800) 688-4697.*
www.parentsinapinch.com

TOURS AND HISTORICAL SIGHTS

Boston by Foot
77 North Washington Street.
Map 2 D2.
Tel *(617) 367-2345.*
www.bostonbyfoot.com

Boston Harbor Cruises
Long Wharf. **Map** 2 E3.
Tel *(617) 227-4321.*
www.bostonharborcruises.com

Fenway Park
4 Yawkey Way.
Tel *(617) 236-6666.*

MUSEUMS

Sports Museum of New England
TD Garden. **Map** 1 C2.
Tel *(617) 624-1234.*
www.sportsmuseum.org

Capybara, some of the many fascinating animals at Franklin Park Zoo

AQUARIUMS, ZOOS, AND PARKS

Visitors are greeted by a group of harbor seals at the entrance to the **New England Aquarium** *(see pp76–7)*, but once inside, all eyes are transfixed by the huge 200,000 gallon (900,000 liter) saltwater tank, which teems with tropical fish, sharks, sea turtles, and even the occasional scuba diver. The gently inclined wheelchair-friendly ramp winds up and around the three-story cylin-drical tank, giving a fascinating view of this simulated marine environment. Young children will also enjoy getting their hands wet in the huge indoor tide pool and watching the penguins and the harbor seals. Families can take a whale watching cruise or just watch a film on the enormous screen in the IMAX Theatre. Animal lovers will want to head directly to **Franklin**

Park Zoo *(see p102)*, with its collection of native and exotic fauna. Don't miss the African Tropical Forest, a re-created savanna with gorillas, monkeys, and pygmy hippos, the Children's Zoo, and Bird's World. For a wildlife trip in the middle of town, no visit to Boston is complete without a ride on the famous **Swan Boats** *(see p46)* in the Boston Public Garden. Immortalized in Robert McCloskey's 1941 children's classic, *Make Way for Ducklings (see p46)*, the pedal propelled boats gently circle a lovely pond as ducks clamor alongside for a snack. Nearby are large bronze sculptures of Mrs. Mallard and family. Crossing Charles Street, visitors will come to **Boston**

Bronze duck sculpture, Boston Public Garden

Common *(see pp46–7)*, which separates Downtown from Beacon Hill and Back Bay. There is a playground here, as well as Frog Pond, which is a huge wading pool in the summer and a skating rink in the winter. Boston's most attractive park, the highlight of the Emerald Necklace, is **Arnold Arboretum** *(see p102)*, in Jamaica Plain. With plenty of opportunity for exploration, it is a good place for children to let off steam.

CHILDREN'S THEATER

Children's theater thrives in Boston. The **Boston Children's Theater** celebrated its 50th season in 2000, with its acclaimed "live theater for children by children." Main-stage productions run from December through April, and its Stagemobile takes performances outside to Boston's parks in the summer. The **Wheelock Family Theater**, another highly acclaimed company, uses multi-ethnic and inter-genera-tional casting, with performances on most weekends from September to May. Fables and fairy tales come to life at the **Puppet Showplace Theatre**, with shows for pre-schoolers on Wednesday and Thursday, and performances for families on weekends from September to May.

Swan Boats on a relaxing cruise around the pond, Boston Public Garden

Marionettes on stage at the Puppet Showplace Theatre

CHILDREN'S SHOPPING

While keeping children entertained can often be a challenge, in Boston you will find that even shopping can hold their interests. With enticing window displays, and stores overflowing with desirable products, do not, however, expect to survive such an outing without spending any money. In Cambridge, **Susie's Gallery** has bright and innovative goods with a sense of whimsy, and **Henry Bear's Park** across the street is especially well-stocked with toys graded by age.

In Harvard Square, **Curious George Books & Toys** carries one of the country's most complete stocks of children's books, while **Calliope** has a menagerie of cuddly stuffed animals and hand puppets. **Newbury Comics** features the best selection of comic books in Boston. **Games People Play** stocks a huge assortment of toys and games. The latest in cool clothing can be found at **Baby Gap**, and there's a wide selection of

outdoor gear at **Patagonia**. It is well worth the trip to Brookline Village for **The Children's Book Shop**, which has an excellent selection of books for infants to young-adults, and to Jamaica Plain for the bubbly **Boing – JP's Toyshop**. Kids will also enjoy the shops, stalls, and street vendors at **Quincy Market** *(see p64)*.

EATING OUT WITH CHILDREN

Though children never seem to tire of fast food, adults generally long for something more substantial and memorable. Both needs can be catered for in many of Boston's restaurants. Children will enjoy sampling Chinese delicacies at **China Pearl** in Chinatown. For pizza in an authentic Italian atmosphere, try the North End's **Pizzeria Regina**. In Cambridge, **The Cheesecake Factory** has an incredibly vast menu of casual fare as well as its eponymous sweets and is sure to please every family member. In the Huron Avenue shopping district in Cambridge, the friendly restaurant **Full Moon** has a play area as well as a varied kid's menu.

Popcorn, a favorite snack

DIRECTORY

CHILDREN'S THEATER

Boston Children's Theater
316 Columbus Ave.
Map 3 C3. **Tel** (617) 424-6634. www.boston childrenstheater.org

Puppet Showplace Theatre
32–33 Station St., Brookline. **Tel** (617) 731-6400. www. puppetshowplace.org

Wheelock Family Theater
200 The Riverway, Brookline. **Tel** (617) 879-2000. www.wheelock.edu/wft

CHILDREN'S SHOPPING

Baby Gap
Copley Place, 100 Huntington Ave. **Map** 3 C3. **Tel** (617) 247-1754.

Boing – JP's Toy Shop
729 Centre St., Jamaica Plain. **Tel** (617) 522-7800.

Calliope
33 Brattle St., Cambridge. **Tel** (617) 876-4149.

The Children's Book Shop
237 Washington St., Brookline. **Tel** (617) 734-7323.

Curious George Books & Toys
1 JFK St., Cambridge. **Tel** (617) 498-0062.

Games People Play
1100 Massachusetts Ave., Cambridge. **Tel** (617) 492-0711.

Henry Bear's Park
361 Huron Ave., Cambridge. **Tel** (617) 547-8424.

Newbury Comics
332 Newbury St. **Map** 3 A3. **Tel** (617) 236-4930.

Patagonia
346 Newbury St. **Map** 3 A3. **Tel** (617) 424-1776.

Susie's Gallery for Children
348 Huron Ave., Cambridge. **Tel** (617) 876-7874.

EATING OUT WITH CHILDREN

The Cheesecake Factory
100 Cambridgeside Place, Cambridge. **Tel** (617) 252-3810.

China Pearl
9 Tyler St. **Map** 4 F2. **Tel** (617) 426-4338.

Full Moon
344 Huron Ave., Cambridge. **Tel** (617) 354-6699.

Pizzeria Regina
11½ Thacher St. **Map** 2 D2. **Tel** (617) 227-0765.

SURVIVAL
GUIDE

PRACTICAL INFORMATION 174–179
TRAVEL INFORMATION 180–185
BOSTON STREET FINDER 186–191

PRACTICAL INFORMATION

Logo for Greater Boston Convention and Visitors Bureau

More than most American cities, Boston is built to human scale. With the main parts of the city all within a relatively small area, Boston is ideal for the visitor, with walking not only possible, but often preferable, despite a modern and efficient transit system. Boston is also one of the safest cities in the U.S., and one of the friendliest, making it very easy to feel at home here and comfortable exploring. So long as visitors take a few sensible precautions, they should enjoy a trouble-free stay. Boston's visitor information centers help people get the most from their stay, and the city also deals better than most with the needs of children and the disabled.

VISAS AND PASSPORTS

Citizens of visa waiver countries – the U.K., most western European countries, Australia, New Zealand, Japan, Canada, Mexico, and Caribbean nations (except Cuba) – need a valid, machine-readable passport and must register (and pay a small charge) before traveling with the Electronic System for Travel Authorization (ESTA) at https://esta.cbp.dhs.gov. The ESTA authorization is for a maximum stay of 90 days in the U.S. and remains valid for travel within two years. Foreign visitors should check with their American consulate for details about passport and visa procedures.

Citizens of all other countries need a valid passport and a tourist visa, which can be obtained from a U.S. consulate or embassy.

TOURIST INFORMATION AND OPENING HOURS

Visitor information desks at the airport can provide guides and maps, answer questions, and make hotel reservations.

The **Greater Boston Convention and Visitors Bureau** offers a more comprehensive service, and can help with arrangements before you travel. Major hotels also have helpful guest service desks. All of these places also hold a range of discount tickets offering savings at many of Boston's major museums and attractions, nightlife spots, theaters, and restaurants.

Attraction and store opening hours vary greatly, so be sure to check with your destination. In general, most shops and attractions are open daily from 10am–6pm, with reduced hours on Sundays. Many shops stay open later on Thursdays, while key attractions, like the Museum of Fine Arts *(see p104–105)*, offer extended hours one night per week.

TAX AND TIPPING

In Boston and the surrounding area, taxes will be added to hotel and restaurant charges and most retail purchases, all clothing items and groceries priced under $175. State sales tax is 6.25 percent, and hotel tax in the Boston metropolitan area is 14.45 percent.

Tipping is expected for most services: in restaurants tip 15–20 percent of the bill, and give $1 per bag to porters and $2 to valet parking attendants. Bartenders expect $1–2 per drink.

ALCOHOL AND SMOKING

The legal minimum age for drinking alcohol in Boston is 21; most young people will be required to show photo identification (I.D.) as proof of age in order to get into bars and to purchase alcohol. It is illegal to drink in public spaces, and penalties for driving under the influence of alcohol are severe. The legal age for buying cigarettes is 18, and I.D. may also be required. It is illegal to smoke in public buildings and in all bars and restaurants *(see p139)*.

TRAVELERS WITH SPECIAL NEEDS

Massachusetts and U.S. law mandate accessibility for persons with handicaps, but wheelchair accessibility is sometimes limited in Boston's historic buildings. Most hotels and restaurants, however, are wheelchair accessible. **Very Special Arts – Massachusetts** provides useful information on disabled-accessible entertainment. For other information, contact the **Society for Accessible Travel and Hospitality**.

Visitor Information Center on Boston Common

◁ Charles River Back Bay

TRAVELING WITH CHILDREN

Boston is in general a child-friendly city, boasting its own Children's Museum *(see p75)*, as well as numerous other museums and a variety of attractions that offer interesting hands-on exhibits and activities for children *(see pp168–71)*.

Families with children will find that the casual and fast-food restaurants cater best to their needs, with menus often tailored to children's tastes and appetites. Children are welcome at most of Boston's restaurants, however.

TRAVELING ON A BUDGET

Boston hosts a large number of free attractions, exhibitions, and performances. For details, consult the websites of *The Boston Globe* and *The Boston Phoenix (see p158)*.

Students from abroad should purchase an **International Student Identity Card (I.S.I.C.)** before traveling, since there are many discounts available to students in Boston. The I.S.I.C. handbook lists places and services offering discounts to card-holders, including hotels, hostels, museums, tours, attractions, restaurants, and theaters. The **Student Advantage Card** is a similar card available to all American undergraduates.

International Student Identity Card, recognized student I.D. in America

SENIOR TRAVELERS

Anyone over the age of 65 is eligible for various discounts with proof of age. Contact the **American Association of Retired Persons** for further information. Also the international senior travel organization **Elderhostel**, offers group vacations, courses and events in Boston.

ELECTRICITY

Electricity flows at 110–120 volts, and a two-prong plug is used. Non-U.S. appliances will need an adaptor and a voltage converter. Most hotel rooms have hairdriers, as well as sockets for electric shavers.

Cycling along the Charles River

RESPONSIBLE TOURISM

Long considered one of the U.S.'s most environmentally conscious cities, Boston continues to gain national acclaim for its forward-thinking policies, such as requiring all taxicabs to go hybrid by 2015.

It is easy to be green while in Boston. Recycling bins have become quite common, and most new buildings boast Earth-friendly features with respect to energy, lighting, and water supplies. The organization **Boston Green Tourism** aims to guide visitors toward green-certified hotels, restaurants, and shops, and the whole "green movement" has spread throughout the city's economic landscape.

Thousands of college students help boost the area's environmental causes, as do the passionate masses that make a living off of the region's seacoast and farms, while selling their wares at community farmers' markets or family-owned shops.

Seasonal farmers' markets pop up everywhere, from small town parks to Boston's City Hall Plaza *(see p62)*. The best way to check when and where the next event will be is to consult www.massfarmers markets.org. For a permanent destination, the family-run Wilson Farm (www.wilson farm.com) has been luring visitors to Lexington *(see p119)* for its fresh apples, corn, and pumpkin since 1884.

Personal Security and Health

Hospital sign

Boston is one of the U.S.'s safest cities's and its crime rate continues to drop. This has made its police force and community relations programs models for other American cities. Nonetheless, it is still prudent to take a few simple precautions and to keep to the tourist areas. The main sights are all located in safe parts of the city with lots of people and where serious crime is rare. If you are unfortunate enough to be taken ill during your visit, healthcare in Boston is world class. This does not come cheaply, however, and it is essential to have adequate insurance coverage before you travel.

LAW ENFORCEMENT AND POLICE

The most visible uniformed law enforcement personnel in Boston are the National Park Service (or Boston Park Service) rangers, usually dressed in olive green or khaki, and the members of the Boston Police Department (BPD), dressed in blue. You will also see City Parking and Traffic officers, who deal exclusively with traffic violations.

Should you encounter any trouble as a visitor, approach any of the blue-uniformed BPD officers who regularly patrol the city streets. Park rangers can often help with directions and general information.

If you need to report a crime, call the Boston **Police non-emergency line** or call 911 in an emergency.

WHAT TO BE AWARE OF

Serious crime is rarely witnessed in the main sightseeing areas of Boston. However, avoid wandering into areas that are off the beaten 'track, during the day or at night. Police officers regularly patrol the tourist areas, but it is still advisable to use common sense, and to stay alert. Try not to advertise the fact that you are a visitor; prepare the day's itinerary in advance, and study your map before you set off. Avoid

Boston police officer

wearing expensive jewelry, and carry your camera or camcorder securely. Only carry small amounts of cash; credit cards are the most secure option.

Before you leave home, take a photocopy of all important documents, including your passport and visa, and keep them and any other valuables in your hotel safe. Keep an eye on your belongings at all times, whether checking into or out of the hotel, standing in the airport, or sitting in a bar or restaurant.

EMERGENCIES

If you are involved in a **medical** emergency, go to a hospital emergency room. Should you need an ambulance, call 911 (toll-free) and one will be sent. Also call 911 for **police** or **fire** department assistance.

If you have your medical insurance properly arranged, you need not worry about medical costs. Depending on the limitations of your insurance, it is better to avoid the overcrowded city-owned hospitals listed in the phone book Blue Pages, and opt instead for one of the private hospitals listed in the Yellow Pages. Alternatively, ask at your hotel desk or at the nearest pharmacy for information on your nearest hospital. For **dental referrals** contact the Massachusetts Dental Society. You can also ask your hotel to call a doctor or dentist to visit you.

If you lose your credit cards, most card companies, for example **American Express**, have toll-free numbers for reporting a loss or theft.

LOST PROPERTY

Although the chances of retrieving lost property are slim, you should report all stolen items to the police. Use the **Police Non-Emergency Line**. Make sure you keep a copy of the police report, which you will need for your insurance claim. In case of loss, it is useful to have a list of your valuables' serial numbers or a photocopy of any relevant documents or receipts as proof of possession. This should be kept separately. It is also useful to try and remember the taxi companies or bus routes you use, as it might make it easier to retrieve lost items. If your passport is lost or stolen, get in touch with your country's embassy or consulate immediately.

Mounted Boston Park Service ranger, Copley Square

Fire engine

Ambulance

Police car

HOSPITALS AND PHARMACIES

Comprising one of the country's most renowned medical communities, Boston's hospitals are primarily clustered around the Fenway and near Beacon Hill, with several other facilities dotted around the city. Patients come from all over the world to seek treatment at legendary institutions like **Children's Hospital Boston** and **Massachusetts General Hospital** (both private). Regardless of one's insurance situation, hospital emergency rooms are required to treat all patients; however, waiting times can reach several hours and costs can be exorbitant. The Massachusetts General Hospital also maintains an **International Patient Center** for those in need of interpreting services, as well as dedicated housing and financial arrangements.

Plan in advance: if you take medication, bring a back-up supply with you. However, if you need a prescription dispensed, there are plenty of pharmacies (drugstores) in and around the city, some staying open 24 hours a day. Ask your hotel for the nearest one. **CVS Pharmacy** is a popular chain of drugstores. The larger pharmacies, such as CVS, can also be a helpful resource for those with basic medical questions and concerns, from an upset stomach to an allergy.

Those needing dental assistance should check first to see if their travel insurance covers dental aid; like emergency medical fees, unforeseen dentist visits can break the bank. An inexpensive option for those without coverage is to visit a clinic such as the **Tufts University School of Dental Medicine** where practicing students work.

TRAVEL INSURANCE

Travel insurance is not compulsory but strongly recommended when traveling to the U.S. It is important to have insurance for emergency medical and dental care, which can be expensive,even in city-owned hospitals and clinics. Even with coverage you may have to pay for the services, then claim reimbursement from your insurance company.

In addition, it is advisable to make sure your personal property is insured and to obtain coverage for lost or stolen baggage, travel documents, and accidental death or injury.

DIRECTORY

EMERGENCIES

American Express
Tel (212) 758-6510.
www.americanexpress.com

Dental Referrals
Tel (800) 342-8747.
www.massdental.org

Medical Referrals
Tel (781) 893-4610
or *(800) 322-2303.*

Police, Fire, Medical (all emergencies)
Tel 911 (toll-free).

LOST PROPERTY

Police Non-Emergency Line
*Tel Boston
(617) 343-4200.*
*Tel Cambridge
(617) 349-3300.*

CONSULATES

Australia
150 East 42nd St.,
34th floor, New York,
NY 10017.
Tel (212) 351-6500.
www.australianyc.org

Canada
3 Copley Place.
Map 3 C3.
Tel (617) 262-3760.
www.boston.gc.ca

Ireland
535 Boylston St. **Map** 3
C2. *Tel (617) 267-9330.*
www.irelandemb.org

New Zealand
37 Observatory Circle,
NW Washington, DC
20008.
Tel (202) 328-4800.
www.nzembassy.com

United Kingdom
1 Memorial Drive,
Cambridge.
Tel (617) 245-4500.
www.britainusa.com

HOSPITALS AND PHARMACIES

Children's Hospital Boston
300 Longwood Ave.
Tel (617) 355-6000.
www.childrenshospital.org

CVS Pharmacy
155 Charles St.
Map 1 B3. *Tel (617) 523-1028.* (Pharmacy open
8am–8pm daily.
Store open 24 hours.)

35 White St., Cambridge.
Tel (617) 876-5519.
(Open 24 hours.)

Massachusetts General Hospital
50 Blossom St. **Map** 1 B3.
Tel (617) 726-2000.
www.mgh.harvard.edu

MGM International Patient Center
55 Fruit St., Blake 180.
Map 1 B3.
Tel (617) 726-2787.

Tufts University School of Dental Medicine
1 Kneeland St. **Map** 4 F2.
Tel (617) 636-6828.

Banking and Currency

Throughout Boston there are various places to access and exchange your money, from the numerous banks and ATMs to the foreign currency exchanges. The most important things to remember are not to carry all your money and credit cards with you at one time, and to be aware that most banks and currency exchanges are closed on Sundays.

One of Bank of America's many branches in Boston

BANKING AND CURRENCY EXCHANGE

Boston has branches of numerous national banking chains, including **Bank of America**, **Citizens Bank**, and **TD Bank**. Most banks are open Monday through Friday from 9am to 3pm, although some may open earlier and close later. Most banks also open Saturday mornings from 9am to noon or 1pm. All banks are closed on Sundays and Federal holidays *(see p37)*.

Always ask if there are any special fees or commission charges before you make your transaction. At most banks, traveler's checks in U.S. dollars can be cashed with any form of photo identification, although a passport is usually required if you want to exchange any foreign money. Foreign currency exchange is available at the main branches of large banks, which often have a separate dedicated area or teller window for foreign exchange.

Foreign currency exchanges are generally open weekdays from 9am to 5pm, but some – especially those in busy shopping districts – may have extended opening hours. Among the best-known companies are **American Express Travel Service** and **Travelex Currency Services**, both of which have several branches in and around Boston. Most currency exchanges charge a fee or commission, so it is worth looking around to get the best value rates. Hotels may also exchange money, but their fees will usually be much more expensive.

ATMS

ATMs (cash machines) can be found throughout Boston. They are usually located near the entrance to banks, and sometimes inside convenience stores and supermarkets. The most widely accepted types of bank cards include Cirrus, Plus, NYCE, and some credit cards such as VISA and MasterCard. Note that a fee may be levied on your cash withdrawal depending on the bank. Before you travel, ensure you check with your bank which machines your card can access and the various fees charged.

American Express charge cards

To minimize the risk of robbery, always be aware of your surroundings and the people around you when using an ATM. Avoid using ATMs in isolated areas. Make sure you shield your PIN and, if available, use a machine located within a bank. Be careful when removing your card from the machine.

CREDIT CARDS AND DEBIT CARDS

American Express, VISA, MasterCard, Diner's Club, and the Discover Card, as well as most debit cards, are accepted almost everywhere in Boston, from theaters and hotels to restaurants and shops.

Besides being a much safer alternative to carrying a lot of cash, credit and debit cards offer some useful additional benefits, such as insurance on your purchases and access to the daily exchange rate. They are also essential if you want to reserve a hotel or book a rental car. Credit cards can also be useful in emergencies when cash may not be readily available.

Before traveling it would be wise to phone your card provider and inform them that you will be abroad, or you risk finding that your card gets blocked when you start using it in Boston.

DIRECTORY

BANKING AND CURRENCY EXCHANGE

American Express Travel Service
1 State Street.
Map 2 D3.
Tel (617) 723-8400.
39 J.F.K. Street, Cambridge.
Tel (617) 868-2600.

Bank of America
100 Federal Street.
Map 2 D4.
Tel (617) 434-3412.
www.bankofamerica.com

Citizens Bank
73 Tremont Street. **Map** 1 C5.
Tel (617) 422-8295.
www.citizensbank.com

TD Bank
579 Boylston Street.
Map 1 A5.
Tel (617) 266-0740.
www.tdbank.com

Travelex Currency Services
Logan Airport, Terminal E.
Tel (617) 567-1030.
www.travelex.com

Communications and Media

Phone company logo

Boston's communications infrastructure is modern and well developed. Public payphones can still be found on some streets and in hotel lobbies. Visitors will find the city is well supplied with cell phone stores, Internet cafés, and public access to computers and Wi-Fi. News is readily available from Boston's many television and radio stations, newspapers, and magazines, and the postal service is quick and efficient – whether you are sending mail within the U.S. or abroad.

TELEPHONES

Public telephones are found on some street corners and in many hotels. Most accept coins as well as phonecards, which can be purchased at gas stations, convenience stores, and newsstands. Local calls cost 50 cents to $1 from payphones; long-distance call rates vary. All numbers with a 1-800, 866, 877, or 888 prefix, however, are free of charge. Direct calls can also be made from hotel rooms but usually carry hefty surcharges. Unless you are using your own international telephone card, it is cheaper to use the payphone in the lobby.

For directory assistance, dial 411 (local) or 00 (international); for operator assistance, dial 0 (local) or 01 (international.) All operator-assisted calls carry a surcharge. For emergency services (police, fire, or ambulance) call 911.

CELL PHONES

In America, there are several cell phone systems (AT&T is one of the largest). Check with your service provider to learn about your options when abroad. Some phones require a chip or need to be unlocked for international usage, while others carry hefty roaming charges. Renting a cell phone while in America (try Cell Hire) is an attractive, and often cheaper, option for many international visitors.

AREA CODES

Central Boston's area code is 617 or 857; include this when dialing local calls. If dialing out of the local area (but within the U.S. or Canada) dial 1, then the area code.

For international calls, dial 011, then the country code, the area code (minus the first 0), and the local number.

INTERNET AND EMAIL

From neighborhood coffee shops and hotel lobbies to parks, Wi-Fi hotspots dot the city. Those traveling without their computers or Internet-enabled devices can visit a library – **Boston Public Library**'s main branch has several Internet terminals for public use – or an Internet café.

POSTAL SERVICE

Post offices are open from 9am to 5pm, Monday through Friday, and most are also open Saturday from 9am to noon. They close on Sundays and for all Federal holidays.

If the correct postage is attached, letters and parcels of less than 13 oz (370 g) can be put in any blue mailbox. Pick-up times are written inside the lid. Always use a zip code to ensure delivery, and send all overseas mail by airmail to avoid long delays.

Boston post office, Charles Street

NEWSPAPERS AND MAGAZINES

The most widely read newspaper in the Boston area is *The Boston Globe (see p158)*, which is thought of as one of the best newspapers in the U.S. The other widely available local daily is *The Boston Herald* tabloid (www.boston herald.com). The Thursday and Friday editions of *The Boston Globe*, and *The Boston Phoenix (see p158)*, published on Thursdays, contain listings of entertainment and cultural events in Boston.

TELEVISION AND RADIO

The Boston media market is highly competitive. Major network television stations include CBS (channel 4), ABC (channel 5), NBC (channel 7), and Fox (channel 25). Public television station PBS is on channel 2. Popular radio stations include NPR (National Public Radio) on WBUR (90.9 FM), WFNX (101.7 FM) for rock music, WCRB (99.5 FM) for classical music, and WMJX (106.7 FM) for easy listening.

DIRECTORY

CELL PHONES

AT&T
www.wireless.att.com

Cell Hire
www.cellhire.com

INTERNET AND EMAIL

Boston Public Library
700 Boylston St.
Map 3 C2.
www.bpl.org

POST OFFICES

Financial District
31 Milk St.
Map 2 D4.
Tel (617) 482-1956.

North End
217 Hanover St.
Map 2 E2.
Tel (617) 723-6397.
www.usps.gov

TRAVEL INFORMATION

American Airlines plane

Arriving in Boston is fairly easy. The city is served by Logan International Airport as well as by the smaller satellites in Manchester, NH, and near Providence, RI, which are both located within 50 miles (80 km) of the city center. Amtrak trains come into Boston's South Station, as do bus carriers. From here, the subway, known as the "T," connects to almost every part of the city. Boston also makes an ideal base from which to take day or weekend trips to the numerous places of interest throughout the New England area.

Control Tower at Boston's Logan International Airport

ARRIVING BY AIR

Situated in East Boston, **Logan International Airport** is the major airport serving Boston and the surrounding area, although some international charter flights and several domestic carriers use the smaller and less crowded **Manchester New Hampshire Airport** and **T.F. Green Airport** in Warwick, Rhode Island. Both are a bus ride of around an hour from Boston.

Boston is served by almost all North American airlines and by most international airlines, either directly or in partnership with U.S. carriers. Often the least expensive flights, especially between continental Europe and Boston, require making a connection in New York. There are frequent non-stop flights available between Boston and the United Kingdom

and Ireland on U.S. carriers, as well as British Airways and Aer Lingus.

Logan International lies within Boston city limits on an island across the inner harbor from the central city. Harbor tunnel crossings tend to act as a bottleneck, which slows taxi services between the airport and downtown. At busy times, a taxi ride ($20–30) can take 30 minutes or more, with much of the trip spent in bumper-to-bumper traffic. The least expensive means of getting from the airport to downtown Boston is via the M.B.T.A. subway (see pp182–3). This takes 18–25 minutes. Free

City Water Taxi, running from Logan Airport to Central and Long wharves

buses connect the airport's air terminals to its subway terminal. There is also a bus service that runs between the airport and Boston's South Station. Arguably the most scenic approach into Boston is the **City Water Taxi**, with stops at Logan Airport, and Central and Long wharves. The journey takes about 20–25 minutes.

AIR FARES

For cheap air fares, search online on websites such as www.lastminute.com and www.expedia.com. The more you shop around, the better deal you will get, and it is worth taking the time to do some research. For inexpensive consolidated tickets, contact **Kayak.com** online or give **Airline Consolidator.com** a try. The easiest way to find the best fare is to use the website **Cheaptickets.com**.

High season runs from June to August, as well as around Easter and Christmas, when flights are at their most expensive. Travelers should also be aware of price hikes when scheduling a visit around large events like the Boston Marathon (see p34) and university commencement ceremonies. May, September, and October are generally less expensive, and any other time of the year is considered off-peak. Flights are usually least expensive for travel from Tuesday to Thursday. APEX tickets, usually the best deal, must be booked a few weeks in advance. However, note that these tickets must include a Saturday night.

PACKAGE DEALS

Boston packages are sometimes available in the U.S. as part of a fall foliage bus tour or through the AAA (American Automobile Association; *see p185*). Several airlines arrange packages including travel and lodging. Boston hotels generally post their special event packages on the website of the Greater Boston Convention and Visitors Bureau (*see p175*).

ARRIVING BY CAR

Boston is not called "The Hub" for nothing, as most routes in the northeast converge here. The principal routes from the north are I-95 from the coast and I-93 from northern New England. I-90 comes in from the west as the Massachusetts Turnpike. I-93 approaches from the south as the Southeast Expressway, while I-95, formerly known as Rte 128, circumvents Boston. Exits from the roadway to parts of downtown come up quickly, so check your exit number in advance.

ARRIVING BY TRAIN

A train service between New York and Boston via coastal Connecticut and Rhode Island is provided by **Amtrak**. Conventional train services take 4–5 hours, and arrive at and depart from

Amtrak train waiting to depart from Boston's South Station

Boston's South Station. A high-speed service that takes 3 hours is also available but is more expensive. The Amtrak service extends north to Maine and south to Philadelphia, Washington, D.C., and beyond.

ARRIVING BY BUS

Although taking a bus is easily the slowest and usually cheapest way to get to Boston, it need not be unpleasant. **Greyhound Bus Lines** and **Peter Pan Trailways** both serve the city of Boston as long-distance carriers, sharing quarters at the South Station bus terminal. Both offer routes around the country and provide discounts for children, senior citizens, and U.S. military personnel on active duty. Both also offer bargain excursion tickets for unlimited travel within a certain time period for a single fixed rate.

Discount carriers include the modern **BoltBus** and **MegaBus**, as well as several no-frills companies that depart from Boston's Chinatown.

Greyhound Bus Lines logo

DIRECTORY

ARRIVING BY AIR

City Water Taxi
Tel (617) 422-0392.
www.citywatertaxi.com

Logan International Airport
East Boston, Massachusetts.
Tel (617) 561-1800
or (800) 23-LOGAN.
www.massport.com/logan

Manchester New Hampshire Airport
Tel (603) 624-6556.
www.flymanchester.com

T.F. Green Airport
Warwick, Rhode Island.
Tel (401) 737-8222.
www.pvdairport.com

AIR FARES

AirlineConsolidator.com
Tel (888) 468-5385.
www.airlineconsolidator.com

Cheaptickets.com
Tel (312) 260-8100.
www.cheaptickets.com

Kayak.com
55 North Water St, Ste 1, Norwalk, CT 06854.
Tel (203) 899-3100.
www.kayak.com

ARRIVING BY TRAIN

Amtrak
South Station, 700 Atlantic Ave.
Map 2 D5. *Tel (800) 872-7245.*
www.amtrak.com

ARRIVING BY BUS

BoltBus
South Station, 700 Atlantic Ave.
Map 2 D5. *Tel (877) 265-8287.*
www.boltbus.com

Greyhound Bus Lines
South Station, 700 Atlantic Ave.
Map 2 D5. *Tel (617) 526-1800*
or (800) 231-2222.
www.greyhound.com

MegaBus
South Station, 700 Atlantic Ave.
Map 2 D5. *Tel (877) 462-6342.*
www.megabus.com

Peter Pan Trailways
South Station, 700 Atlantic Ave.
Map 2 D5. *Tel (800) 343-9999.*
www.peterpanbus.com

Main concourse of Boston's South Station

Getting Around Boston

Public transportation in Boston and Cambridge is very good. In fact, it is considerably easier to get around by public transportation than by driving, with the added benefit of not having to find a parking space. All major attractions in the city are accessible on the subway, by bus, or by taxi. The central sections of the city are also extremely easy to navigate on foot.

M.B.T.A. commuter bus, with distinctive yellow paintwork

GREEN TRAVEL

Boston's moniker of "America's Walking City" hints at how easy it is to tour the city in this environmentally friendly way. Those needing to cover some serious ground can lean on one of the U.S.'s leading public transportation systems. The **M.B.T.A.** has worked with the Environmental Protection Agency on projects like locomotive engine pollution-control devices, while replacing its diesel-powered bus fleet with natural gas-powered buses. Visitors can reach almost anywhere in the metro area – from the historic towns of Lexington and Concord to the scenic Boston Harbor Islands – using public transportation. Websites like **HopStop** offer public transit and walking directions to just about any-where in the city. The 17-mile (27-km) Esplanade trail along the **Charles River** (where you can rent canoes and kayaks) and the Minuteman Bikeway *(see p164)* offer ample opportunities for bikers, joggers, and walkers.

FINDING YOUR WAY

The Greater Boston Convention and Visitors Bureau *(see p175)* provides a helpful contact point. To find out about any upcoming cultural events, check the websites for Boston CitySearch and *The Boston Globe (see p158)*.

Most of Boston is laid out "organically" rather than in the sort of strict grid found in many American cities. When trying to orient yourself, it helps to think of Boston as enclaves of neighborhoods around a few central squares. In general, uphill from Boston Common is Beacon Hill, downhill is Downtown. Back Bay begins west of Arlington Street. The North End sticks out from the north side of Boston, while the Waterfront is literally that, where Boston meets the sea.

M.B.T.A. SUBWAY AND TROLLEY BUSES

Boston's subway system is the oldest in North America, but it has been vastly expanded and modernized since the first cars rolled between Park Street and Boylston Street in 1897. The street trolley system began in 1846 with trolleys drawn along tracks by horses. In 1889, the system was electrified.

Charlie Card, valid on Boston's public transit network

Combined, the subway and trolley lines are known as the "T." The "T" operates 5–12:45am Monday through Saturday, and 6–12:45am Sunday. Weekday service is officially every 3–15 minutes; on weekends it is less frequent.

There are five lines: the Red Line runs from south of the city to Cambridge, and the Green Line runs from the Museum of Science westward into the suburbs. The Blue Line begins near Government Center and goes to Logan Airport and on to Revere, while the Orange Line connects the northern suburbs to southwest Boston. The Silver Line, a surface bus, runs from Roxbury to Logan Airport via South Station. Maps of the system are available at the Downtown Crossing M.B.T.A. station.

Admission to subway stations is via turnstiles into which you insert a paper Charlie ticket or touch your plastic CharlieCard on the reader. Day or week LinkPasses for unlimited travel can be purchased at stations and Airport "T" stops, and can be loaded on to Charlie tickets or CharlieCards.

M.B.T.A. BUSES

The bus system complements the subway system and in effect enlarges the entire transit network to cover more than 1,000 miles (1,600 km). However, buses are often crowded, and schedules can be hard to obtain. Two useful routes for sightseeing are Charlestown–Haymarket, (from Haymarket, near Quincy Market, to Bunker Hill) and Harvard–Dudley (from Harvard Square via Massachusetts Avenue, through Back Bay and the South End, to Dudley Square in Roxbury). Cash, a Charlie ticket, or a plastic CharlieCard is required for the fare.

WALKING IN BOSTON

Boston is considered North America's premier walking city – partly because it is so compact, and partly because virtually all streets are flanked by sidewalks. It is nonetheless essential to wear comfortable walking shoes with adequate cushioning and good support.

Because Boston is principally a city of neighborhoods, it is often simplest to use public transportation to get to a particular neighborhood, and then to walk to soak up the atmosphere. Walking also allows you to see parts of the city that are impractical to explore by car because the streets are too narrow – for example, Beacon Hill, parts of the North End, and Harvard Square.

Boston parkland, ideal for walking

TAXIS

Taxis can be found at taxi stands in tourist areas or be hailed on the street. They may pick up fares only in the city for which they are licensed – Cambridge taxis in Cambridge, and Boston taxis in Boston. It is possible to call a taxi company and arrange a pick-up time and place.

Rates are calculated by both mileage and time, beginning with a standard "pickup" fee (around $3) when the meter starts running. Taxis in Boston and Cambridge are generally more expensive than in other U.S. cities. Taxis to Logan International charge an airport use fee (around $3), while those coming from the airport charge for the harbor tunnel toll (around $6). Additional surcharges may apply late at night. A full schedule of fares should be posted inside the vehicle. The driver's photo-graph and permit and the taxi's permit number will also be posted inside all legitimate taxicabs, along with directions for reporting complaints.

CYCLING

Boston and Cambridge have an extensive network of bike paths. Cycling on the highways is illegal, city streets can be hazardous, and cycling on sidewalks is discouraged, but dedicated bike paths are gen-erally very safe. Cycling is a fun way to see some of the outlying sights. Cycle shops and some newsstands carry the Boston Bike Map, which details trails and paths across the metropolitan region. For more on cycling, *see p164*.

GUIDED TOURS

Many city tours, including **Old Town Trolley Tours** and theme tours (such as ghosts or chocolate), depart from the Visitor Information Center on Boston Common. The **Boston Duck Tours** use an open-air amphibious vehicle that tours the streets and navigates the Charles River. Also, **National Park Service** rangers offer free walking tours of Boston's parks, the Freedom Trail *(see pp124–7)*, and the Black Heritage Trail *(see p49)*.

THE BOSTON "T"

Boston traffic by night with the Financial District in the background

and public holidays, and many downtown areas allow parking in loading zones on Sunday as well. Read posted signs carefully. Parking in a public lot or garage can cost more than $10 per hour or $40 per day, but it is sometimes the only choice. Valet parking is available at some restaurants, hotels, and malls for a fee.

In order to avoid traffic congestion in the city center, visitors may consider parking near a "T" or bus stop in the suburbs, and continuing their journey into town by public transportation.

DRIVING

Despite heavy traffic and restricted parking, having your own vehicle in Boston can, at times, be an undeniable convenience. For example, visiting some of the outlying sights of Boston *(see Getting Out of Boston p185)*, which may be difficult to reach by public transportation, is much easier with a car. Many U.S. visitors to the city arrive with their own cars, and overseas visitors can rent one quite easily. Even so, driving in and around Boston requires patience, humor, reliable maps, good driving skills, and the ability to read the road swiftly and take decisive actions.

Despite Boston's comparatively small size, its traffic can at times rival that of much larger cities such as Rome or New York. Boston has far too many vehicles for its roads, and the city's many one-way streets can prove confusing to everyone except the locals, who will honk at befuddled visitors. Although the work to move the I-93 under the city is now complete, expect detours as construction continues in the Waterfront area. Use the Street Finder *(see pp188–91)* or another good map (the best show the direction of one-way streets) to help you get around. Also avoid the rush hours of 8–9:30am and 4–6pm and plan your route in advance so you can concentrate on traffic.

RULES OF THE ROAD

The highway speed limit in the Boston area is 55 mph (88 km/h) – much lower than in many European countries. In residential areas, the speed limit ranges from 20 to 35 mph (32–48 km/h). Near schools, it can be as low as 15 mph (24 km/h). It is important to obey all signs or you will risk getting a ticket. If you are stopped by the police, be courteous or you may face a larger fine. In addition, all drivers are required to carry a valid driver's license and registration documents for their vehicle.

PARKING

Curbside parking is hard to find at the most popular locations, and during morning and afternoon rush hours curbside parking is banned altogether in some areas. If you do manage to find a space on the street, be sure to feed the meter, or you might face a hefty fine. Vehicles parked near fire hydrants, alleyways, in spaces reserved for the handicapped, or at overland "T" and bus stops may be towed away, and you will be able to retrieve them only at considerable cost and inconvenience. Parking at meters is free on Sundays

"Tow Zone" sign

GAS

Compared to much of the rest of the world, gas (petrol) is less expensive in the U.S. However, with the large engines that are often found in older American cars, any savings on fuel may be partially offset. Gas comes in three grades: economy, super, and premium. There are many gas stations in and around Boston, and they often have self-service pumps. The gas at these is often a few cents cheaper per gallon than at pumps with attendants.

BREAKDOWNS

In the unlucky event of a breakdown, the best course of action is to pull off the road completely and put on the hazard lights to alert other drivers that you are stationary. There are emergency phones along some major interstate highways, but in other situations, it is best to contact breakdown services or even the police from land or cell phones. In the event of a breakdown, drivers of rental cars should contact the car rental company first. Members of the **American Automobile Association (AAA)** can contact the association to have their car towed to the nearest service station to be repaired.

CAR RENTAL

You must be at least 21 years old with a valid driving license (plus an international driver's license if from outside the U.S.) to rent a car. Drivers under 25 may be charged additional fees. All rental agencies require a credit card or a cash deposit. Collision and liability insurances are recommended, but they are sometimes offered free with credit cards. Return the car with a full tank of gas to avoid inflated agency fuel prices. Save paying airport fees by picking up and dropping off your car downtown.

GETTING OUT OF BOSTON

Boston holds enough treasures to satisfy even the most finicky of tourists, but any visitor would be wise to escape the city in order to appreciate the area's historical sites, stunning natural beauty, and world-class dining and entertainment options. Fortunately, most of this can be achieved without the use of a car, as public transportation options abound. Nearby cities like Cambridge (*see pp108–14*), and Charlestown (*see p115*), are all easily accessible using

the M.B.T.A.'s subway and bus lines, and the M.B.T.A. commuter rail service links the city with farther-out destinations, including historic Salem and Gloucester, as well as the scenic waterfronts and beaches of Newburyport and Cohasset. The commuter boat system also ferries passengers from the city's waterfront to various stops along the South Shore. Consider renting a bike (which you can bring along on the bus, boat, or train) to explore the historic sites and battlefields in Concord (*see pp116–18*) and Lexington (*see p119*), or the area's scenic coastline. Several bike shops offer daily rentals, and there are a few companies, such as **Urban AdvenTours**, that offer guided bike tours.

Many visitors to the Boston area also take advantage of seasonal excursions. For the summer, Cape Cod and its islands (Martha's Vineyard and Nantucket), not to mention Rhode Island's stunning coastline, are within a 2 hour journey from the city. It's possible to reach these destinations by plane, bus, or boat, but visitors will have an easier time using a rental car. When fall arrives, the areas north of the city – extending up into Vermont, New

Hampshire, and Maine – lure leaf-peepers from all over the world to see breathtaking foliage. Again, to see this region, a car is necessary. Except in the very high season, traffic and parking aren't much of a problem for these getaways.

Amtrak (*see p181*) provides a scenic, albeit slower and usually more expensive, option when it comes to escaping north – the Down-easter service travels along Maine's rugged coastline up to inviting Portland, and south to Rhode Island and Connecticut.

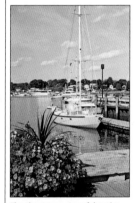

The picturesque, peaceful marina at Newburyport

DIRECTORY

GREEN TRAVEL

Charles River Canoe & Kayak
Kendall Sq., Cambridge.
Tel (617) 492-0941.
www.paddleboston.com

HopStop
www.hopstop.com

M.B.T.A.
10 Park Plaza.
Tel (617) 222-3200.
www.mbta.com

TAXIS

Boston Cab Dispatch, Inc.
Tel (617) 262-2227.

Checker Cab Co. of Cambridge
Tel (617) 497-9000.

Town Taxi
Tel (617) 536-5000.

Yellow Cab
Cambridge.
Tel (617) 547-3000.

GUIDED TOURS

Boston Duck Tours
Prudential Center. **Map** B3. **Tel** (617) 267-3825.
www.ducktours.com

National Park Service
Tel (617) 242-5642.
www.nps.gov/bost

Old Town Trolley Tours
Boston Common Visitors' Center. **Map** 1 C4.
Tel (617) 269-7010.
www.trolleytours.com

BREAKDOWNS

American Automobile Association (AAA)
125 High St., Boston.
Tel (800) 222-4357 or (617) 443-9300.
www.AAA.com

CAR RENTAL

Alamo
Tel (877) 222-9075.
www.alamo.com

Avis
Tel (800) 331-1212.
www.avis.com

Budget
Tel (800) 527-0700.
www.budget.com

Dollar
Tel (800) 800-4000.
www.dollar.com

Enterprise
Tel (800) 736-8222.
www.enterprise.com

Hertz
Tel (800) 654-3131.
www.hertz.com

Thrifty Car Rental
Tel (800) 847-4389.
www.thrifty.com

GETTING OUT OF BOSTON

Urban AdvenTours
103 Atlantic Ave.
Map 2 E3.
Tel (617) 670-0637.
www.urbanadventours.com

BOSTON STREET FINDER

The key map below shows the area of Boston covered by the *Street Finder* maps, which can be found on the following pages only. Map references, given throughout this guide, for sights, restaurants, hotels, shops, and entertainment venues refer to the grid on the maps. The first figure in the map reference indicates which *Street Finder* map to turn to (1 to 4), and the letter and number that follow refer to the grid reference on that map.

KEY

▪	Major sight
▪	Place of interest
▪	Other building
⛴	Ferry boarding point
🚆	Main railroad station
Ⓣ	"T" station
🚌	Bus station
🚕	Taxi rank
P	Parking
ℹ	Tourist information
✚	Hospital with A&E unit
◆	Police station
✝	Church
✉	Post Office
═══	Railroad
——	One-way street
⋯⋯	Pedestrian street

0 meters 1000
0 yards 1000

SCALE OF MAPS 1–4

0 meters 250
0 yards 250

A

A Street	4 F4
Acorn Street	1 B4 & 4 D1
Adams Place	1 B3
African Meeting House	1 C3
Albany Street	4 D5
Anderson Street	1 B3
Appleton Street	3 C3
Arch Street	2 D4 & 4 F1
Arlington Street	1 A4 & 4 D1
Ash Street	2 D4 & 4 F1
Ash Street	4 E3
Athens Street	4 F4
Atlantic Avenue	2 D5 & 4 F2
Avenue De Lafayette	1 C5 & 4 F2
Avery Street	1 C5 & 4 E2

B

B Street	4 F5
Back Bay Station	3 C3
Battery Street	2 E2
Battery Wharf	2 E2
Batterymarch Street	2 D4
Beach Street	1 C5 & 4 E2
Beacon Street	1 A4 & 3 A2
Beaver Place	1 A4 & 4 D1
Bedford Street	2 D5 & 4 F2
Bell Atlantic Building	2 D4
Belvidere Street	3 A3
Benton Street	3 A5
Berkeley Street	1 A4 & 3 C1
Blackstone Block	2 D3

Blackstone Square	3 C5
Blackstone Street	2 D3
Blagden Street	3 C3
Blossom Court	1 B2
Blossom Street	1 B2
Bond Street	4 D4
Boston Athenaeum	1 C4
Boston Center for the Arts	4 D3
Boston Globe Store	2 D4 & 4 F1
Boston Public Library	3 C2
Boston Tea Party Ship	2 E5
Bosworth Street	1 C4 & 4 F1
Bowdoin Street	1 C4
Bowker Street	1 C3
Boylston Street	1 A5 & 3 B3
Braddock Park	3 B3
Bradford Street	4 D4
Branch Street	1 B4 & 4 D1
Brattle Book Shop	1 C4 & 4 E1
Bridge Court	1 B3
Bristol Street	4 E4
Broad Street	2 E4
Broadway	4 F3
Bromfield Street	1 C4 & 4 F1
Burbank Street	3 A4
Burke Street	3 A5
Byron Street	1 B4 & 4 D1

C

Cambria Street	3 A3
Cambridge Street	1 B3
Camden Street	3 B5
Canal Street	2 D2
Cardinal O'Connell Way	1 B2

Causeway Street	1 C2
Cedar Lane Way	1 B4
Center Plaza	1 C3
Central Wharf	2 E3
Chandler Street	4 D3
Charles Street	1 B2
Charles Street Meeting House	1 B4
Charlesbank Park	1 A2
Charlestown Avenue	1 A1
Charter Street	2 D2
Chatham Street	2 D3
Chauncy Street	1 C5 & 4 F2
Chester Park	3 B5
Chestnut Street	1 A4 & 4 D1
Children's Museum	2 E5
Christian Science Center	3 B3
Christopher Columbus Park	2 E3
Church Street	4 D2
City Square	1 C1
Claremont Park	3 B4
Clarendon Street	1 A5 & 3 C1
Clark Street	2 E2
Clearway Street	3 A3
Clinton Street	2 D3
Clough House	2 E2
Colonial Theater	1 B5 & 4 E2
Columbia	2 D5 & 4 F2
Columbus Avenue	1 B5 & 3 A5
Commercial Avenue	1 A2
Commercial Street	2 D1
Commercial Street	2 E3
Commercial Wharf	2 E3
Commonwealth Avenue	3 B2

Concord Street	3 C5
Congress Street	2 D3
Cooper Street	2 D2
Copley Place	3 C3
Copley Square	3 C2
Copp's Hill Burying Ground	2 D2
Cortes Street	4 D3
Cotting Street	1 C2
Court Houses	1 C3
Court Street	2 D3
Coventry Street	3 A5
Cross Street	2 D3
Cross Street	2 E3
Cunard Street	3 A5
Custom House	2 E3
Cutler Majestic Theater	1 C5 & 4 E2

D

Dalton Street	3 A3
Dartmouth Place	3 C3
Dartmouth Street	3 C2
Davenport Street	3 B5
Dedham Street	4 D4
Derne Street	1 C3
Devonshire Street	2 D5 & 4 F1
Dorchester Avenue	4 F5
Dwight Street	4 D4

E

East Street	2 D5 & 4 F2
East Berkeley Street	4 D3
East Brookline Street	4 D5

East Canton Street 4 D5
East Concord Street 3 C5
East Dedham Street 04 D5
East Newton Street 3 C4
East Rutland Street 4 D5
Eastern Avenue 2 E2
Edgerly Road 3 A3
Edinboro Street 2 D5 & 4 F2
Eliot Street 1 B5 & 4 D2
Embankment Road 1 A4
Endicott Street 2 D2
Essex Street 1 C5 & 4 E2
Exchange Place 2 D4
Exeter Street 3 B2

F

Fairfield Street 3 B2
Faneuil Hall 2 D3
Farnsworth Street 2 E5
Fayette Street 4 D3
Federal Street 2 D4 & 4 F1
Filene's Department
  Store 1 C4 & 4 F1
First Baptist Church 1 A5 & 3 C2
Fleet Street 2 E2
Foodmart Road 4 E5
Foster Street 2 D2
Foundry Street 4 F4
Franklin Square 4 D5
Franklin Street 2 D4 & 4 F1
Friend Street 1 C2
Frog Pond 1 B4 & 4 E1
Fruit Street 1 B3
Fulton Street 2 E3

G

Gainsborough Street 3 A4
Garden Court 2 E2
Garden Street 1 B3
Garrison Street 3 B3
Gibson House
  Museum 1 A4 & 3 C1
Gloucester Street 3 A2
Gold Street 4 F4
Government Center 2 D3
Gray Street 4 D3
Greenwich Park 3 B4
Greenwich Street 3 B5
Gridley Street 2 D4
Groton Street 4 E4
Grove Street 1 B3

H

Hamilton Place 1 C4 & 4 E1
Hammond Street 3 B5
Hancock Street 1 C3
Hanover Avenue 2 E2
Hanover Street 2 D3
Hanson Street 4 D4
Harcourt Street 3 B3
Harris Street 2 E2
Harrison Avenue 1 C5 & 3 C5
Harrison Gray Otis House 1 C3
Harvard Street 4 D4
Hatch Shell 1 A4 & 3 C1
Haverhill Street 2 D2
Haviland Street 3 A3
Hawes Street 2 D4
Hawkins Street 1 C3
Hayden Planetarium 1 B2
Hemenway Street 3 A3
Hepzibah Swan
  Houses 1 B4 & 4 E1
Herald Street 4 D3
Hereford Street 3 A2
High Street 2 D5 & 4 F2
Holyoke Street 3 C3
Hoosac Pier 2 D1
Hudson Street 4 F3
Hull Street 2 D2
Huntington Avenue 3 A4
Hynes Convention
  Center 3 B3

I

India Street 2 E3
Industrial Park Road 1 B1
Institute of
  Contemporary Art 3 A3
Irving Street 1 B3
Isabella Street 4 D3

J

J. F. K. Federal Office
  Building 2 D3
Jacob Wirth's 1 B5 & 4 E2
James J. Storrow
  Memorial Drive 3 A2
John Hancock Tower 3 C2
Joy Street 1 C3

K

Keany Square 2 D2
Kendall Street 3 B5
King's Chapel and
  Burying Ground 1 C4
Kingston Street 2 D5 & 4 F2
Kneeland Street 4 F2
Knox Street 4 D3

L

Lagrange Street 1 C5 & 4 E2
Lancaster St 1 C2
Lawrence Street 4 D3
Lechmere Square 1 A1
Lenox Street 3 B5
Lewis Wharf 2 E3
Lime Street 1 A4 & 4 D1
Lincoln Place 3 C5
Lincoln Street 2 D5 & 4 F2
Lincoln Wharf 2 E2
Lombard Place 2 D2
Long Wharf 2 E3
Louisburg Square 1 B4
Lowell Street 1 C2
Lynde Street 1 C3
Lynn Street 2 D2

M

Malden Street 4 D5
Margaret Street 2 D2
Margin Street 2 D2
Marginal Road 4 E3
Marlborough Street 3 A2
Martha Road 1 B2
Mason Street 1 C5 & 4 E1
Massachusetts Avenue 3 A2
Massachusetts State House 1 C4
Massachusetts State Transpor-
  tation Building 1 B5 & 4 E2
Melrose Street 4 D3
Merrimac Street 1 C2
Milford Street 4 D4
Milk Street 2 D4 & 4 F1
Monsignor Reynolds Way 4 D4
Montgomery Street 3 C4
Moon Street 2 E2
Mount Vernon
  Street 1 A4 & 4 D1
Museum of Science 1 A2
Myrtle Street 1 B3

N

Nashua Street 1 C2
Nassau Street 4 E3
New City Hall 2 D3
New England Aquarium 2 E3
New Street 2 F1
New Sudbury Street 1 C3
Newbury Street 1 A5 & 3 A3
Newland Street 3 C4
Nichols House Museum 1 B4
North Bennett Street 2 E2
North End Playground 2 D1
North Grove Street 1 B3
North Square 2 E2
North Station 1 C2

North Street 2 D3
North Street 2 E2
North Washington Street 2 D2
Northampton Street 3 B5
Northern Avenue 2 E5
Northern Traffic Road 1 A2
Norway Street 3 A3

O

Oak Street 4 E3
Old City Hall 2 D4
Old Colony Avenue 4 F5
Old Granary Burying
  Ground 1 C4 & 4 E1
Old North Church 2 E2
Old Northern Avenue 2 E4
Old South Meeting
  House 2 D4 & 4 F1
Old State House 2 D4
Old West Church 1 C3
Oliver Street 2 D4
Omni Parker House 1 C4 & 4 E1
Opera House 1 C5 & 4 E1
Otis Place 1 A4 & 4 D1
Otis Street 2 D5 & 4 F1
Oxford Street 1 C5 & 4 F2

P

Parmenter Street 2 D2
Park Place 1 C4 & 4 E1
Park Plaza 1 B5 & 4 D2
Park Square 1 B5 & 4 D2
Park Street 1 C4 & 4 E1
Park Street Church 1 C4 & 4 E1
Parkman Street 1 B3
Paul Place 4 D3
Paul Revere House 2 E2
Paul Revere Mall 2 E2
Pearl Street 2 D4
Pemberton Square 1 C3
Pembroke Street 3 C4
Perry Street 4 E4
Phillips Street 1 B3
Piedmont Street 4 D2
Pinckney Street 1 B3
Pine Street 4 E3
Pittsburgh Street 2 F5
Plympton Street 4 D5
Portland Street 1 C2
Post Office Square 2 D4
Prince Street 2 D2
Providence Street 1 A5 & 3 C2
Prudential Center 3 B3
Purchase Street 2 D5

Q

Quincy Market 2 D3

R

Randolph Street 4 E4
Revere Street 1 B3
Richmond Street 2 E3
Ridgeway Lane 1 C3
River Street 1 B4 & 4 D1
Rowes Wharf 2 E4
Rutland Street 3 C4

S

Salem Street 2 D2
Sargents Wharf 2 E2
Savoy Street 4 E4
School Street 2 D4 & 4 F1
Science Park 1 A2
Scotia Street 3 A3
Shawmut Avenue 3 C5
Sheafe Street 2 D2
Shubert Theater 1 C5 & 4 E2
Silver Street 4 F4
Sleeper Street 2 E5
Snow Place 2 D4 & 4 F1
Snow Hill Street 2 D2
Somerset Street 1 C4
South Charles Street 1 B5 & 4 E2
South Russell Street 1 B3

South Station 2 D5
South Street 2 D5 & 4 F2
Springfield Street 3 B5
St. Botolph Street 3 A4
St. Cecelia Street 3 A3
St. Charles Street 4 D3
St. George Street 4 D5
St. Germain Street 3 A3
St. James Avenue 1 A5 & 3 C2
St. Paul's Cathedral 1 C4 & 4 E1
St. Stephen Street 3 A4
St. Stephen's Church 2 E2
Stanhope Street 4 D3
Staniford Street 1 C3
State Street 2 D3
Stillings Street 2 F5
Stillman Street 2 D2
Stuart Street 1 B5 & 4 D2
Summer Street 2 D5 & 4 F1
Sumner Street 2 F1
Symphony Hall 3 A4
Symphony Road 3 A4

T

Taylor Street 4 D4
TDBankNorth Garden 1 C2
Temple Place 1 C4 & 4 E1
Temple Street 1 C3
Thatcher Street 2 D2
Thayer Street 4 E4
Tileston Street 2 E2
Traveler Street 4 E4
Traverse Street 1 C2
Tremont Street 1 C5, 3 A5,
  & 4 E2
Trinity Church 1 A5 & 3 C2
Trinity Place 3 C2
Tufts Street 2 D5 & 4 F2
Tyler Street 1 C5 & 4 E3

U

Union Park 4 D4
Union Park Street 4 D4
Union Street 2 D3
Union Wharf 2 E2
Unity Street 2 E2
Upton Street 4 D4
Utica Street 2 D5 & 4 F2

W

W. E. Mullins Way 4 E3
Walnut Street 1 B4 & 4 E1
Waltham Street 4 D4
Wang Center for the
  Performing Arts 4 E2
Wareham Street 4 D5
Warrenton Street 1 B5 & 4 E2
Warren Avenue 3 C4
Warwick Street 3 B5
Washington Street 1 C5 & 3 C5
Water Street 2 D1
Water Street 2 D4 & 4 F1
Wellington Street 3 B4
West Street 1 C4 & 4 E1
West 2nd Street 4 F4
West 4th Street 4 F4
West 5th Street 4 F4
West 6th Street 4 F5
West 7th Street 4 F5
West Brookline Street 3 C4
West Canton Street 3 C3
West Cedar Street 1 B4
West Newton Street 3 B3
West Rutland Square 3 B4
Westland Avenue 3 A4
Widett Circle 4 E5
Winchester Street 4 D2
Winter Street 1 C4 & 4 E1
Worcester Square 3 C5
Worcester Street 3 C5

Y

Yarmouth Street 3 C3

General Index

Page numbers in **bold** type
refer to main entries

A

Aalto, Alvar 109
Abbey, Edward 97
Abiel Smith School 49, 169
Academy of Music 87
Accessories shops 155
Adams, Abigail 22
Adams, John 22, 31
Adams, John Quincy 22, 31
Adams, Samuel 30
  Boston Tea Party 59, 75
  Faneuil Hall 63
  grave of 48
  Hancock-Clarke House
    (Lexington) 119
  Massachusetts State House 50
  Paul Revere's ride 21
  "Sons of Liberty" 20
  statue of 63
Aeolian-Skinner Company 98
African Meeting House 23, 49
Agassiz, Louis 114
Air travel **180**, 181
AirlineConsolidator.com
  180, 181
Airports 180, 181
Alamo 185
Alan Bilzerian 154, 155
Alberts-Langdon Inc 156, 157
Alcohol **174**
  in restaurants 139
Alcott, Louisa May 31
  Orchard House
    (Concord) 118
  Sleepy Hollow Cemetery
    (Concord) 118
  The Wayside
    (Concord) 118
Algonquin Indians 17
Along the Battle Road
  (Rush) 116
Ambulances 177
American Apparel 154, 155
American Association of Retired
  Persons (A.A.R.P.) 175
American Automobile
  Association (AAA) 185
American Express Travel
  Service 178
American Federation of Labor
  (A.F.L.) 24
American football **166**, 167
American Meteorological
  Society 45
American Repertory Theater
  160, 161
American Revolution **20–21**
  Boston Tea Party 75
  Concord 116–17
  Copp's Hill Burying Ground
  70

American Revolution (cont.)
  Dorchester Heights
    Monument 122
  Freedom Trail 124–7
  Harvard Yard 110
  Lexington 119
  Liberty Tree 83
  Old North Church 71
American Unitarian
  Association 22
Ames Hotel 133
Amtrak 181
An Tua Nua 162, 163
Andover Shop 154, 155
Andros, Sir Edmund 18, 19
Angelino, Fra
  (Christ on the Cross) 113
Angell, George Thorndike 64–5
Ann Taylor 154, 155
Annual Festival Betances 35
Annual Lantern Celebration 34
Anthem 143
Anthropologie 154, 155
Antico Forno 143
Antiques
  Ellis Memorial Antiques
    Show 36
  shops **156**, 157
Aquariums, New England
  Aquarium 11, 27,29, **76–7**, 170
Arboretums, Arnold
  Arboretum **102–3**, 170
Archaeology, Peabody
  Museum of Archaeology and
  Ethnology (Cambridge) 114
Architecture 32–3
Area codes, telephones 179
Arnold Arboretum **102–3**
  Children's Boston 170
  Lilac Sunday 34
Ars Libri Ltd 156, 157
Art Deco architecture 33
Artful Hand Gallery 157
Arts First 34
Artù 142
ATMs (Automated Teller
  Machines) 178
August Moon Festival 35, 79
Australian Consulate 177
Avis 185

B

B & G Oysters 146
Baby Gap 171
Back Bay Bicycles 164, 165
Back Bay Fens 103
Back Bay Hotel 135
Back Bay and South End **88–99**
  architecture 33
  area map 89
  hotels 134–6
  restaurants 146–8
  Street-by-Street map 90–91
  Trinity Church 94–5

Baez, Joan 108
Ball, Thomas 46
Ballet **160–61**
  Boston Ballet Season 36
  José Mateo's Ballet Theater
    161
Banana Republic 154, 155
Bank of America 178
Bank of America Pavilion 159
Banking 178
Banner, Peter 48
Barking Crab 144
Barney's New York 154, 155
Bars **151**, **162–3**
  gay clubs and bars 163
  tipping in 174
Bartholdi, Auguste 92
Baseball 34, **166**, 167
Basketball 36, **166**, 167
Bastille Day 35
Bates, Katharine Lee 48
Bauhaus 113
Bay Village 85
Beaches 122, 164
Beacon Hill Hotel and Bistro
  132, 142
Beacon Hill Skate Shop 165
Beacon Hill and West End
  27, **40–53**
  architecture 32
  area map 41
  Boston Common and Public
    Garden 46–7
  Hidden Gardens of Beacon
    Hill 34
  hotels 132
  Massachusetts State House
    50–51
  Mount Vernon Street 44
  restaurants 142–3
  Street-by-Street map 42–3
Beacon Press 45
Beacon Street **45**
  Street-by-Street map 43
BeanTown Jazz Festival 36
Beanpot Tournament 37
Beckmann, Max 113
Bed and breakfast (B&B) 131
Bed and Breakfast Agency
  of Boston 131
Bed and Breakfast Associates
  Bay Colony Ltd 131
Beech Tree Inn 136
Bell, Alexander Graham 31, **65**
  Government Center 62
  Verizon Building 65
Ben and Jerry's 150, 151
Benjamin, Asher 32
  African Meeting House 49
  Charles Street Meeting
    House 44
  Old West Church 52
  William Hickling Prescott
    House 45

Beranek 31
La Berceuse (Van Gogh) 106
Berenson, Bernard 103
Bergman, Ingrid 86
Berkeley Perk 150, 151
Berklee Performance Center **97**, 162, 163
Berk's 155
Berlin, Irving 84
Bernhardt, Sarah 86
Bernini, Gian Lorenzo, Model 112
Best Western 131
Best Western Roundhouse Suites 136
Betsey Jenney 154, 155
Betty's Wok & Noodle 148
Bicycling **164**, 165, **183**
Bin 26 Enoteca 142
Bina Osteria 145
Black Heritage Trail **49**, 169
Black Masons 126
Blackall, Clarence H.
    Colonial Theater 84
    Metropolitan Theater 86
Blackstone Block 63
Blackstone Memorial Tablet 47
Blackstone, William 19
    Boston Common and Public Garden 46
Blaschka, Leopold and Rudolph 114
Blue Ginger 149
Blue Hills Ski Area 165
Blues music **162**, 163
Boats and ships
    Boat Programs (New England Aquarium) 76
    Boston Tea Party Ship 29, 66, **74–5**, 169
    Charlestown Navy Yard **115**, 127
    Dragon Boat Festival 35
    Head of the Charles Regatta 36
    rowing 167
    U.S.S. *Constitution* (Charlestown) 115
    water sports **164**, 165
Bobby from Boston 155
Bogart, Humphrey 86
Boing – JP's Toy Shop 171
BoltBus 181
Bond 143
Bond, Charles 86
Bookshops
    Boston International Antiquarian Book Fair 36
    Brattle Book Shop 80, **83**
Booth, John Wilkes 58
BosTix 158, 159
Boston Antique Cooperative I and II 156, 157
Boston Athenaeum 22, **49**

Boston Athletic Club 165
Boston Ballet Company 36, 160–61
Boston Bruins 166, 167
Boston by Foot 168, 169
Boston Cab Dispatch Inc. 185
Boston Caribbean Carnival 35
Boston Celtics 166, 167
Boston Center for the Arts **99**, 160, 161
Boston Children's Museum 169, 175
Boston Children's Theater 170, 171
Boston City Hall 62
Boston CitySearch 175, 182
Boston Common and Public Garden 10, 11, 27, 34, **46–7**
    Children's Boston 170
    Emerald Necklace 103
    Freedom Trail 124
Boston Duck Tours 11, 168, 183
Boston Fashion Week 36
The Boston Globe 179, 182
Boston Granite style architecture **32**, 53
Boston Green Tourism 175
Boston Harbor (Lane) 106
Boston Harbor Cruises 168, 169
Boston Harbor Hotel 133
Boston Harbor Islands National Park Area 165
Boston Harborfest 35
Boston International Antiquarian Book Fair 36
Boston International Youth Hostel 131
Boston Jewish Film Festival 36
Boston Landing 152, 153
Boston Latin School 18, 19
Boston Lyric Opera 160, 161
Boston Marathon 34, **167**
    Copley Square 96
Boston Massacre (1770) 20, **61**, 75
    Freedom Trail 125
    Reenactment of Boston Massacre 34
Boston Open Studios 36
Boston Park Plaza 134
Boston Parks and Recreation Department 165
Boston Police Strike (1919) 24
Boston Pops 34
    Annual Fourth of July Concert and Fireworks 35, 92
Boston Pride 35
Boston Public Garden
    see Boston Common and Public Garden
Boston Public Library **96–7**
    architecture 32
    history 22, 23
    Street-by-Street map 90

Boston Red Sox 25, 34, 166, 167
Boston Restaurant Week 35
"Boston School" 106
Boston Symphony Orchestra 11, 36, 160, 161
    history 24
Boston Tea Party (1773) 20, **75**
    Liberty Tree 83
    Old South Meeting House 59
    Reenactment of the Boston Tea Party 37
Boston Tea Party Ships & Museum **74–5**
    Children's Boston 169
Boston University 24
Boston Wine Expo 37
Bouchée 146
Boylston Street 10, **96**
    Street-by-Street map 90
Bradford, William 18
Bradstreet, Anne 31
Brahmins, Boston 30, 45
Brando, Marlon 89
Brasserie Jo 146
Brattle Book Shop 80, **83**, 156, 157
Brattle Theater 161
Breakdowns **184**, 185
Breakfast 138
    in hotels 130
Brewer Fountain 47
Bricco 144
Bridges, Lagoon Bridge 46
Brinks Robbery (1950) 72
The Bristol Lounge 150, 151
British Consulate 177
Bromfield Pen Shop 156, 157
Brooks Brothers 154–5
Brooks, Phillips 95
Bryn Mawr Bookstore 156, 157
Buckman Tavern (Lexington) 119
Budget (car rental) 185
Budget hotels 131
Bulfinch, Charles 32, **53**
    Beacon Hill 44
    Bulfinch Pavilion and Ether Dome 53
    Faneuil Hall 63
    Federal Street Theater 87
    Harrison Gray Otis House 29, 52
    Harvard University 110
    Hepzibah Swan Houses 43, 45
    Massachusetts State House 50, 51, 124
    Mount Vernon Street 44
    Nichols House Museum 45
    St. Paul's Cathedral 82
    St. Stephen's Church 69, 72
Bulfinch Hotel 132

Bunker Hill, Battle of
  (1775) 20
  Bunker Hill Day 37
  Bunker Hill Monument
    (Charlestown) **115**, 127
  Bunker Hill Weekend 35
  Central Burying Ground 47
  Freedom Trail 127
Burberry 154, 155
Burgoyne, General John 59
Burne-Jones, Edward 94, 95
The Burren 162, 163
Burying Grounds
  see Cemeteries.
Busch-Reisinger Museum
  (Cambridge) 112–13
Buses 181, 182
Business travelers, hotels 131

C
Cabot, Edward Clarke 49
Cabot, John 17
Cabot Family 22, 30
Café Pamplona 150, 151
Café Vanille 150, 151
Cafés **150–51**
Caffè Pompei 150, 151
Caffè Vittoria 150, 151
Calder, Alexander 11, 121
Caldwell, Sarah 83
Calliope 171
Cambridge 101, **108–14**
  Four Great Days in Boston 11
  Harvard University museums
    11, **112–14**
  Harvard Yard 11, **110–11**
  map 109
  restaurants 148–9
Cambridge Antiques Market
  156, 157
Cambridge Artist's Cooperative
  157
Cambridge Athletic Club 165
Cambridge Carnival 36
Cambridge Common 108
Cambridge Office for Tourism
  175
Cambridge River Festival 35
Cambridgeside Galleria
  152, 153
Canadian Consulate 177
Cantab Lounge 162, 163
Carmen 144
Carpenter Center for the
  Visual Arts (Cambridge) **111**
  architecture 33
Cars **184–5**
  breakdowns **184**, 185
  driving to Boston 181
  gas **184**
  hotel parking 130
  parking **184**
  rental **185**
Carson Beach 122

Carver, Governor John 18
Casablanca
  (Cambridge) 149
The Cask 'N' Flagon 163
Castle Island 123
Cathedrals, St Paul's Cathedral
  80, **82**
Celebrity Series 160, 161
Cemeteries
  Central Burying Ground 47
  Copp's Hill Burying Ground
    68, **70**, 126
  King's Chapel and Burying
    Ground 56, **58**, 124
  Old Granary Burying
    Ground **48**, 124
  Sleepy Hollow Cemetery
    (Concord) 118
Center Plaza 62
Central Burying Ground 47
Chain hotels 131
Chandler Inn Hotel 134
Chanel 154, 155
Channing, William Ellery
  American Unitarian
    Association 22
  statue of 46
Charles I, King of England 18
Charles II, King of England
  18, 19
Charles Hayden Planetarium
  53
Charles Hotel 137
Charles River Canoe & Kayak
  Center 164, 165, 185
Charles Street **44**
  Street-by-Street map 42
Charles Street Inn 132
Charles Street Meeting House
  44
  Street-by-Street map 42
Charlesmark Hotel 135
Charlestown 101, **115**
  Freedom Trail 127
  restaurants 149
Charlestown Navy Yard **115**
  architecture 32
  Freedom Trail 127
Charlie card 182
Charlie ticket 182
Chau Chow City 145
Cheaptickets.com 180, 181
Checker Cab Co of Cambridge
  185
Cheesecake Factory, The 171
Chestnut Street,
  architecture 32
Children **168–71**, 175
  Four Great Days in Boston 11
  in hotels 131
  in restaurants 139
Children's Book Shop 171
Children's Museum 11, **75**
China Pearl 171

Chinatown and Theater
  District **78–87**
  area map 79
  Chinatown 84–5
  History of Boston's
    Theater District 87
  hotels 134
  Liberty Tree 83
  restaurants 145
  Street-by-Street map 80–81
Chinese New Year 37
Christ Church
  (Cambridge) 108
Christ Episcopal Church
  see Old North Church
Christian Science Center 98–9
Christina's 150, 151
Christmas 37
Christopher Columbus Park
  10, **73**
Church of England 18
Churches
  Christ Church
    (Cambridge) 108
  Christian Science Center
    98–9
  Church of the Covenant 93
  First Baptist Church 33, 91,
    92–3
  King's Chapel 10, **124**
  Memorial Church
    (Cambridge) 111
  New Old South Church 96
  Old North Church 10, 27,
    34, 68, **71**, 126
  Old West Church 52
  Park Street Church 48, 124
  St. Stephen's Church 69, **72**
  Trinity Church
    10, 27, 32, 33, 91, **94–5**
  see also Cathedrals; Meeting
    houses
Ciao Bella 146
Cigarettes 174
Cinema 161
Citizens Bank 178
City Hall *see* New City Hall;
  Old City Hall
City Sports 164, 165
City Square (Charlestown) 115
City Water Taxi 180, 181
Civil War 23, 24
  Soldiers and Sailors
    Monument 47
Classical music **160**, 161
Clayton & Bell 94
Climate 34–5
Clio 147
Clothes, fashion shops 154–5
Clothware 154, 155
Clough, Ebenezer 68, 70
Clough House **70**
  Street-by-Street map 68
Club Passim 162, 163

Clubs
  comedy clubs 163
  gay clubs and bars 163
  nightclubs **162**, 163
Cobb, Henry 97
Coconut Grove 85
College sports 167
Colonial Boston,
  Street-by-Street map 56–7
Colonial Theatre
  11, **84**, 160, 161
Colonnade Hotel 135
Columbus, Christopher
  Christopher Columbus Park
  73
  statue of 44
Columbus Day 37
Columbus Day Parade 36
Comedy clubs 163
Comedy Connection 163
Commonwealth Avenue **93**
  architecture 33
  Street-by-Street map 91
Commonwealth Court Guest
  House 131, 134
Commonwealth Shakespeare
  Company 159
Communications 179
Community Bicycle Supply
  164, 165
Community Boating 164, 165
Concierge of Boston 152–3
Concord 101, **116–18**
  map 117
Concord Museum 117
Constitution, U.S.S.
  (Charlestown) **115**
  Freedom Trail 127
Constitution Inn 136
Constitutional Convention
  (1787) 22
Consulates 177
Continental Army
  Cambridge Common
  (Cambridge) 108
  Christ Church
  (Cambridge) 108
Continental Congress (1774)
  21
Coolidge, Calvin 31
Cooperatives, antiques
  156, 157
Copley, John Singleton
  Copley Square 96
  Museum of Fine Arts, Boston
  106
  *Portrait of John
  Hancock* 104
Copley Place 10, **99**
  shopping mall 152, 153
Copley Square 10, **96**
  Street-by-Street map 90
Copley Square Hotel 135
Copp, William 70

Copp's Hill, Freedom Trail 126
Copp's Hill Burying Ground **70**
  Freedom Trail 126
  Street-by-Street map 68
Cornwallis, General 21
Cornwell, Dean, *Telephone
  Men and Women at Work* 65
Cortereal, Miguel 17
CRAFTBOSTON Holiday 37
Crafts shops 157
Craigie on Main (Cambridge)
  149
Crease, Thomas 59
Credit cards **178**
  in restaurants 139
  security 176
  in shops 152
Crema Café 150, 151
Crime 176
Curious George Books & Toys
  171
Curley, James Michael 25, 31
  Beacon Hill 45
  elected mayor 24
  L Street Bath House 122
  Old City Hall 59
Currency exchange 178
Custom House 54, **64**, 73, 74
Cutler Majestic Theater
  159, 161
CVS Pharmacy 168, 177
Cycling **164**, 165, **183**

D

Dado Tea 150, 151
Dallin, Cyrus 72
Dance **160–61**
  Boston Ballet Season 36
Dance at Bougival
  (Renoir) 105
Dance Complex 161
Danish Country 156, 157
Davis, Stuart 106
Days Hotel Boston 136
Days Inn 131
Declaration of Independence
  21
Decor International 156, 157
Degas, Edgar
  Fogg Art Museum
  (Cambridge) 112
  Museum of Fine Arts, Boston
  106
Dentists 177
Department of Conservation
  and Recreation 164, 165
Department stores **152–3**
  Macy's 81
Dickens, Charles 58
Disabled visitors **174**
  entertainment 159
  in hotels **131**
  in restaurants 139
Discos **162**, 163

Discounts
  air travel 180
  clothes shops 154–5
  discount stores 153
  hotels 131
  students 175
Dix, Dorothea 30
DKNY 154, 155
Doctors 177
Dollar (car rental) 185
Dorchester Heights Monument
  122
Douglass, Frederick
  African Meeting House 49
  anti-slavery speeches 23
Dove, Arthur 106
Downtown Crossing **82**
  Street-by-Street map 81
Dragon Boat Festival 35
Drinks
  see Food and drink
Driving in Boston **184–5**
Drowne, Shem 63
Drugstores 177
Druid 163
Duckling Day Parade 34
Dukakis, Michael 25
Durgin-Park 10, **143**
Dyer, Mary 18, 19, 30

E

Eakins, Thomas 106
East Coast Grill
  (Cambridge) 149
East India Company
  Boston Tea Party 20, **75**
  Boston Tea Party Ship 74
Easy Chairs 156, 157
Eddie Bauer 154, 155
Eddy, Asa Gilbert 98
Eddy, Mary Baker 98
Edgerton, Harold 109
Electricity 175
Eliot Suites Hotel 135
Ellis Memorial Antiques Show
  36
Email 179
Emerald Necklace 11, **103**
Emergencies 176, 177
Emerson, Ralph Waldo 22, 31
  Concord Museum 117
  Emerson House
  (Concord) 116
  First Baptist Church 92
  Old Corner Bookstore 59
  The Old Manse (Concord) 117
  Omni Parker House 58
  Sleepy Hollow Cemetery
  (Concord) 118
Emmanuel Church 93
Emmanuel Music 160, 161
Enterprise (car rental) 185
Entertainment **158–63**
  general information 158–9

Epstein, Leslie 31
Erikson, Leif 17, 93
Ernesto's Pizzeria 143
The Esplanade 92
Ether Monument 46
Etheridge, Melissa 97
Etiquette
   in restaurants 139
Eugene Galleries 156, 157
Evacuation of Boston (1776) 21
Evacuation Day 37
Exploritas 175

F

463 Beacon Street
   Guest-House 134
Fairmont Battery Wharf 133
Fairmont Copley Plaza Hotel
   135
Fall in Boston 36
La Famiglia Giorgio 144
Faneuil, Peter
   Faneuil Hall **63**, 125
   grave of 48
Faneuil Hall **63**
   Freedom Trail 125
Farragut, David, statue
   120, **122**
Fashion shops 154–5
Fast food 139
Feast of Saints Cosma &
   Damiano 36
Federal Street Theater 87
Federal style architecture 32
Feininger, Lyonel 113
Fenollosa, Ernest 107
Fenway Park
   Children's Boston 168, 169
   history 24, 25
Festivals 34–7
Fielder, Arthur 92
Fields, W.C. 86
XV Beacon 133
Figs 142
Filene's Basement 153, 154, 155
Finale 150, 151
Financial District
   see Old Boston and
   the Financial District
Fire Service 177
First Baptist Church **92–3**
   architecture 33
   Street-by-Street map 91
First Night 37
First Public School,
   Freedom Trail 125
Fitcorp 165
Fitness Facilities 165
Fitzgerald, John F. "Honey Fitz"
   elected mayor 24, 25
   Old City Hall 59
Flour Bakery & Café 150, 151
Fogg Art Museum (Cambridge)
   112–13

Folk music **162**, 163
Food and drink
   alcohol 139, **174**
   Flavors of Boston 140–41
   What to Drink 141
   see also Restaurants
Foot Paths 155
Ford, Henry 86
Fort Independence 123
Fort Wagner, Battle of (1861)
   23
Four Great Days in Boston
   10–11
Four Seasons 134
Fourth of July 35
Franklin, Benjamin 48
   Blackstone Block 63
   statue of 59
   Unity Street 70
Franklin Park 103
Franklin Park Zoo **102**, 170
Freedom Trail 124–7
Freeport Merchants
   Association 153
French, Daniel Chester 96
   Minute Man statue
   (Concord) 116
   Sleepy Hollow Cemetery
   (Concord) 118
French and Indian War (1754)
   19
Fresh Pond Golf Course 165
A Friendly Inn 136
Fritz Lounge 163
Frog Pond,
   Ice Skating on Frog Pond 36
Full Moon 171
Fuller, Margaret,
   Old Corner Bookstore 59

G

Galbraith, John Kenneth 31
Galleries
   see Museums and galleries
Games People Play 171
Gap 154, 155
Gardens
   see Parks and gardens
Gardner, Cato 49
Gardner, Isabella Stewart 24
   Isabella Stewart Gardner
   Museum 28, **103**
Garrison, William Lloyd 30
   abolition of slavery 23
   The Liberator 23
   Museum of African American
   History 49
   Park Street Church 48
   statue of 93
Gas 184
Gay clubs and bars 163
Gehry, Frank, Stata Center 121
George III, King of England 70
George Middleton House 49

George Washington Statue 46
Gershwin, George 87
Getting out of Boston **185**
Gibson, Catherine Hammond
   92
Gibson, Charles Hammond Jr.
   92
Gibson House Museum **92**
   architecture 33
Gift shops 157
Gilbert and Sullivan 87
Gilman, Arthur 93
Giorgio Armani 154, 155
Gloss, Kenneth 83
Golf **164**, 165
Gompers, Samuel 24
The Good Life 151
Gosnold, Bartholomew 17
Government Center 62
Granary Burying Ground see
   Old Granary Burying Ground
Grand Canal (nightclub) 162,
   163
Grant, Cary 86
Great Brinks Robbery (1950) 72
Great Fire of Boston (1872) 24
Greater Boston Convention
   and Visitors' Bureau
   174, 175, 181, 182
El Greco 106
Greek Revival architecture 32
Green Street Studios 161
Green travel **182**, 185
Greyhound Bus Lines 181
Greyhound racing 167
Grill 23 147
Grolier Poetry Book Shop
   156, 157
Gropius, Walter 33
   Busch-Reisinger Museum
   (Cambridge) 113
Guided tours 183
Gullager, Christian 71
Gund, Graham 97
Gyms 165
Gypsy Bar 162, 163

H

H & M 154, 155
Hadzi, Dmitry 62
Hale, Edward Everett,
   statue of 46
Hall, Prince, grave of 70, 126
Hamersley's Bistro 147
Hancock, John
   Continental Congress 21
   grave of 48, 124
   Hancock-Clarke House
   (Lexington) 119
   Old State House 61
   portrait of 104
Handel, George Frideric 87
Handel & Haydn Society
   160, 161

Hanover Street,
  Street-by-Street map 69
Harborside Inn 132
Harrison Gray Otis House
  architecture 32
  see also Otis House Museum
Harrison, Peter 108
Harrison, Rex 86
Hart Nautical Gallery
  (Cambridge) 109
Hartt, Edmund, grave of 70
Harvard, John
  Harvard University 19, 110
  John Harvard Mall
  (Charlestown) 115
  statue of 110
Harvard Film Archive 161
Harvard Medical School 53
Harvard Museum of Natural
  History (Cambridge) 114
Harvard Square (Cambridge)
  108
Harvard Square Hotel 136
Harvard University
  architecture 32
  Arnold Arboretum 102–3
  Boston's Top Ten 27
  Harvard Yard 11, **110–11**
  history 18, 19, 24
  museums 11, 28, **112–14**
  Visitors' Checklist 111
Harvard's Hasty Pudding Club
  Parades 37
Hatch Memorial Shell 92
  Performing Arts Series at the
  Hatch Shell 35
Hawthorne, Nathaniel 22
  Longfellow National Historic
  Site (Cambridge) 108
  Old Corner Bookstore 59
  The Old Manse (Concord)
  117
  Omni Parker House 58
  The Scarlet Letter 58
  Sleepy Hollow Cemetery
  (Concord) 118
  The Wayside (Concord) 118
Hayden, Harriet 49
Hayden, Lewis 23, 49
Haynes, W.S. 85
Head of the Charles Regatta
  36, 167
Head Island light pavilion 123
Health care 177
Healy, *Liberty and Union,
  Now and Forever* 63
Helen's Leather 155
Henry Bear's Park 171
Hepzibah Swan Houses **45**
  architecture 32
  Street-by-Street map 43
Here-There (Noland) 121
Heritage on the Garden
  152, 153

Hertz 185
Hidden Gardens of Beacon
  Hill 34
Higginson, Major Henry Lee 30
Hilton Boston Financial District
  133
Historic New England 52
Historical Society Houses
  (Lexington) 119
History 17–25
Ho Chi Minh 30
  Omni Parker House 58
Hockey 36
Holiday Inn Express 136
Holiday Inn Select
  Government Center 132
Holidays, Public 37
Holmes, Oliver Wendell
  22, 30, **45**
  Massachusetts State House 50
Holmes Alley 49
Holyoke Center, architecture 33
Homer, Winslow 106
HopStop 182, 185
Horse racing 166
Hospitals 177
  Massachusetts General
  Hospital 53
Host Homes of Boston 131
Hostels 131
Hotel 140 135
Hotel Commonwealth 137
Hotel Indigo 136
Hotel Marlowe 137
Hotel Onyx 132
Hotel Tria 137
Hotel Veritas 137
Hotels **130–37**
  Back Bay and South End
  134–5
  Beacon Hill and West End 132
  Chinatown and Theater
  District 134
  Farther afield 136–7
  general information 130–31
  North End and Waterfront
  133–4
  Old Boston and Financial
  District 132–3
  taxes 130, 174
  tipping in 174
House of Blues 162, 163
Howe, Elias 31
Howe, Julia Ward 30
  Old Corner Bookstore 59
Howe, Dr Samuel Gridley 45
Howells, William Dean,
  Old Corner Bookstore 59
Hungry Mother 148
Huntington Theater
  10, **160**, 161
Hutchinson, Anne 30
  banished from Boston 18, 19
Hutchinson, Thomas 75

Hyatt Harborside 137
Hyatt Regency Boston
  Financial District 134
Hynes Convention Center 96

I

Ice cream parlors 150–51
Ice hockey **166**, 167
Ice skating 165
  Ice Skating on Frog Pond 36
Il Casale 149
Independence Day 37
The Independent
  (nightclub) 162, 163
Inn at Harvard 137
Institute of Contemporary Art
  29, 66, 74
Insurance 177
InterContinental Hotel 134
International Poster Gallery 157
International Student Identity
  Card (I.S.I.C.) 175
Internet 179
  useful websites 175
Irish Consulate 177
Irish Famine memorial **59**
  Street-by-Street map 56
Irving House 137
Isaac Harding House 137
Isabella Stewart Gardner
  Museum 10, 100, 101, **103**
  Boston's Best: Museums 28
Italian Feast Days 35

J

J. Press 154, 155
Jackson, Lydia 116
Jacob Wirth **85**, 145
  bar 151
Jacques 163
Jamaica Pond 103
James, Henry,
  Mount Vernon Street 44
James I, King of England 17
James II, King of England 18, 19
James, Henry 31
James, Thomas 86
James, William 31
Jasper White's Summer Shack
  146
Jazz **162**, 163
  Boston Globe Jazz and Blues
  Festival 35
Jews, New England Holocaust
  Memorial 63
JMW Gallery 156, 157
Joe Moakley Park 122
Jogging 164
John F. Kennedy Library and
  Museum 25, **102**
  Boston's Best: Museums 29
John F. Kennedy National
  Historic Site 103
John Hancock Tower 27, **97**

John Harvard Mall
(Charlestown) 115
John Jeffries House 132
Johnny D's Uptown Restaurant
& Music Club 162, 163
Johnson, Philip 97
Joie de Vivre 157
Jones, Quincy 97
Jordan Hall 159
Jos. A. Bank Clothiers 154, 155
José Mateo's Ballet
Theater 161
J.P. Licks 150, 151
Judith Dowling Asian Art
156, 157

K

Kallmann, McKinnell and
Knowles 62
Kandinsky, Wassily 113
Kate Spade 154, 155
Kayak.com 180, 181
Keayne, Robert 60
Keayne Hall 60
Keezer's 155
Keith, B.F. 83
Kellet, Rev. P. 70
Kendall Hotel 136
Kendall Square Cinema 161
Kennedy, Edward M. 25, 31
Kennedy, John F. 25, 31
assassination 62
John F. Kennedy Library
and Museum 25, 29, **102**
John F. Kennedy National
Historic Site 103
Union Oyster House 63
Kennedy, Robert F. 25, 31
John F. Kennedy Library
and Museum 102
Kennedy, Rose Fitzgerald
103
Kent, Corita 123
King and I 142
King, Martin Luther Jr,
Walden Pond State
Reservation (Concord) 118
King's Chapel and Burying
Ground 10, **58**
Freedom Trail 124
Street-by-Street map 56
Kings 163
Kittery Outlets 153
Klee, Paul 113
Kokoschka, Oskar 113
Kresge Auditorium and Chapel
33

L

L'Espalier 148
L Street Bath House 122
L.A. Burdick's Handmade
Chocolates 150, 151
Labor Day 37

Ladder District **82–3**
Street-by-Street map 81
LaFarge, John, Trinity Church
94, 95
Lafayette, Marquis de 85
Lagoon Bridge 46
Lala Rokh 142
Lamb, Thomas 83
Land, Edwin H. 31
Lane, Fitz Hugh, *Boston
Harbor* 106
Langham Boston Hotel 133
Lannan Ship Model Gallery
156, 157
Law enforcement 176
Le Corbusier, Carpenter Center
for the Visual Arts
(Cambridge) 33, 111
Le Méridien (Cambridge) 137
Le's (Cambridge) 148
Lee, General Robert E. 23
Legal assistance 177
Legal Sea Foods 145
Lehane, Dennis 31
Lenox Hotel 135
Lewis and Clark expedition 114
Lewis and Harriet Hayden
House 49
Lewitt, Sol 114
Lexington 101, **119**
Lexington Battle Green 119
Liberty Hotel 132
Liberty Tree **83**
*Liberty and Union, Now and
Forever* (Healy) 63
Libraries
Boston Athenaeum 49
Boston Public Library
22, 23, 32, 90, **96–7**
John F. Kennedy Library and
Museum 25, 29, **102**
Widener Library
(Cambridge) 110
Life is Good 154, 155
Light-Space Modulator
(Moholy-Nagy) 112
Lilac Sunday 34
Lincoln, Abraham
assassination 23, 58
Civil War 23
List Visual Arts Center
(Cambridge) **109**, 121
Little, Malcolm
see Malcolm X
Live Nation Tickets 158, 159
Lizzy's Ice Cream 150, 151
L.L. Bean 153
Locke-Ober 145
Lodge family 22
Loews Boston Common 83
Loews Theaters 161
Logan International Airport
123, 180, 181
Long Wharf 74

Longfellow, Henry Wadsworth 31
First Baptist Church 92
Longfellow Birthday
Celebration 37
Longfellow National Historic
Site (Cambridge) 108
Old Corner Bookstore 59
Omni Parker House 58
poem about Paul Revere 73
Tales of a Wayside Inn 21, 22
Longfellow National Historic
Site (Cambridge) 108
Longwood Cricket Club 167
Lost property 176, 177
Louis Boston 154, 155
Louis Philippe,
King of France 63
Louisburg Square **44**
Street-by-Street map 42
Lowell, Amy 30
Lowell, James Russell 22, 30
Old Corner Bookstore 59
Lowell, Robert 30
Lowell family 22, 30
Lulu's Bake Shop 150, 151
Luther Standing Bear, Chief,
Walden Pond State
Reservation (Concord) 118
Lyric Stage 160, 161

M

McCloskey, Robert
Boston Common and Public
Garden 46
Duckling Day Parade 34
Swan Boats 170
McCormack, John W. 65
McKay, Donald 30
memorial 123
McKim, Charles 32, 90, 96, 97
Macy's 153
Street-by-Street map 81
Magazines 179
Maginnis, Charles 94
Mailboxes 179
Malcolm, Daniel, grave of 126
Malcolm X 30
Omni Parker House 58
Manchester New Hampshire
Airport 180, 181
Mandarin Oriental 135
Manet, Edouard
Fogg Art Museum
(Cambridge) 112
Museum of Fine Arts,
Boston 106
Skating 113
Mapparium 99
Maps
Back Bay 90–91
Back Bay and South End 89
Beacon Hill 42–3
Beacon Hill and West End 41
Boston 12–13

Maps (cont.)
Boston Common
and Public Garden 46–7
Boston and environs 13
Boston Street Finder 186–91
Boston "T" 183
Boston transportation
see Back Endpaper
Boston's Best: Museums
28–9
Cambridge 109
Chinatown and Theater
District 79
Colonial Boston 56–7
Concord 117
farther afield 101
Freedom Trail 124–7
Greater Boston 14–15
Modern Art & Architecture
at MIT 121
North America 12
North End Street-by-Street
68–9
North End and the
Waterfront 67
Old Boston and the
Financial District 55
South Boston: Carson Beach
to Castle Island 122–3
Three Guided Walks 120–23
Washington Street 80–81
Marathon 34, **167**
Copley Square 96
Marc, Franz 113
Maria's Pastry Shop 150, 151
Marika's Antiques Shop
156, 157
Mario Radziki Oriental Rugs
156, 157
Market 145
Markets, antiques **156**, 157
Marriott Long Wharf 134
Marsalis, Branford 97
Marshall's 154, 155
Martin Luther King Day 37
Mary II, Queen of England 19
Mary Prentiss Inn 136
Masa 146
Mason, Jonathan 44
Massachusetts Bay Colony
18–19
John Harvard Mall
(Charlestown) 115
Massachusetts Bay Company 18
Massachusetts General
Hospital 53
Massachusetts Institute
of Technology (M.I.T.,
Cambridge) 11, 24, **109**
architecture 32
M.I.T. Museum
(Cambridge) 109
Modern Art & Architecture
at MIT 121

Massachusetts Network of
Information Providers for
People with Disabilities 131
Massachusetts Society for the
Prevention of Cruelty to
Animals 64–5
Massachusetts State House
27, 40, **50–51**, 53
Freedom Trail 124
Massachusetts State
Transportation Building 84
Massasoit, Chief 18
Mather, Cotton, grave of 70
Mather, Increase, grave of 70
Mather, Samuel, grave of 70
Mather family 126
Matisse, Henri 103
Maurizio's Ristorante Italiano 144
Max Mara 154, 155
May Fair 34
Mayflower 18
"Mayflower Compact" 18
M.B.T.A. 185
buses 182
subway and trolley buses 182
Meacham, George F. 46
Media 179
The Media Test Wall 121
Medical emergencies 177
Medical insurance 177
Meeting houses
African Meeting House 23, 169
Charles Street Meeting
House 42, 44
Old South Meeting House
10, 57, **59**
MegaBus 181
Memorial Day 37
Memorials *see* Monuments
Men's fashion **154**, 155
Meritage 144
Metropolitan Theater 86
Middle East 162, 163
Middlesex Fells Reservation 165
Midtown Hotel 135
Mike's City Diner 146
Mike's Pastry 150, 151
Millennium Boston 133
Millet, Pierre François 106
Million Year Picnic 156, 157
Mills Gallery 99
Minute Man National Historic
Park – Minute Man Visitor
Center (Lexington) 119
Minute Man National
Historical Park – North
Bridge Visitor Center
(Concord) 116
Minute Man statue
(Concord) 116
Mistral 162, 163
M.I.T. (Cambridge)
see Massachusetts
Institute of Technology

Mobile phones 179
Mobilia 157
Modernist architecture 33
Mohican Indians 17
Moholy-Nagy, Laszlo
Busch-Reisinger Museum
(Cambridge) 113
Light-Space Modulator 112
Monet, Claude, Museum of
Fine Arts, Boston 106
Money 178
Monument Square
(Concord) 116
Monuments
Blackstone Memorial Tablet 47
Bunker Hill Monument
(Charlestown) **115**, 127
Donald McKay memorial 123
Dorchester Heights
Monument 122
Ether Monument 46
Irish Famine memorial 56, **59**
New England Holocaust
Memorial 63
Shaw Memorial 47
Soldiers and Sailors
Monument 47
see also Statues
Morison, Samuel Eliot 30
Morris, William 94, 95
Motherwell, Robert 62
Mount Vernon Street **44**
Street-by-Street map 43
Mr. Bartley's Burger and Salad
Cottage (Cambridge) 148
Munch, Edvard, Fogg Art
Museum (Cambridge) 111
Munroe Tavern (Lexington) 119
Museums and galleries
Boston's Best: Museums **28–9**
Children's Boston 169
Boston Children's Museum
169, 175
Boston Tea Party Ships &
Museum **74–5**, 169
Bunker Hill Pavilion
(Charlestown) 115
Busch-Reisinger Museum
(Cambridge) 112–13
Carpenter Center for Visual
Arts (Cambridge) 111
Children's Museum 11, **75**
Clough House 68, **70**
Concord Museum 117
Constitution, U.S.S.
(Charlestown) 117
Custom House 64
Fogg Art Museum
(Cambridge) 112–13
Gibson House Museum 33, **92**
Hart Nautical Gallery
(Cambridge) 109
Harvard Museum of Natural
History (Cambridge) 114

Museums and galleries (cont.)
Harvard University museums
28, **112–14**
Institute of Contemporary
Art 29, 74
International Poster Gallery
157
Isabella Stewart Gardner
Museum 10, 28, 100, 101, **103**
John F. Kennedy Library and
Museum 25, 29, **102**
List Visual Arts Center
(Cambridge) **109**, 121
M.I.T. Museum
(Cambridge) 109
Museum of African American
History 23, **49**, 169
Museum of Fine Arts, Boston
(MFA) 10, 24, 27, 28, 49,
104–7, 159, 169
Museum of Science and
Science Park 28, **53**, 169
Nichols House Museum 29,
43, **45**
Old South Meeting House 59
Old State House 57, **60–61**
Otis House Museum 29, **52**
Paul Revere House
69, **73**, 125
Peabody Museum of
Archaeology and Ethnology
(Cambridge) 114
Sackler Museum
(Cambridge) 114
Sports Museum of New
England 169
Verizon Building 65
William Hickling Prescott
House 45
Music
Boston Ballet Season 36
Boston Globe Jazz and Blues
Festival 35
Boston Pops 34, 35
Boston Symphony Orchestra
Season 36
classical music **160**, 161
folk and world music
162, 163
Hatch Memorial Shell 35, 92
jazz and blues **162**, 163
opera **160**, 161
rock music **162**, 163

N

National Historic Landmarks,
Walden Pond State
Reservation (Concord) 118
National Historic Parks
Minute Man National
Historical Park (Concord) 116
Minute Man National
Historical Park
(Lexington) 119

National Historic Sites
John F. Kennedy National
Historic Site 103
Longfellow National
Historical Site
(Cambridge) 108
The Wayside (Concord) 118
National Park Service 183
Boston Harbor Islands
National Park Area 165
Natural History, Harvard
Museum of Natural History
(Cambridge) 114
Nauset Indians 17
Neiman Marcus 153
Nevelson, Louise 121
New Balance Factory Outlet
154, 155
New England Aquarium
11, 27, **76–7**, 170
Boston's Best: Museums 29
New England Conservatory of
Music 11, 24, 159, 160, 161
New England Holocaust
Memorial 63
New England Patriots 166, 167
New England Revolution
166, 167
New England Spring Flower
Show 34
New England Telephone
Building 65
architecture 33
"New Guinea",
Freedom Trail 126
New Old South Church 96
New Year's Day 37
New Year's Eve 37
New Zealand Consulate 177
Newbury Comics 171
Newbury Guest-House 135
Newbury Street 10, **93**
Street-by-Street map 91
Newman, Robert
grave of 70
Old North Church
71, 126
Paul Revere's ride 21
Newspapers **179**
children's events 168
Nichols, Rose Standish 43, 45
Nichols family 44
Nichols House Museum **45**
Boston's Best: Museums 29
Street-by-Street map 43
Nick's Comedy Stop 163
Nightclubs **162**, 163
Niketown 155
Nine Zero 133
Nixon, Richard M. 102
No. 9 Park 142
Noland, Kenneth,
Here-There 121
Nolde, Emil 113

Nomad 154, 155
North America, map 12
North of Boston Convention
and Visitors' Bureau 131
North Bridge Visitor Center
(Concord) 116
North End and the Waterfront
66–77
area map 67
Four Great Days in Boston 10
Freedom Trail 126
hotels 133–4
New England Aquarium
76–7
restaurants 143–4
Street-by-Street map 68–9

O

Oak Room 148
O'Brien, Hugh 24
Oceanaire 143
Oilily 154, 155
Oishii 148
O'Keefe, Georgia 106
Old Boston and
the Financial District **54–65**
architecture 33
area map 55
hotels 132–3
Old State House 60–61
restaurants 143
Street-by-Street map 56–7
Old City Hall 59
Street-by-Street map 56
Old Corner Bookstore **59**
Freedom Trail 125
Street-by-Street map 57
Old Granary Burying Ground
48, **48**
Freedom Trail 124
The Old Manse (Concord) 117
Old North Church 10, 27, **71**
Annual Lantern Celebration 34
Freedom Trail 126
Street-by-Street map 68
Old South Meeting House 10, **59**
Freedom Trail 125
Street-by-Street map 57
Old State House 10, 27, **60–61**
Freedom Trail 125
Street-by-Street map 57
Old Town Trolley Tours 183
Old West Church 52
Oleana 149
Oliver, Andrew 83
Olives (Charlestown) 149
Olmsted, Frederick Law 103
Omni Parker House **58**, 133
Street-by-Street map 56
1369 Coffeehouse 150, 151
O'Neill, Eugene 87
O'Neill, Thomas "Tip" 31
Oona's 154, 155
Open-air entertainment 159

Opening hours 174
  banks 178
  restaurants 138
  shops 152
Opera **160**, 161
Opera House **83**, 160, 161
  Street-by-Street map 80
Orchard House (Concord) 118
Oriental Tea Company 62
Orinoco 146
Orpheum Theater 162, 163
Otis, Harrison Gray
  Beacon Hill 45
  Second Harrison Gray Otis
    House 44
Otis House Museum **52**
  Boston's Best: Museums 29
Outlet stores 153

P
Pain, Elizabeth, grave of 58
Paine, Robert Treat, grave of 48
Palladio, Andrea 49
Panificio 142
Paper Source 157
Paramount Deli-Restaurant 142
Parents-in-a-Pinch 168, 169
Paris, Treaty of (1783) 21
Parish Café 146
Park Street Church **48**
  Freedom Trail 124
Parker, Harvey D. 58
Parker, Robert 31
Parker's Bar 151
Parking 130, 184
Parkman Bandstand 47
Parkman, Dr. George
  Beacon Street 45
  Parkman Bandstand 47
Parkman House 45
Parks and gardens
  Arnold Arboretum 34, **102–3**,
    170
  Boston Common and Public
    Garden 11, 34, **46–7**, 170
  Christopher Columbus Park
    10, **73**
  Copley Square 96
  Emerald Necklace 11, **103**
  The Esplanade 92
  Fenway Park 24, 25
  Fort Independence Park 123
  Franklin Park 103
  Hidden Gardens of Beacon
    Hill 34
  Joe Moakley Park 122
  Minute Man National
    Historical Park (Concord) 116
  Minute Man National
    Historical Park
    (Lexington) 119
  Thomas Park 122
Parris, Alexander 32
  Charlestown Navy Yard 115

Parris, Alexander (cont.)
  Massachusetts General
    Hospital 53
  St. Paul's Cathedral 82
Passports 174
  security 176
Patagonia 154, 155, 171
Patrick, Deval 25
Patriot's Day 37
Patriot's Day Parade 34
Paul A. Duggan Co. 156, 157
Paul Revere House **73**
  Freedom Trail 125
  Street-by-Street map 69
Paul Revere Mall **72**
  Street-by-Street map 69
Peabody Museum of
  Archaeology and Ethnology
  (Cambridge) 114
Peach Farm 145
Peale, Charles Wilson 106
Pei, I.M.
  Government Center 62
  John F. Kennedy Library and
    Museum 102
  Museum of Fine Arts, Boston
    104
Pennacook Indians 17
Pennell, H.B. 84
Performing Arts Series
  at the Hatch Shell 35
Personal security 176
Peter Pan Trailways 181
Petit Robert Bistro 148
Pharmacies 177
Philippoteaux, Paul 99
Phillips, Wendell 23
Phips, Governor William 19
Phoenix Landing Bar and
  Restaurant 162, 163
Picasso, Pablo 121
Pierce-Hichborn House 73
Pilgrim Fathers 18
Pino, Tony 72
Pinsky, Robert 31
Pizzeria Regina's 171
Planetarium, Charles Hayden
  Planetarium 53
Pleasure Bay 122–3
Pleasure Bay Causeway 123
Plymouth Company 17
Pocumtuc Indians 17
Poe, Edgar Allen 123
  birthplace 85
Police **176**, 177
Police Non-Emergency Line
  176, 177
Pollock, Jackson 106
Polo/Ralph Lauren 154, 155
Pomodoro **144**
Post 390 146
Post Office 33
Post Office Square 64–5
Postal Service 179

Precinct 162, 163
President's Day 37
Preston, William G. 46
Prezza 144
Prudential Center 10, 96, **98**
Public holidays 37
Public transportation
  181, 182–3
Publick Theater 159
Puppet Showplace Theater
  170, 171
Puritans 17–19
Purple Shamrock 151
Puvis de Chavannes, Pierre 96–7

Q
Quakers 19
Quincy, Josiah 64
  statue of 59
Quincy Market 10, **64**, 168, 171
  architecture 32

R
Racing
  greyhound racing 167
  horse racing 166
Radcliffe Institute for
  Advanced Study
  (Cambridge) 24, **109**
Radio 179
Radius 143
Rail travel 181
Rainfall 37
Ramada Inn Boston 136
Real Deal Jazz Club 162, 163
Reenactment of Boston
  Massacre 34
Reenactment of the
  Boston Tea Party 37
Regal Fenway 13 161
Regatta Bar 162, 163
Rembrandt
  Isabella Stewart Gardner
    Museum 103
  Museum of Fine Arts, Boston
    106
Renaissance Revival
  architecture 32
Renoir, Pierre-Auguste
  Dance at Bougival 105
  Fogg Art Museum
    (Cambridge) 112
  Museum of Fine Arts, Boston
    106
Renting cars **185**
Reside 156, 157
Responsible tourism **175**
Restaurants **138–49**
  Back Bay and South End 146–8
  Beacon Hill and West End
    142–3
  Cambridge 148–9
  Charlestown 149
  Children's Boston 171

Restaurants (cont.)
Chinatown and the Theater District 145
Flavors of Boston 140–41
general information 138–9
Jacob Wirth **85**, 145
North End and the Waterfront 143–4
Old Boston and the Financial District 143
taxes 138, 174
tipping in 174
Revere, Paul
church bells 58, 73
Concord Museum 117
grave of 48, 124
King's Chapel 58
Massachusetts State House 50
midnight ride 21, 22, 73
Old North Church 68, 71
Patriot's Day Parade 34
Paul Revere House 69, **73**, 125
Paul Revere Mall 69
St. Stephen's Church 72
silverware 104, 106
statues of 69, 72, 126
Revere, Rachel 73
Rialto (Cambridge) 149
Riccardi 154, 155
Richardson, Henry Hobson 32–3
First Baptist Church 91, 92
Harvard University 111
Trinity Church 91, 94–5
Richardson Romanesque architecture 32–3
Ritz-Carlton Boston Common 82, 134
Riverway 103
Rocca 148
Rock music **162**, 163
Rodgers and Hammerstein 84, 87
Romberg, Sigmund 84
Ron's Gourmet Homemade Ice Cream & Bowling 151
A Room with a Vieux Antiques 156, 157
Rowes Wharf 74
Rowing 167
Royal Sonesta Hotel 137
Royale 162, 163
Rubens, Peter Paul 106
Rush, John,
Along the Battle Road 116
Ruth, Babe 25
Ryles Jazz Club 162, 163

S

Saarinen, Eero, Kresge Auditorium and Chapel 33, 109
Sackler, Arthur M. 114

Sackler Museum (Cambridge) 114
Safety **176**
driving in Boston 185
Sailboats 164
St. Patrick's Day Parade 34
St. Paul's Cathedral **82**
Street-by-Street map 80
St. Stephen's Church **72**
Street-by-Street map 69
Saks Fifth Avenue 153
Salem 19
Sales 153
Sales tax 152, 174
Sandrine's Bistro (Cambridge) 11, **149**
Santayana, George 31
Saratoga, Battle of (1777) 21
Sargent, John Singer
Boston Public Library 90, 97
Isabella Stewart Gardner Museum 103
Museum of Fine Arts, Boston 104, 105, 106
Scampo 143
Schoenhof's Foreign Books 156, 157
Science, Museum of Science and Science Park 28, **53**, 169
Scooper Bowl 35
Scullers Jazz Club 162, 163
Seaport Hotel 133
Seasons 34–7
Second Time Around 155
Security 176
Sel de la Terre 11, 144
Senior travelers 175
Sensing 144
Sert, Josep Lluis 33
Settebello 154, 155
The Sevens 151
Shabu-Zen 145
Shaw, Colonel Robert Gould 30
Battle of Fort Wagner 23
Shaw Memorial 47
Shay, Daniel 22
Shay's Pub and Wine Bar 151
Sheraton Commander 137
Ships *see* Boats and ships
Shoe shops 155
Shopping **152–7**
antiques, fine crafts and gifts 156–7
Children's Boston 171
fashion 154–5
general information 152–3
opening hours 174
Shopping malls **152**, 153
Shops at Prudential Center 152, 153
Shreve, Crump & Low 96
architecture 33
Shubert Theatre **86**, 160, 161
Shure, Robert 59

Sibling Rivalry 147
Sidney, Margaret,
The Wayside (Concord) 118
Skating **164**, 165
Skating (Manet) 113
Ski and Snowboard Expo 36
Skidmore, Owings & Merrell 74
Skiing 165
Skinner Inc. 156, 157
Skywalk 98
Slavery
abolition movement 23
"Underground Railroad" 49
Sleepy Hollow Cemetery (Concord) 118
Small Pleasure 156, 157
Smith, Captain John 17, 18
Smith, John J. 23
Smoking 174
in restaurants 139
Soccer 166
Society for Accessible Travel and Hospitality 174, 175
Society of Arts and Crafts 157
Sofra 148
Sola Men 155
Soldiers and Sailors Monument 47
Somerset Club 45
Sons of Liberty 20
Liberty Tree 83
Old South Meeting House 59
Sonsie 147
Sorellina 148
South End
see Back Bay and South End
Spectator sports 166–7
Speed limits 184
Speedwell 18
Sportello 144
Sports 164–7
Sports Depot 163
Sports Museum of New England 169
Spring in Boston 34
Stanford Calderwood Pavilion 99
Stata Center 121
Statues
Christopher Columbus 44
David Farragut 120, **122**
Edward Everett Hale 46
George Washington Statue 46
John Harvard 110
Minute Man statue (Concord) 116
Paul Revere 69, 72, 126
Samuel Adams 63
William Ellery Channing 46
William Garrison 93
Stella, Frank 121
Stephanie's on Newbury 147
Steve's Greek Restaurant 146
Stirling, James 114

Stowe, Harriet Beecher 59
Street Performers Festival 34
Stuart, Gilbert
  Boston Athenaeum 49
  grave of 47
  Museum of Fine Arts, Boston
  106
Stuart Weitzman 155
Student Advantage Card 175
Students 175
Sturgis, William Bigelow 107
Subway 24, 182
Suffolk Downs 166, 167
"Sugar Bowl" beach 122–3
Summer in Boston 35
Sumner, Charles
  anti-slavery speeches 23
  Longfellow National
  Historical Site
  (Cambridge) 108
  Park Street Church 48
Sunshine 35
Susi's Gallery for Children 171
Swan, Hepzibah 45
Swan Boats 170
Swimming 164

T
"T" 24, 182
  map 183
Taiwan Café 145
Taj Boston Hotel 135, 150, 151
Talbots 154, 155
Tandy, Jessica 87
Tanjore 148
The Tannery 155
Tapeo 147
A Taste of Culture 154, 155
Taxes **174**
  in restaurants 138, 174
  sales tax 152, 174
Taxis **183**
Tchaikovsky, Pyotr 87
TD Bank 178
TD Garden 162, 163
Tea rooms **150**, 151
Tealuxe 150, 151
Teatro 145
Telephone Men and Women at
  Work (Cornwell) 65
Telephones 179
Television 179
Temperatures 36
Temple Bar (Cambridge) 149
Tennis **164**, 165, 167
Terramia 144
T.F. Green Airport 180, 181
Thanksgiving 18, 37
Theater **160**, 161
  Berklee Performance
  Theater **97**
  Children's Boston **170**, 171
  Colonial Theater
  11, **84**, 160, 161

Theater (cont.)
  History of Boston's Theater
  District 87
  Huntingdon Theater
  10, **160**, 161
  Opera House 83
  Shubert Theatre 86
  Stanford Calderwood
  Pavilion 99
  Wang Theatre 86
Theater District see Chinatown
  and Theater District
Theft 176
Thomas Park 122
Thompson, Benjamin &
  Associates 64
Thoreau, Henry David 22, 31
  Concord Museum 117
  Old Corner Bookstore 59
  The Old Manse (Concord)
  117
  Omni Parker House 58
  Sleepy Hollow Cemetery
  (Concord) 118
  Walden Pond State
  Reservation (Concord) 118
Thrifty Car Rental 185
Ticketmaster 158, 159
Ticknor & Fields 59
Tiffany, Louis Comfort 93
Tipping 174
  in restaurants 138–9
Titian 103, 106
Top Ten Attractions 27
Toro 147
Tory Row 149
Toscanini's 150, 151
Tourist information **174**, 175
Tours **183**
  Children's Boston 168
  Town Taxi 185
Townshend Acts 20
Trains 181
Transcendental Club 22
Travel **180–85**
  air travel **180**, 181
  Back Bay and South End 89
  Beacon Hill and West End
  41
  buses 181, 182
  cars 181, 184–5
  Chinatown and Theater
  District 79
  insurance 177
  map
  see Back Endpaper
  M.B.T.A. Subway 182
  North End and the
  Waterfront 67
  Old Boston and the
  Financial District 55
  taxis 183
  trains 181
  trolley buses 182

Traveler's checks
  security 176
  in shops 152
Travelers with special needs
  174, 175
  see also Disabled visitors
Travelex Currency Services 178
Traveling on a budget **175**
Trees, Arnold Arboretum 102–3
Tremont 647 147
Tremont Estates Building 99
Trevisiani, Francesco 111
Trinity Church 10, 27, **94–5**
  architecture 32, 33
  Street-by-Street map 91
Trolley buses 182
Troquet 151
Truth, Sojourner 49
Twain, Mark 30
Twentieth Century Ltd
  156, 157
21st Amendment 151

U
"Underground Railroad" 49
Union Bar & Grill 147
Union Oyster House 63, 143
Union Park 99
Unitarian Universalist
  Association 45
United Kingdom Consulate 177
Universities
  Boston University 24
  college sports 167
  Harvard University
  18, 19, 24, 27, 32, **110–11**
  Massachusetts Institute
  of Technology (M.I.T.,
  Cambridge) 24, 32, **109**
  Radcliffe Institute for
  Advanced Study
  (Cambridge) 24, **109**
Upstairs Downstairs 156, 157
Urban AdvenTours 164, 165
Urban Outfitters 154, 155
U.S.S. Constitution
  (Charlestown)
  see Constitution, U.S.S.

V
Van Gogh, Vincent 107
  La Berceuse 106
Venu 162, 163
Veronese, Paolo 106
Very Special Arts –
  Massachusetts 159, 174, 175
Veterans Day 37
Veterans Day Parade 36
Via Matta Plaza 147
Victorian architecture 33
Vikings 17
Vinland 17
Vintage clothes 154–5
Visas 174

W

W Boston 134
Wadsworth, Henry
  First Baptist Church 92
  Omni Parker House 58
Walden Pond State
  Reservation (Concord) 118
Walk for Hunger 34
Walking **182**
  Freedom Trail **124–7**
  Modern Art & Architecture
  at MIT 121
  South Boston:
  Carson Beach to Castle Island
  122–3
Wally's 162, 163
Wang Theatre **86**, 160, 161
War of 1812 22, 48
Warren, Dr Joseph 115
Washington, George 85
  Boston Athenaeum 49
  Bunker Hill Monument
  (Charlestown) 115
  bust of 71
  Cambridge Common
  (Cambridge) 108
  Christ Church
  (Cambridge) 108
  Dorchester Heights
  Monument 122
  Evacuation of Boston 21
  Fort Independence 123
  George Washington Statue 46
  Harvard Yard 110
  Longfellow National Historic
  Site (Cambridge) 108
  Massachusetts State House 51
  presidential inauguration 22

Washington, Martha 108
Washington Street,
  Street-by-Street map 80–81
Watch and Ward Society 87
Water sports **164**, 165
Waterfront *see* North End
  and the Waterfront
Watson, Thomas 65
The Wayside
  (Concord) 118
Weather 35–7
Websites 175
Webster, Daniel 63
Webster, Dr John 45
Welton Beckett & Associates
  62
West End
  see Beacon Hill and West End
West, Mae 86
Western Front 162, 163
Westin Boston Waterfront 133
Wheatley, Phillis 30, 31
Wheelchair access *see*
  Travelers with special needs
Wheelock Family Theater
  159, 170, 171
Whistler, James McNeill 103
Whitehill, Walter Muir 97
Widener, Harry Elkins 110
Widener Library
  (Cambridge) 110
Wilbur Theater 87, 160, 161
Wildlife *see* Aquariums; Zoos
Willard, Solomon 82
William III, King of England
  19, 49

William Hickling Prescott
  House 45
William J. Devine Golf Course
  164, 165
Williams, Tennessee 87
Wine, Boston Wine Expo 37
Winter in Boston 37
Winter sports 165
Winthrop, John 18, 19
  City Square (Charlestown) 115
  grave of 58, 124
Wirth, Jacob 85
witchcraft 19
Women's fashion **154**, 155
Wonderland Park 167
Woodward 143
Woody's L Street Tavern 122
World Music **162**, 163
Wren, Sir Christopher
  Old North Church 71
  Old South Meeting House 125
  Park Street Church 48
Wrentham Village Premium
  Outlets 153

X

Xinh Xinh 145

Y

Yellow Cab 185

Z

Ziegfeld Follies 84, 87
Zoos
  Franklin Park Zoo **102**, 170
  see also Aquariums
Zurbarán, Francisco de 106
Les Zygomates 149, 151

Acknowledgments

Dorling Kindersley would like to thank the following people whose contributions and assistance have made the preparation of this book possible.

Main Contributors

Patricia Harris and David Lyon are journalists and critics. They review art and restaurants and write extensively about travel, food, and popular culture from their home in Cambridge, Massachusetts. In addition to their books on art and travel, their essays, narratives, and photographs have appeared in a wide variety of online and print publications, including Expedia.com, *The Boston Globe*, the *Los Angeles Times, American Craft, Arthur Frommer's Budget Travel, The Robb Report*, and *Boston Magazine*.

Tom Bross has lived in Massachusetts since 1965 and now lives in Boston's North End, virtually next door to Old North Church. During the past 25 years as a freelance travel journalist Tom has written extensively about U.S., Canadian, and overseas destinations for various guidebooks, national magazines, newspapers, newsletters, and on-line publications. His domestic specialties are New England and California; overseas, Germany, Belgium, and Austria. He is, in addition, a professional photographer and spent several years in the 1980s as staff photographer of his home city's American League baseball team, the Boston Red Sox.

Kem Sawyer lives in Washington DC and has written children's books, feature articles, and book reviews. She particularly enjoys writing about history and has written the history feature for the *DK Eyewitness Travel Guide to Washington DC* as well as for this guide.

Additional Contributors Brett Cook, Eric Grossman, Carolyn Heller, Juliette Rogers.

Additional Illustrations Christopher King.

Additional Photography Peter Anderson, John Coletti, Patricia Harris, David Lyon, Ian O'Leary, Stephen Oliver, Susannah Sayler, Clive Streeter.

Managing Editor Helen Townsend.

Managing Art Editor Kate Poole.

Art Director Gillian Allan.

Design and Editorial Assistance Mark Bailey, Eleanor Berman, Marta Bescos, Sam Borland, Jo Gardner, Claire Jones, Priya Kukadia, Esther Labi, Carly Madden, Sam Merrell, Katherine Mesquita, Mary Ormandy, Catherine Palmi, Marianne Petrou, Pete Quinlan, Rada Radojicic, Mani Ramaswamy, Lynne Robinson, Sands Publishing Solutions, Meredith Smith, Brett Steel, Rachel Symons, Ros Walford, Hugo Wilkinson.

Proofreader Stewart J. Wild.

Indexer Hilary Bird.

Researcher Timothy Kennard.

Special Assistance

Aimee O'Brien at the Greater Boston Convention and Visitors Bureau, who provided invaluable assistance with many Boston sights. Rosemary Barron for acting as food consultant and for food preparation..

Photography Permissions

Dorling Kindersley would like to thank the following for their assistance and kind permission to photograph at their establishments:

Courtesy COMMONWEALTH OF MASSACHUSETTS ART: *George Washington* Sir Francis Chantrey, 1827 – 51bl; *Civil War Army Nurses Memorial* Bela Pratt, 1911 – 51ca; *John Hancock Memorial* artist unknown, 1915 – 21cl; *Return of the Colours to the Custody of the Commonwealth*, December 22, 1986, mural by Edward Simmons, 1902 – 51tl; Stained glass window, Main Stair Hall, 1900/details: *Magna Carta seal* 41, *Seal of the Commonwealth* (pre-1898) 50b.

Museum of Fine Arts, Sackler Museum, Harvard Museum of Natural History, the Fogg Art and Busch- Reisinger Museums, and Franklin Park Zoo.

All other churches, museums, hotels, restaurants, shops, galleries and sights too numerous to thank individually.

Picture Credits

t = top; tl = top left; tlc = top left centre; tc = top centre; tr = top right; cla = centre left above; ca = centre above; cra = centre right above; cl = centre left; c = centre; cr = centre right; clb = centre left below; cb = centre below; crb = centre right below; bl = bottom left; b = bottom; bc = bottom centre; bcl = bottom centre left; br = bottom right; d = detail.

Works of art have been reproduced with the permission of the following copyright holders: *Here-There Wall* by Kenneth Noland 1985 (c) DACS, London/VAGA, New York 2006 121bc.

The publisher would like to thank the following individuals, companies and picture libraries for permission to reproduce their photographs.

ALAMY IMAGES: ANDRE Jenny 120bl, 141tl; Alan Myers 123br; William Owens 10cl; Chuck Pefley 11tc; Swerve 10tc, 123tl; Jeff Titcomb 121tr; ALLSPORT USA: 166t/c/b; AMERICAN AIRLINES: 180tc; THE ART ARCHIVE: 87bc; AT&T INC.: 179tl; AXIOM: 34cl; LAURA BARISONZI PHOTOGRAPHY/ WWW.PHOTOGRAPHERSDIRECT.COM: 122bl; BERKLEE COLLEGE OF MUSIC: Nick Balkin 97bc; Boston Ballet: Farnsworth/ Blalock Photography 158cr; BOSTONIAN SOCIETY/OLD STATE HOUSE: 53b, 87cb; *Boston Harbor*, 1853, John White Allen Scott. Purchase 1884 – 8-9.

CITY WATER TAXI: 180bc; CORBIS: 24t; Bettmann 25t, 31t/b, 72b, 87cra/bl, 98b; Edifice, Philippa Lewis 126c; Kevin Fleming 10br, 37b, 158b, 184t; Todd Gypstein 170b; Robert Holmes 140cl, 100; Hulton-Deutsch Collection 45t; Richard T. Nowitz 73c; Lee Snider 1; CONCORD MUSEUM www.concord museum.org: *A View of Town of Concord April 19, 1775 (1775-1825)* Artist Unknown, oil on canvas, bequest of Mrs. Stedman Buttrick, Sr. 117cr; CULVER PICTURES, INC.: 22c, 24c.

FOURTHREE MEDIA: Justine Flute 178tl; Getty Images: Photonica 141c; GRANGER COLLECTION, NEW YORK: 9 (insert), 16, 17t, 18t/c/b, 19t/c/b, 20tr/cl/b, 20-21c, 21t/ cra/crb, 22t, 23t/c, 25cl, 30t/b, 31c, 39 (insert), 65tl, 75b/c, 83b, 173 (insert); GREATER BOSTON CONVENTION & VISITORS BUREAU: 174tc; US Photo-Group/Leslie Wood 185cr; GREYHOUND LINES INC.: 181c.

HARVARD UNIVERSITY ART MUSEUMS: © President and Fellows of Harvard College, courtesy of Fogg Art Museum, Alpheus Hyatt Purchasing and Friends of the Fogg Art Museum Funds *Kneeling Angel* Gian Lorenzo Bernini, c.1674-1675 -112cr; courtesy of the Busch-Reisinger Museum, Gift of Sibyl Moholy-Nagy, *Light-Space Modulator*, Laszlo Moholy-Nagy, 1930 © Hattula Moholy-Nagy/DACS, London 2006 - 112b; courtesy of Fogg Art Museum, The Hervey E. Wetzel Bequest Fund *Christ on the Cross between the Virgin and Cardinal Torquemada and St. John the Evangelist* Fra Angelico, c.1446 -113b; courtesy Fogg Art Museum, Bequest: Collection of Maurice Wertheim *Skating* Edouard Manet, 1877 - 113cl; HULTON GETTY COLLECTION: 58b; HYATT REGENCY: 130br.

IMAGE BANK: Archive Photos 30c; INSTITUTE OF CONTEMPORARY ART, BOSTON: Iwan Baan 29cr, 66; IRVING HOUSE: 131c. MAGGIE JANIK/www. photographersdirect.com: 120tc, 122cla.

LEBRECHT COLLECTION: The Rodgers & Hammerstein Organization 87t/br; JAMES LEMASS: 6cl, 18 tc, 25crb, 34t/b, 35t/c/b, 36b, 37t, 54, 78, 91crb, 118tl, 119br, 164c, 165, 167t, 168c/b, 172-173.

MARY EVANS: 129 (insert); MASSACH-USETTS TRANSPORTATION AUTHORITY: 183b; MINUTE MAN NATIONAL HISTOR-ICAL PARK: 119cla; MUSEUM OF FINE ARTS BOSTON: Gift of Egypt Exploration Fund *Egypt, Deir el-Bahri* painted wood 24b; HU-MFA Expedition *Shawabtis of Taharka* 28b; 104t; Bequest of Mrs. Beatrice Constance (Turner) Maynard in Memory of Winthrop Sargent *Revere Silver Teapot* 104ca; Egypt Exploration Fund *Inner Coffin of Nes-mut-aat-neru* 104cb; Picture Fund *Dance at Bougival* Pierre-Auguste Renoir, 1883 -105t; Ruth and Carl J. Shapiro Colonnade and Vault *John Singer Sargent Murals* 105c; Francis Bart-lett Donation of 1900 *Head of Aphrodite*, Greek Late Classical or Early Hellenistic period -105b; George Nixon Black Fund *Ewer and basin* 106t; M. and M. Karolik Collection of American Paintings, 1815 – 1865, by exchange, *Boston Harbor* Fitz Hugh Lane 106c; Bequest of John T. Spaulding *La Berceuse* Vincent van Gogh, 1889 – 106b; Maria Antoinette Evans Fund *Babylonia:Nebuchadnezzar II* 107t; Gift by Contribution *Horse, early 8th century, China* 107c; Richard Norton Memorial Fund *Fragment of fresco from villa at Contrada Bottaro* 107b; MUSEUM OF SCIENCE: George Kiley 169t; Andrew Brilliant 169b; Kindra Clineff 28t; NEW ENGLAND AQUARIUM: 76cl, Bob Kramer 76t/b, 77tc, 77cra; DAVID NOBLE: 38-39.

OLD NORTH CHURCH, BOSTON: 71cl; OMNI PARKER HOUSE: 56clb; Used by Permission of Orchard House / The Louisa May Alcott Memorial Association: 118c; PAUL O'SHAUGHNESSY: 119ca.

PEABODY MUSEUM OF ARCHAEOLOGY AND ETHNOLOGY/HARVARD UNIVERSITY: © President and Fellows of Harvard College 1976. All Rights Reserved. Photos Hillel Burger 114c. Courtesy Paul Revere Memorial Association: 73t; PUPPET SHOWCASE THEATRE: Marionettes by Paul Vincent Davis 171tl.

SCIENCE PHOTO LIBRARY: Cnes, 1986 Distribution Spot Image 13t; STA TRAVEL GROUP: 175clb; SWISSOTEL BOSTON: © René Staud 130b.

TOPHAM PICTUREPOINT: 25b. UNITED AIRLINES: 180t.

FRONT ENDPAPER: All special photography except INSTITUTE OF CONTEMPORARY ART, Boston: Iwan Baan cr; JAMES LEMASS: bl/bc.

JACKET

Front – PHOTOLIBRARY: Roy Rainford. Back – ALAMY IMAGES: JLImages bl; Megapress tl; DORLING KINDERSLEY: Demetrio Carrasco clb; Linda Whitwham cla. Spine – PHOTOLIBRARY: Roy Rainford t.

All other images ©Dorling Kindersley. See www.dkimages.com for further information.

SPECIAL EDITIONS OF DK TRAVEL GUIDES

DK Travel Guides can be purchased in bulk quantities at discounted prices for use in promotions or as premiums. We are also able to offer special editions and personalized jackets, corporate imprints, and excerpts from all of our books, tailored specifically to meet your own needs.

To find out more, please contact: (in the United States) **SpecialSales@dk.com** (in the UK) **travelspecialsales@uk.dk.com** (in Canada) DK Special Sales at **general@tourmaline.ca** (in Australia) **business.development@pearson.com.au**

Further Reading

Non-Fiction

A Guide to Public Art in Boston: from Newburyport to Plymouth. Carlock, Marty. (Harvard Common Press, 1993.)

AIA Guide to Boston. Southworth, Michael and Susan. (Globe Pequot Press, 1996.)

All about Boston Harbor Islands. Kales, Emily and David. (Hewitts Cove Publishing Co. Inc., 1983.)

Boston Sites and Insights. Wilson, Susan. (Beacon Hill Press, 1994.)

Exploring in and Around Boston on Bike and Foot. Sinai, Lee. (Appalachian Mountain Club Books, 1996.)

Gaining Ground: A History of Landmaking in Boston. Seasholes, Nancy. (Mit Press, 2003)

Imagining Boston: A Literary Landscape. O'Connell, Shaun. (Beacon Press, 1990.)

Paul Revere's Ride. Fischer, David Hackett. (Oxford University Press, 1994.)

The Fitzgeralds and the Kennedys: an American Saga. Goodwin, Doris Kearns. (Simon and Schuster, 1987.)

26 Miles to Boston: the Boston Marathon Experience from Hopkinton to Copley Square. Connelly, Michael. (Parnassus Imprints, 1998.)

Fiction

The Godwulf Manuscript. Parker, Robert. (Delacorte Press, 1974.)

Make Way for Ducklings. McCloskey, Robert. (Viking Press, 1941.)

Mortal Friends. Carroll, James. (Little Brown & Company, 1978.)

The Last Hurrah. O'Connor, Edwin. (Little Brown & Company, 1956.)